Lecture Notes in Computer Science 13130

More information about this subseries at https://link.springer.com/bookseries/7408

Sérgio Campos · Marius Minea (Eds.)

Formal Methods: Foundations and Applications

24th Brazilian Symposium, SBMF 2021
Virtual Event, December 6–10, 2021
Proceedings

Editors
Sérgio Campos (iD)
Departamento de Ciência da Computação
Universidade Federal de Minas Gerais
Belo Horizonte, MG, Brazil

Marius Minea
College of Information and Computer
Sciences
University of Massachusetts
Amherst, MA, USA

ISSN 0302-9743   ISSN 1611-3349 (electronic)
Lecture Notes in Computer Science
ISBN 978-3-030-92136-1   ISBN 978-3-030-92137-8 (eBook)
https://doi.org/10.1007/978-3-030-92137-8

LNCS Sublibrary: SL2 – Programming and Software Engineering

This Springer imprint is published by the registered company Springer Nature Switzerland AG
The registered company address is: Gewerbestrasse 11, 6330 Cham, Switzerland

Preface

This volume contains the papers presented at SBMF 2021: the 24th Brazilian Symposium on Formal Methods. The conference was held online during December 6–10, 2021.

The Brazilian Symposium on Formal Methods (SBMF) is an event devoted to the development, dissemination, and use of formal methods for the construction of high-quality computational systems, aiming to promote opportunities for researchers and practitioners with an interest in formal methods to discuss the recent advances in this area. SBMF is a consolidated scientific-technical event in the software area. Its first edition took place in 1998, reaching the 24th edition in 2021. The proceedings of the last editions have been published mostly in Springer's Lecture Notes in Computer Science series as volumes 5902 (2009), 6527 (2010), 7021 (2011), 7498 (2012), 8195 (2013), 8941 (2014), 9526 (2015), 10090 (2016), 10623 (2017), 11254 (2018), and 12475 (2020)

The conference included four invited talks, given by Jeannette Wing (Columbia University, USA), Orna Grumberg (Technion, Israel), Fritz Vaandrager (Radboud University, The Netherlands), and Vander Alves (Universidade de Brasília, Brazil). A total of eight papers were presented at the conference and are included in this volume. They were selected from 15 submissions that came from authors in seven different countries: Argentina, Brazil, India, Norway, South Africa, the UK, and the USA.

The Program Committee was comprised of 31 members from the national and international community of formal methods. Each submission was reviewed by three Program Committee members. Submissions, reviews, deliberations, and decisions were handled via EasyChair, which provided good support throughout this process.

We are grateful to the Program Committee and to the additional reviewers for their hard work in evaluating submissions and suggesting improvements. We are very thankful to the general chair of SBMF 2021, Tiago Massoni (Universidade Federal de Campina Grande, Brazil), who made everything possible for the conference to run smoothly. SBMF 2021 was organized by the (Universidade Federal de Campina Grande, Brazil), and promoted by the Brazilian Computer Society (SBC). We would like to thank Springer for agreeing to publish the proceedings as a volume of Lecture Notes in Computer Science.

October 2021

Sérgio Campos
Marius Minea

Organization

General Chair

Tiago Massoni   Universidade Federal de Campina Grande, Brazil

Program Committee Chairs

Sérgio Campos   Universidade Federal de Minas Gerais, Brazil
Marius Minea   University of Massachusetts, Amherst, USA

Steering Committee

Tiago Massoni   Universidade Federal de Campina Grande, Brazil
Mohammad Mousavi   University of Leicester, UK
Adolfo Duran   Universidade Federal da Bahia, Brazil
Phillip Wadler   University of Edinburgh, UK
Gustavo Carvalho   Universidade Federal de Pernambuco, Brazil
Volker Stolz   Western Norway University of Applied Sciences, Norway

Program Committee

Aline Andrade   Universidade Federal da Bahia, Brazil
Haniel Barbosa   Universidade Federal de Minas Gerais, Brazil
Luis Barbosa   Universidade do Minho, Portugal
Christiano Braga   Universidade Federal Fluminense, Brazil
Manfred Broy   Technische Universität München, Germany
Sérgio Campos   Universidade Federal de Minas Gerais, Brazil
Gustavo Carvalho   Universidade Federal de Pernambuco, Brazil
Ana Cavalcanti   University of York, UK
Márcio Cornélio   Universidade Federal de Pernambuco, Brazil
Jim Davies   University of Oxford, UK
David Déharbe   CLEARSY Systems Engineering, France
Clare Dixon   University of Liverpool, UK
José Fiadeiro   University of Dundee, UK
Rohit Gheyi   Universidade Federal de Campina Grande, Brazil
Juliano Iyoda   Universidade Federal de Pernambuco, Brazil
Thierry Lecomte   CLEARSY Systems Engineering, France
Michael Leuschel   Universität Düsseldorf, Germany
Patrícia Machado   Universidade Federal de Campina Grande, Brazil
Tiago Massoni   Universidade Federal de Campina Grande, Brazil

Ana Melo	Universidade de São Paulo, Brazil
Sidney Nogueira	Universidade Federal Rural de Pernambuco, Brazil
Marcel Oliveira	Universidade Federal do Rio Grande do Norte, Brazil
Leila Ribeiro	Universidade Federal do Rio Grande do Sul, Brazil
Augusto Sampaio	Universidade Federal de Pernambuco, Brazil
Adenilso Simão	Universidade de São Paulo, Brazil
Volker Stolz	Western Norway University of Applied Sciences, Norway
Sofiène Tahar	Concordia University, Canada
Leopoldo Teixeira	Universidade Federal de Pernambuco, Brazil
Maurice ter Beek	Istituto di Scienza e Tecnologie dell'Informazione, Italy
Nils Timm	University of Pretoria, South Africa
Jim Woodcock	University of York, UK

Additional Reviewers

Alexandre Mota
Blair Archibald
Andrea Vandin
Mohamed Zaki
Adrian Rutle
Michele Sevegnani
Ionut Tutu

Contents

A Two-Level Approach Based on Model Checking to Support Architecture Conformance Checking

Bruno Menezes[1]([✉]) , Ana Teresa Martins[1] , and Thiago Alves Rocha[2]

[1] Universidade Federal do Ceará, Fortaleza, Brazil
brunomenezesr@alu.ufc.br, ana@dc.ufc.br
[2] Instituto Federal de Educação, Ciência e Tecnologia do Ceará IFCE,
Maracanaú, Brazil
thiago.alves@ifce.edu.br

Abstract. We propose a Model Checking based method to aid Architecture Conformance Checking, which is a fundamental analysis to ensure software quality, dependability and maintainability. In this work, a new logic, which combines temporal logic, hybrid logic and a new logical operator in order to formalize software specifications, is proposed. The method described in this paper uses two structures, namely call graphs and software version graphs. The first one is used to check specifications related to classes and methods and we apply it intending to analyze a specific software version. The latter one gives us an overview of the software development process and we employ it to check global software requirements. These two graphs allow us to design a two-level checking method. The first level deals with specifications of a single software version that must be inspected in the call graph. The second level handles the global requirements throughout all software versions. Using our new operator and a function, we are able to use the same logic in both levels, allowing them to communicate with each other and handle the verification process in a neat and uniform manner. Our two-level approach is the great differential of this work, since the current approaches available in the literature focus on an unique software version at a time. We also present the general idea of an algorithm, which has polynomial time complexity, to perform Model Checking for our proposed temporal logic.

Keywords: Formal verification · Model Checking · Architecture Conformance Checking · Temporal logic · Hybrid logic

1 Introduction

The current paper is inserted in the context of Architecture Conformance Checking. In order to understand it, one needs to be aware of what software

This research was supported by the Brazilian National Council for Scientific and Technological Development (CNPq) under the grant number 424188/2016-3.

S. Campos and M. Minea (Eds.): SBMF 2021, LNCS 13130, pp. 1–16, 2021.
https://doi.org/10.1007/978-3-030-92137-8_1

architecture is. We present a definition by synthesizing a few definitions found in [21, 25, 26].

Definition 1. *Software architecture consists in:*

1. *Software components and their requirements;*
2. *The relationships between these components;*
3. *The communication interfaces between the components and external software systems;*
4. *The documentation regarding the definitions and the design of the points above.*

When developing a software, its architecture is defined by the software architects. The developers must implement this exact architecture. However, throughout the implementation phase, disagreements between the documented architecture and the coded architecture arise. These disagreements prejudice the software quality. Hence, they should be avoided. This problem is known as Architecture Erosion [20, 21, 25]. Some issues induced by Architecture Erosion include loss of planned scalability, reduced maintainability (which makes it difficult to update and fix the software), loss of dependability and reusability.

Architecture Conformance Checking [20, 21, 25] aims to avoid disagreements induced by Architecture Erosion. This analysis measures the accordance level between the design architecture and the coded architecture. The architecture conformance is achieved when there is no disagreements between the real architecture, implemented in the source code, and the architecture which has been designed and documented by the architects. We give a high-level abstraction definition below:

Definition 2. *Architecture Conformance Checking is the process of verifying if the decisions, the definitions and the specifications made during design architecture phase are indeed being implemented when the software is coded. This verification should be constantly done while the software is implemented by the developers.*

Conformance checking is a complex process, since it involves analysing design decisions and software artifacts in some levels:

1. Higher abstract level:
   - Modules;
   - Software connectors;
   - Communication interfaces.
2. Deeper implementation level:
   - Methods;
   - Classes;
   - Class packages;
   - Control flow structures.

We develop a formal verification method aiming to aid Architecture Conformance Checking. As we explain in Sect. 2, we focus on requirements related to classes and methods. This analysis is applied to a specific software version. We extend this analysis to a global point of view, gathering all software versions. Summarizing the problem we are dealing with:

Given a software model and a set of specifications related to its methods relationships, we aim to check if the model satisfies such specifications along its several versions.

The goal of this work is:

To propose a Formal Verification Method able to solve the problem above while allowing the analysis of the specifications throughout the software development process, i.e., along its various versions, aiming to be applied in Architecture Conformance Checking.

We list below the key ideas of the method we propose:

1. A Formal Verification method to be used by Architecture Conformance Checking in order to verify specifications related to classes and methods of a software;
2. The analysis of the behavior of these specifications along the software development process;
3. A logic with a new operator to represent specifications;
4. The application of Model Checking to verify if the specifications are satisfied by the system. Call graphs and version graphs are used to model the system, allowing that we can use the formal method pointed out.

Taking into account the global level, i.e., considering several software versions and not only one in the analysis, is the great differential of this work. The works found in the literature, such as [1–4,11,14,16–19,24], focus on a particular software version at a time. We aim to allow the user to assesses specifications across all software versions.

Section 2 gives the background to support and contextualize this work. Section 3 presents our method, explains the structures we use, the semantics of our logic and gives some examples. We also give an overview of the Model Checking algorithm. Section 4 is the conclusion, followed by suggestions for future works.

2 Theoretical Background

2.1 Model Checking

In this work, we use Model Checking, a Formal Verification method. Model Checking [5,23] is a method which allows us to analyse if a system satisfies desired specifications by modeling it and inspecting the states of the model. It is an efficient technique to find flaws in systems design. The desired specifications are written in some formal language, e.g., a logic. Thus, the problem consists of checking if the model satisfies a set of formulas from an initial state.

Definition 3. *Model Checking is the following problem: given a model M and a specification properly formalized α, we ask if M satisfies α from an initial state s. We denote this as $M, s \models \alpha$.*

A pretty common structure used to model systems is the so called Kripke structure [5,23]. We adopt it here and present their definition:

Definition 4. *A Kripke structure is a tuple $M = (V, \rightarrow, L, PROP, v_0)$, where:*

1. *V is a set of states;*
2. *$\rightarrow \subseteq (V \times V)$ is a transition relation;*
3. *$L: V \rightarrow 2^{PROP}$ is a label function;*
4. *PROP is a set of propositional atoms;*
5. *v_0 is an initial state.*

The notion of path in a Kripke structure is used to define the semantics of our proposed logic. Thus, we present its definition below:

Definition 5. *A path in a Kripke structure $M = (V, \rightarrow, L, PROP)$ is an infinite sequence of states $v_1, v_2, v_3, ... \in V$ such that for each $i \geq 1$, we have $v_i \rightarrow v_{i+1}$.*

2.2   Temporal Logic and Hybrid Logic

Temporal logic is a kind of modal logic such that the modality is time [5,12,23]. These logics have proved to be really useful when it comes to writing system requirements [5,12]. Since systems change their states through time, we need a logic capable to represent temporal concepts.

As the system runs, properties are satisfied and then are not. This dynamic aspect is captured by temporal logic, while first order logic and propositional logic are not able to capture it, since they are static. There are temporal logics to fulfill several purposes. These logics are classified according to how they treat time. Time can be linear, treat as a set of paths, with each path being a succession of instants in time. LTL is an instance of temporal logic which treats time as linear [23]. Time can also be treat as a tree. In this case, the root represents the present instant and branches are the possible futures. CTL treats time this way [23]. Time can also be discrete or continuous, finite or infinite.

Our proposed logic follows CTL. Thus, we deal with infinite, discrete, branching time. With discrete time, we have a set of instants, represented by states. Infinite time means that each state has at least one successor. Thus, time never stops. We can have a finite number of states, but since each one of them has a successor, the paths are infinite, hence, the time is infinite.

CTL allows to explicitly quantify on paths by means of the quantifiers A (all paths) and E (there is a path) that works with temporal operators. For example, EFq means "there is a path such that at some moment satisfies the atom q" and stands for the property "There is a reachable state which satisfies q".

Hybrid logic [7] have a special type of propositional atoms, the nominals, used to identify states of a model. The idea is that each nominal is true only in a unique state. Thus, using them allow us to refer to a certain state in an easy manner.

We combine connectives from a temporal logic known as CTL [5,6,23] and from a simple hybrid logic which can be found in [7] to create a new logic. Besides theses connectives, we propose a new one, namely IN, as a means to permit the communication between our two levels of verification. The details are explained in Sect. 3.

2.3 Software Versioning

Software systems are incrementally developed. We gradually add new modules, resources, bug fixes until we get a version meeting all requirements. In this process, it is fundamental to organize the versions to facilitate management and understand how the software evolves. Even after a final version is delivered to the client, a neat development history is necessary as a means to maintain and update the system. To do so, software versioning is used.

Software versioning is the process of organizing each development state in a version and giving unique identifiers to them. Hence, software engineers, project managers and stakeholders are able to keep track of where and when changes were made. Users can easily find the newest versions to keep their systems updated.

A common way to identify the versions is the semantic versioning [22]. We are not going to get into details here, but basically we have a hierarchy following the pattern x.y.z, with x, y, z $\in$ N. We begin at version 1.0.0 and the values are incremented according to the versions evolution and the depth of the changes. The meaning of x, y and z suggested in [22] is:

1. x stands for the major version. It should be incremented when the changes made are incompatible with the API (Application Programming Interface) of the software;
2. y stands for the minor version. It should be incremented when a new functionality is added;
3. z stands for the patch version. It should be incremented when bug fixes are added.

We use software version graphs [15], or just version graphs for the sake of brevity, as a means to maintain the history of versions. These structures synthesize the different development branches and how they evolve through time. This history can be stored and managed by Version Control Systems (VCS), such as Git [8].

Definition 6. *A version graph is a directed cycle free graph which the vertex set represents the versions of a software and the edges set is the succession relation between the versions.*

Version graphs are cycle free graphs, since it is not possible that a version released in a day x be followed by a version released in a day before x. Thus, we can travel only forward, it is not possible to go back to a vertex which has already been visited. There is only one initial version and one final version, which is possible to be extended when the software goes through maintenance or evolution. We assume that we can reach any version from the initial one, since they are derived from it. Each path in this graph stands for a development branch.

3   The Proposed Method

This section presents our method. We show the structures that we use to model the system and in which we apply Model Checking. We define our logic, used to formalize software specifications, and give some examples to demonstrate how our method works and better explain its behavior. We also briefly speak about the Model Checking algorithm for our logic.

Tools to aid Architecture Conformance Checking are fundamental: they reduce the verification time, additional spending and are more reliable than totally human analysis, which is unviable to large systems. In this work, we focus on the analysis of requirements related to methods, classes and class packages in order to propose one of these tools. To fulfill the goal presented in Sect. 1, we create two levels of verification:

Level 1: we deal with a specific software version. With the purpose of doing so, we use call graphs. Each version has its own call graph, which is used to build the model for Model Checking. We refer to this level using the subscript *in*.

Level 2: we deal with the global development process utilizing the version graph. This graph gives us an overview of all version of a system. As in level 1, the version graph is used to build the model for Model Checking. We refer to this level using the subscript *out*.

The connection between these two levels is made by linking the call graph corresponding to a version to the vertex of this version by means of a function. In the logic we create, we put a connective that allows the communication between the two levels. Hence, we are able to deal with these levels in a homogeneous manner. This makes our method a neat solution for the proposed problem.

Summarizing the steps of our proposed method, it follows:

1. Formalize the software specifications using our proposed logic. These specifications should be found in the documentation of the architecture.
2. Model the system according to the structures we explain in the following two sections.
3. Then we have a model of the system and a set of formulas. Thus, we can apply a model checking algorithm to decide if the model satisfies or not the specifications.

Checking if the set of specifications is satisfied or not by the model allows us to verify if the code is indeed implementing the desired architecture. The specifications may change during the development, since the requirements can be changed by the stakeholders, the technology evolves and the software needs to keep updated, among other reasons. Of course, the software interfaces, the methods, the relationships between the components can change in order to comply with the new requirements. Assessing the specifications through all versions gives us a global vision of the development process that facilitate the understanding of the changes, their scope, where and when their happened. This may help new developments, new manages and software engineers in general to understand a software project. It can also help debugging, since one can analyze when a new requirement has been implemented and the impacts that it cause to the software. These are the main advantages of our proposed method that we highlight.

3.1 Call Graphs as Kripke Structures

As mentioned before, we use call graphs as one of the structures to model the system. We define them in this subsection and explain how we represent them as Kripke structures. Call graphs [13] are structures that code the relationships between the methods of a program:

Definition 7. *A call graph is a directed graph which the vertex set represents programming methods and edges mean the call from one method to another. Thus, if a method A invokes a method B, there is a directed edge from the vertex A to the vertex B.*

We convert these graphs in Kripke structures using the following definition:

Definition 8. *Let $M_{in} = (V_{in}, \rightarrow_{in}, L_{in}, PROP_{in}, v_{0in})$ be a Kripke structure with:*

1. *V_{in} is the set of states: it represents the methods present in the software, i.e., the vertex set of a call graph.*
2. *$\rightarrow_{in}$ is the set of transitions: there is an edge from state A to state B if the method represented by A calls the method represented by B. It is the edge set of a call graph.*
3. *L_{in} is the label function: $L_{in} : V_{in} \rightarrow 2^{PROP_{in}}$. We label a state with the method that this state stands for and with the class that has this method.*
4. *$PROP_{in}$ is the set of propositional atoms. We have a propositional atom for each method and for each class being assessed.*
5. *v_{0in} is the initial state: when we apply Model Checking, we take this state as the initial one.*

Note that the call graph is an arbitrary graph. We do not have any special property about it. Thus, the Kripke structure that represents it is also arbitrary. However, in order to fit in the semantics of the proposed logic, we need to add a dead state which receives an edge from states that do not have a successor. By doing so, we guarantee the concept of infinite time. We identify this dead state using a propositional atom.

In case of polymorphism [10], we may use propositional atoms to differentiate the polymorphic methods. Also, we can use a notation alike class::prop_atom and method::prop_atom to enlighten what is each atom in the labels. Please, note that this is not mandatory, you can use whatever notation you want, as long as it is clear what the methods and the classes refer to.

The choice of the initial state is up to the software engineers based on what requirements are under analysis. For instance, suppose we want to check a set of specifications related to a execution flow to print a spreadsheet saved in some storage device. The initial state is the one which stands for the method that triggers the execution flow.

Obtaining the call graphs involves inspecting the source code. We have to go through it, find the methods called by the methods in the execution flow that is under analysis and assemble the call graph. Algorithms to perform this task can be found in [13].

3.2   Version Graphs as Kripke Structures

We use the following enhancement of Kripke structures to codify the version graphs:

Definition 9. *Let $M_{out} = (V_{out}, \rightarrow_{out}, L_{out}, PROP_{out}, v_{0out}, I, GC, N, C)$ be a Kripke structure with I, GC, N, C as additional elements with:*

1. *V_{out} is the set of states of version graph: each vertex represents a software version.*
2. *$\rightarrow_{out}$ is the set of edges of version graph: it says which versions are successors of a particular version.*
3. *L_{out} is the label function: $L_{out} : V_{out} \rightarrow 2^{PROP_{out}}$. Propositional atoms can be used to code extra information about a version graph.*
4. *$PROP_{out}$ is the set of propositional atoms.*
5. *v_{0out} is the initial state, it represents the first version.*
6. *I is the set of nominals used to identify each version.*
7. *GC is the set of call graphs under analysis.*
8. *N is a function that links nominals to its corresponding vertex: $N : I \rightarrow V_{out}$.*
9. *C is a function that links a version graph vertex to the call graph corresponding to the version represented by the vertex: $C : V_{out} \rightarrow GC$.*

The same properties that we mentioned earlier right after version graph Definition 6 are valid to this Kripke structure. However, with the aim of respecting the semantics of our proposed logic, we add a loop in the vertex corresponding to the final version. If the software is updated, this loop will be removed and an edge to the next version will be added. We apply this same procedure to intermediate versions that are discarded during development process. We show an example (Fig. 1):

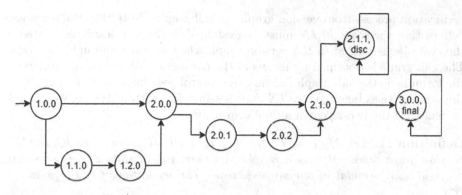

Fig. 1. A version graph. Each path is a development branch. Note the discarded version.

3.3 The Proposed Logic: A Two-Level Temporal Logic for Specifications Checking

We propose a variant of the temporal logic CTL [5,6,23] adding hybrid logic operators. The formulas of this logic are composed of two-levels: the first one is intended to verify specifications based on call graphs. The second one aims to evaluate requirements related to version graphs. As we said before, we use the subscripts *in* and *out* to refer to each of these levels.

Definition 10. *We use the well-known adequate set* $\{\neg, \vee\}$ *for boolean operators and the adequate set* $\{AF, EU, EX\}$ *for temporal operators [23]. We present the syntax of our proposed logic in Backus-Naur form:*

1. *For formulas evaluated based on call graphs, in the first verification level:*
   $\alpha_{in} := p_{in} \| \neg \alpha_{in} \| \alpha_{in} \vee \alpha_{in} \| EX\alpha_{in} \| AF\alpha_{in} \| EU(\alpha_{in}, \alpha_{in}) \| AP(\alpha_{in}) \| EP(\alpha_{in})$
2. *For formulas evaluated based on version graphs, in the second verification level:*
   $\alpha_{out} := p_{out} \| i \| \neg \alpha_{out} \| \alpha_{out} \vee \alpha_{out} \| EX\alpha_{out} \| AF\alpha_{out} \| EU(\alpha_{out}, \alpha_{out}) \| @_i \alpha_{out} \| IN\alpha_{in}$

From now on, we refer to call graph meaning the structure defined in Definition 8 and to version graph meaning the Definition 9. We evaluated our formulas based on this last structure: $M_{out} \models \alpha_{out}$ if and only if $M_{out}, v_{0_{out}} \models \alpha_{out}$, according to the semantics definition given after the next two paragraphs.

The clauses 7 and 8 define the nominal and $@_i$ semantics. We use this to identify and access a specific software version. Thus, we do not need them for call graphs. The clauses 11 and 12 define temporal operators that talk about the past. We use them only for call graphs, because we have found specifications which need to evaluate method calls that take place in the past of the execution flow. We do not need these operators for version graphs. If one finds specifications that need to talk about the past on version graphs, it is easy to extend the logic with them on the second level.

The IN operator, explained in the clause 9, is responsible for allowing the communication between the two verification levels. This operator transfers the verification process from version graphs to call graphs. Note that the semantics defines that the scope of IN must be evaluated in the call graph associated to the state being visited in the version graph when we walk through the graph. The call graph is obtained by means of the C function. When the evaluation of the formula on the call graph finishes, the control goes back to version graph, to the same state as before, since IN does not interfere with it. Hence, we are able to deal with the two-levels in an uniform manner.

Definition 11. *Let $M_{out} = (V_{out}, \rightarrow_{out}, L_{out}, PROP_{out}, v_{0_{out}}, I, GC, N, C)$ a version graph represented as a Kripke structure, v_{out} a state of this structure, α_{in} and α_{out} formulas of our proposed logic. The semantics of this logic is:*

1. *$M_{out}, v_{out} \models p_{out}$ iff $p_{out} \in L_{out}(v_{out})$.*
2. *$M_{out}, v_{out} \models \neg\alpha_{out}$ iff $M_{out}, v_{out} \not\models \alpha_{out}$.*
3. *$M_{out}, v_{out} \models \alpha_{out1} \vee \alpha_{out2}$ iff $M_{out}, v_{out} \models \alpha_{out1}$ or $M_{out}, v_{out} \models \alpha_{out2}$.*
4. *$M_{out}, v_{out} \models EX\alpha_{out}$ iff there is v_{out_2} such that $v_{out} \rightarrow_{out} v_{out_2}$ and $M_{out}, v_{out_2} \models \alpha_{out}$.*
5. *$M_{out}, v_{out} \models AF\alpha_{out}$ iff for all path $v_{out} = v_{out_1} \rightarrow_{out} v_{out_2} \rightarrow_{out} v_{out_3} \rightarrow_{out}$ ... if there is v_{out_i} for $i \geq 1$ along the path such that $M_{out}, v_{out_i} \models \alpha_{out}$.*
6. *$M_{out}, v_{out} \models EU(\alpha_{out_1}, \alpha_{out_2})$ iff there is a path $v_{out} = v_{out_1} \rightarrow_{out} v_{out_2} \rightarrow_{out} v_{out3} \rightarrow_{out}$ ... such that there is $i \geq 1$ with $M_{out}, v_{out_i} \models \alpha_{out_2}$ and for all j such that $1 \leq j \leq i$ - 1, we have $M_{out}, v_{out_j} \models \alpha_{out_1}$.*
7. *$M_{out}, v_{out} \models i$ iff $N(i) = v_{out}$.*
8. *$M_{out}, v_{out} \models @_i\alpha_{out}$ iff $M_{out}, v \models \alpha_{out}$, with $N(i) = v$.*
9. *$M_{out}, v_{out} \models IN\alpha_{in}$, iff $M_{in}, v_{0in} \models \alpha_{in}$, with $C(v_{out}) = M_{in}$.*
10. *The semantics of p_{in}, $\{\neg_{in}, \vee_{in}\}$, and $\{EX\alpha_{in}, AF\alpha_{in}, EU(\alpha_{in}, \alpha_{in})\}$ is analogous to the semantics of the second level.*
11. *$M_{in}, v_{in} \models AP(\alpha_{in})$ iff for all path $v_{0_{in}} = v_{in_1} \rightarrow_{in} v_{in_2} \rightarrow_{in} v_{in_3} \rightarrow_{in}$ ... $\rightarrow_{in} v_{in}$ there is v_{in_i} with $i \geq 1$ along the path such that $M_{in}, v_{in_i} \models \alpha_{in}$.*
12. *$M_{in}, v_{in} \models EP(\alpha_{in})$ iff there is a path $v_{0_{in}} = v_{in_1} \rightarrow_{in} v_{in_2} \rightarrow_{in} v_{in_3} \rightarrow_{in}$ ... $\rightarrow_{in} v_{in}$ there is v_{in_i} with $i \geq 1$ along the path such that $M_{in}, v_{in_i} \models \alpha_{in}$.*

3.4   Examples

We assume the verification on version graph always starts from the initial state, which represents the first version of the software. However, we can skip to specific versions using $@_i$. For call graphs, the verification always starts from the initial state, according to the semantics of our proposed logic. For the examples present in this subsection, let M_{out} be a Kripke structure that represents a version graph, according to Definition 9. We verify if $M_{out} \models \alpha_{out}$, i.e., $M_{out}, v_{0_{out}} \models \alpha_{out}$. Note that this is computed applying Model Checking.

We use all temporal and boolean operators, not only the adequate sets, in the way that they are usually found in the literature [23]:

$\alpha \wedge \beta := \neg(\neg\alpha \vee \neg\beta)$, $\alpha \rightarrow \beta := (\neg\alpha \vee \beta)$, $AX\alpha := \neg EX\neg\alpha$, $EF\alpha := EU(\top, \alpha)$, $AU(\alpha, \beta) := \neg EU(\neg\alpha, (\neg\alpha \wedge \neg\beta)) \wedge AF\beta$, $AG\alpha := \neg EF\neg\alpha$, $EG\alpha := \neg AF\neg\alpha$, with $\top$ being a propositional atom that stands for true.

General Examples of Specifications: we present a few software specifications adapted from [9]. We present a formula, which codifies the desired specification, dividing it into two parts: α_{in} is the formula that must be evaluated on the first level and α_{out} must be evaluated on the second level.

Specification 1: the convertToIntervalXml method of the ConversionFilter class is executed by the software in all versions, but version 5.

- $\alpha_{in} := EF(\text{ConversionFilter} \wedge \text{convertToInternalXml})$: this formula is true if we find a state that satisfies ConversionFilter $\wedge$ convertToInternalXml, according to EF semantics. This means that occurs a call to convertToIntervalXml, so the method is executed by the software.
- $\alpha_{out} := AG((i_5 \rightarrow \neg IN(\alpha_{in})) \wedge (\neg i_5 \rightarrow IN(\alpha_{in})))$: we verify for all version graph states if $(i_5 \rightarrow \neg IN(\alpha_{in})) \wedge (\neg i_5 \rightarrow IN(\alpha_{in}))$ is true in the state. We use implication to check if we are in version 5, using the nominal i_5. If it is the case, then the call graph of this version must not satisfy α_{in}. To do so, we use IN. If we are not in version 5, the call graph must satisfies α_{in}. Thus, we verify if the version graph state satisfies $IN(\alpha_{in})$.

Specification 2: from version 5, if a call to placeOrder method of the CustomerPortalServiceCLientProxy class occurs, then eventually must happen a call to the forwardRequest method of the ApacheCamelBroker class.

- $\alpha_{in} := AG((\text{CustomerPortalServiceClientProxy} \wedge \text{placeOrder}) \rightarrow AF(\text{ApacheCamelBroker} \wedge \text{forwardRequest}))$: the property must be complied by all call graph states. Thus, we use the AG operator. Since the specifications has a if-then structure, we use the implication. Then, if we have a call to placeOrder, which happens if we find a state that satisfies CustomerPortalServiceClientProxy $\wedge$ placeOrder, we must eventually find a call to forwardRequest. Thus, we use the AF operator.
- $\alpha_{out} := @_{i_5} AG(IN\alpha_{in})$: since the property must be satisfied from the version 5, we ignore the versions before and execute the verification from version 5. In order to achieve this, we use the $@_i$ operator. This formula works because a version graph has only edges to the next version, it does not have edges that allow to go back to a version assessed before. The formulas we present in this subsection take into account this property. Considering the fact that α_{in} must be satisfied by all states from the version 5, we use the AG operator. To say that α_{in} must be checked based on call graphs, we apply IN.

Specification 3: for all version must be valid that every call to the generatePDF method of the DocumentGenerationFilter class is preceded for a call to the addAdditionalInformation method of the EnrichmentFilter class.

- $\alpha_{in} := AG((\text{DocumentGenerationFilter} \wedge \text{generatePDF}) \rightarrow AP(\text{EnrichementFilter} \wedge \text{addAdditionalInformation}))$: this specifications has the same structure of Specification 2, but, instead of searching for an occurrence of a call in the future, we search in the past by means of the AP operator.

- $\alpha_{out} := AG(\alpha_{in})$: since the property coded by α_{in} must be true in all version, we use the AG operator. Remember that, according we said in the begin of this subsection, we check this formulas from the initial state.

IN Scope: the aim of this example is to spotlight the behavior of the IN operator and how it gives power for the proposed logic. Consider:

1. $\phi_1 := IN(\alpha_{in}) \wedge \alpha_{out}$: analysing what happens when $M_{out}, v_{out} \models \phi_1$ is evaluated, because of the conjunction semantics, $v_{out} \models IN(\alpha_{in})$, which means that the call graph associated to the state v_{out} satisfies α_{in}. For the same reason, $v_{out} \models \alpha_{out}$, which means that the state v_{out} satisfies α_{out}. To summarize, α_{in} must be satisfied by the call graph, and α_{out} must be satisfied by a version graph state.
2. $\phi_2 := IN(\alpha_{in_1} \wedge \alpha_{in_2})$: the IN operator tells us to verify if the call graph linked to v_{out} satisfies the formulas α_{in_1} and α_{in_2}. To ϕ_2, we do not verify if v_{out} satisfies α_{in_1} or α_{in_2}, like we do to α_{out} of ϕ_1. Due to the scope of the IN operator, we check α_{in_1} and α_{in_2} in the call graph linked to v_{out} by the C function.

This example aims to emphasize the scope of the IN operator: it allows us to define exactly what must be checked in the call graph and what must be checked in the version graph. The operator can be used to walk through the version graph getting into the call graphs when it is necessary and then coming back to the version graph to proceed to the next state.

Properties Related to Layered Architecture: the layered architecture pattern [26] is a pretty common pattern used to build software architecture. We present some specifications related to this pattern and that can be used when we verify a software which follows layered architecture. We use propositional atoms with the same name of the classes and methods they represent. For instance, the atom A refers to the A class. The size of a sequence of method calls is the number of states, which represents the methods, in the sequence.

1. **The A class calls the B class directly**: this is true if we find a method of A that calls a method of B in the call graph. The following formula does the trick:

   $EF(A \wedge EX(B))$: at some point during program execution, some method of A class appears in the call graph and has as successor a method of the B class. Thus, there is a direct call between these classes.
2. **The A class calls the B class indirectly**: this happens if we have a method of the A class followed by a call of a method that is not of the B class and then a series of zero or more calls of methods of another classes until a call to a method of the B class. We get the formula:

EF(A ∧ EX(¬B ∧ EF(B))): there is a call to some method of the A class and at least one successor of this method is not a method of the B class. However, there is a sequence of method calls that eventually reaches a method of the B class.

3. **There is a sequence of calls starting from a m method that reaches a n method:** this situation is just like the indirect call between two classes, but here we have methods instead and there is no problem if the m method calls the n method directly, that is, we can have zero size sequences. The following formula captures our intention:

EF(m ∧ EX EF(n)): this formula copes with the case of zero size sequences and arbitrary size sequences. If we mean to avoid zero size sequences, we have the formula *EF(m ∧ EX EX EF(n))*, forcing the existence of at least one call between m and n.

4. **The A class is in a call loop:** this means that we have a method of A that is followed by a sequence of method calls and, along this sequence, we are able to find an infinite number of methods of the A class. Note that the call graph is finite, but we can have infinite paths on it. The formula to code this specification is a little bit tricky:

EF(A ∧ EX(EGEF(A))): at some point, a method of the A class is called. For at least one successor of this method, we have a path in which is always possible to find a method of the A class. It can be the same method. If this occurs, we say that the A class is in a call loop. In order words, a method of the A class is called. After this call, some method of A is always called while the program is executed.

A Model Checking algorithm for our logic consists in apply a CTL algorithm to verify all subformulas in *IN* operators scope. These subformulas are evaluated in call graphs using a simple algorithm for CTL which can be found in [23]. After this, we have the truth values of the subformulas in *IN* scope and can deal with them as if they were propositional atoms. Then, we apply the CTL algorithm again for temporal and boolean operators in the version graph. Nominals can be treated as propositional atoms, case handled by the CTL algorithm. The satisfiability of $@_i$ can be verified by means of a graph search algorithm and *IN* makes us visit a call graph through a function. These operations take polynomial time in the size of the model. Hence, the algorithm has polynomial complexity. Unfortunately, we do not have space to explain this algorithm in details and describe how we calculate its complexity. However, we present it below:

1. Let n_{out} be the number of states and m_{out}, the number of edges in the version graph, t_{out} be the number of logical and temporal operators.
2. The cost of the checking disregarding the *IN* operator is $v_1 = t_{out} \times n_{out} \times (n_{out} + m_{out})$.
3. Let $n_{max_{in}}$ be the greatest number of states in a call graph, and $m_{max_{in}}$, the greatest number of edges in a call graph in the set of call graphs and $t_{max_{in}}$,

the greatest number of logical and temporal operators in a call graph in the set of call graphs (GC). It does not need to be the same call graph, our goal is to get a upper bound.

4. Let z be the number of IN operators in the formula under analysis. The costs of propositional atoms, nominals and @$_i$ operators are surpassed by the other costs.

5. The cost of the checking regarding the IN operator is $v_2 = n_{out} \times z \times (t_{max_{in}} \times n_{max_{in}} \times (n_{max_{in}} + m_{max_{in}}))$.

6. The complexity of the Model Checking algorithm of our proposed logic is O($v_1 + v_2$).

4   Conclusion and Future Works

The methodology we proposed here formalizes the requirements using a kind of logic that is familiar to software engineers, what makes it easier to apply in real world scenarios than other methodologies found in the literature, like [14]. As we could see in the examples, the size of the formulas are small and they can be easily read by humans. Our two-level approach is an innovation that gives to engineers a manner to analyse the global behavior of the requirements being assessed. This gives a point of view that the current methods cannot give. Thus, we can perform assessments that would not be possible or would require a lot of workaround in other methods, without lost the intuition about the meaning of the requirements. Also, we do not need to develop an algorithm from scratch. By using algorithms that already exists, we save time and still get a polynomial time algorithm. This is fundamental if one intends to apply our methodology in real world. Considering the features we have just spotlighted, we believe that our methodology can be really useful to Architecture Conformance Checking, contributing to the development of reliable and quality systems.

We spotlight our contributions below:

1. We propose a method that deals with two levels of verification in a homogeneous manner. By adding a global level, we are able to check how specifications behave along the history of the development of a system. The current methods deals with only one version at a time.

2. The method we define in this paper utilizes the history versions, kept by VCS. Thus we can take advantage of the management made by VCS.

3. We present a model of the system that links the two structures used in each verification level and a logic that possesses a connective which allows the communication between the two verification levels.

4. Once we have a model of the system and the specifications formalized in the proposed logic, we apply Model Checking. We adapt the algorithms for the two logic that we adopt to create our own. This algorithm has polynomial time complexity.

5. The solution we propose is generic: we use call graph and evaluate specifications related to them. We can switch them to other structures that

code another features of a system and then apply the same methodology we describe here, as long as the structures involved can be converted to Kripke structures. Hence, our solution works like a framework.

As future works, we suggest analysing other structures, such as control flow graphs, in order to enumerate the specifications that can be evaluated based on them. It would be necessary investigate if the proposed logic is suitable to formalize the specifications. If not, we must adjust, whether creating new operators or adopting other logic. We can also try to improve the complexity of the algorithm that performs Model Checking on our proposed logic.

References

1. Cqlinq syntax. https://www.ndepend.com/docs/cqlinq-syntax/#architect. Accessed 4 Aug 2021
2. Lattix architect. https://www.lattix.com/products-architecture-issues/#architect. Accessed 4 Aug 2021
3. Sonargraph-architect (2017)
4. Aldrich, J., Chambers, C., Notkin, D.: ArchJava: connecting software architecture to implementation. In: Proceedings of the 24th International Conference on Software Engineering, ICSE 2002, pp. 187-197. IEEE (2002)
5. Baier, C., Katoen, J.P.: Principles of Model Checking. The MIT Press, New York (2008)
6. Beyersdorff, O., Meier, A., Thomas, M., Vollmer, H., Mundhenk, M., Schneider, T.: Model checking CTL is almost always inherently sequential. In: 2009 16th International Symposium on Temporal Representation and Reasoning (2009)
7. Blackburn, P., de Rijke, M., Venema, Y.: Modal Logic. Cambridge Tracts in Theoretical Computer Science. Cambridge University Press (2002). https://books.google.com.br/books?id=gFEidNVDWVoC
8. Chacon, S., Straub, B.: Pro Git, 2nd edn. Apress, New York (2014)
9. Czepa, C., Tran, H., Zdun, U., Thi Kim, T.T., Weiss, E., Ruhsam, C.: On the understandability of semantic constraints for behavioral software architecture compliance: a controlled experiment. In: 2017 IEEE International Conference on Software Architecture (ICSA), pp. 155-164 (2017)
10. Deitel, P., Deitel, H.: Java How to Program - Early Objects, 10th edn. Prentice Hall Press, Englewood Cliffs (2014)
11. Duszynski, S., Knodel, J., Lindvall, M.: SAVE: software architecture visualization and evaluation. In: 2009 13th European Conference on Software Maintenance and Reengineering, pp. 323-324. IEEE (2009)
12. Fisher, M.: An Introduction to Practical Formal Methods Using Temporal Logic, 1st edn. Wiley Publishing, Chichester (2011)
13. Grove, D., Chambers, C.: A framework for call graph construction algorithms. ACM Trans. Program. Lang. Syst. (TOPLAS) 23(6), 685-746 (2001)
14. Herold, S.: Architectural compliance in component-based systems. Ph.D. thesis, Clausthal University of Technology (2011)
15. Hoffmann, A.B.G., et al.: Um modelo para o controle de versões de sistemas para apoio ao desenvolvimento colaborativo através da web (2002)
16. Hou, D., Hoover, H.J.: Using SCL to specify and check design intent in source code. IEEE Trans. Software Eng. 32(6), 404-423 (2006)

17. Iadarola, G., Martinelli, F., Mercaldo, F., Santone, A.: Call graph and model checking for fine-grained android malicious behaviour detection. Appl. Sci. **10**(22), 7975 (2020)
18. de Lima Meneses Filho, J.: Uma Solução para Verificação Estática de Conformidade Arquitetural do Tratamento de Exceção. Master's thesis, Universidade Federal do Ceará (2016)
19. Mitschke, R., Eichberg, M., Mezini, M., Garcia, A., Macia, I.: Modular specification and checking of structural dependencies. In: Proceedings of the 12th Annual International Conference on Aspect-Oriented Software Development, pp. 85–96 (2013)
20. Passos, L., Terra, R., Valente, M.T., Diniz, R., Mendonça, N.: Static architecture-conformance checking: an illustrative overview. IEEE Softw. **27**(5), 82–89 (2010). https://doi.org/10.1109/MS.2009.117
21. Perry, D.E., Wolf, A.L.: Foundations for the study of software architecture. SIGSOFT Softw. Eng. Notes **17**(4), 40–52 (1992)
22. Preston-Werner, T.: Semantic versioning 2.0.0. https://semver.org/spec/v2.0.0.html. Accessed 4 Aug 2021
23. Ryan, M., Huth, M.: Logic in Computer Science: Modelling and Reasoning about Systems. Cambridge University Press, New York (2004)
24. Schröder, S.: Ontology-based architecture enforcement: defining and enforcing software architecture as a concept language using ontologies and a controlled natural language. Ph.D. thesis, Staats-und Universitätsbibliothek Hamburg Carl von Ossietzky (2020)
25. de Silva, L., Balasubramaniam, D.: Controlling software architecture erosion: a survey. J. Syst. Softw. **85**(1), 132–151 (2012)
26. Sommerville, I.: Software Engineering, 9th edn. Addison-Wesley Publishing Company, Boston (2010)

Statistical Model Checking for Traffic Models

B. Thamilselvam, Subrahmanyam Kalyanasundaram[✉], Shubham Parmar,
and M. V. Panduranga Rao

Department of Computer Science and Engineering, IIT Hyderabad, Sangareddy, India
{cs17resch11005,subruk,m20mtech12002,mvp}@iith.ac.in

Abstract. Statistical Model Checking (SMC) is a popular technique in
formal methods for analyzing large stochastic systems. As opposed to the
expensive but exact model checking algorithms, this technique allows for
a trade-off between accuracy and running time. SMC is based on Monte
Carlo sampling of the runs of the stochastic system, and lends itself to
stochastic discrete event simulators as well.

In this paper, we use SMC to analyze traffic models like car-following
and lane-changing models. We achieve this through an integration of the
SMC tool MultiVeStA with the discrete event simulation software for
urban mobility, SUMO.

As illustration of the approach and the tool chain, we compare the car-
following and lane-changing models against various performance parameters like throughput, emissions and waiting times. Importantly, the use
of formal methods allows for formulating and evaluating complex queries
that can be asked of the model. The results show the utility of such a
tool chain in performing complex quantitative what-if analyses of various
traffic models and policies.

Keywords: Statistical Model Checking · Traffic modeling and
simulation · Car following and lane changing models

1 Introduction

Modeling and simulation is used extensively by traffic engineers for understanding and designing protocols and policies for maximizing traffic flow and min-
imizing jams and emissions. Microscopic traffic flow modeling and simulation,
that operate at the granularity of individual vehicles have attracted attention
in the recent past. The impact of how vehicles follow each other and respond to
the changing dynamics of nearby vehicles, and the way vehicles change lanes in
a moving traffic flow has been accepted to be significant. So much so that two
important examples of microscopic traffic modeling and simulation, the class of
car-following models and *lane-changing* models, have been studied extensively
in the past. Several mathematical models have been proposed, and several simulation tools have been developed on which these models have been implemented.

© Springer Nature Switzerland AG 2021
S. Campos and M. Minea (Eds.): SBMF 2021, LNCS 13130, pp. 17–33, 2021.
https://doi.org/10.1007/978-3-030-92137-8_2

The simulations are studied to draw inferences or validate various predictions of the models. SUMO (Simulation of Urban MObility) is a popular tool that provides the facility to carry out such studies [12].

Given their importance, several studies have been conducted in the past to compare the relative merits of various car-following and lane-changing models [5,10,15,16]. In this work, we study these models from the stand-point of (statistical) model checking. In particular, we pick the following car-following models–Wiedemann [22], Krauss [11] and Intelligent Driver[21], and the following lane-changing models–LC2013 [13] (LC) and SL2015 [9] (SL).

Model checking is a branch of formal methods that is used for analysis of systems against desirable properties. In order to perform this analysis automatically, both the system under analysis and the properties need to be specified in a mathematically precise manner [7]. This technique can be applied for analyzing stochastic systems as well. Generically called probabilistic model checking, there are two important ways to accomplish this–exact model checking and statistical model checking [23]. Statistical model checking (SMC) has emerged as an attractive approach to quantitative analysis of large stochastic systems [3,14,18,24]. While approaches like exact model checking that rely on expensive state space exploration are accurate, SMC offers a trade-off between accuracy and run-time [23]. An additional advantage that we leverage in this paper is that this technique lends itself to black box systems and Stochastic Discrete Event Simulators. MultiVeStA [1] is an example SMC tool that allows for easy integration with (stochastic) discrete event simulators. MultiVeStA supports both temporal logic queries (like PCTL and CSL), as well as (Multi)Quatex (quantitative temporal expression) queries. In this work, we use statistical model checking to study traffic models. Our contributions are twofold:

1. We integrate the statistical model checker MultiVeStA with SUMO.
2. We analyze various car-following and lane changing models for performance parameters using this tool chain.

From the analysis that we report through four illustrative queries in this paper, different combinations of car-following and lane-changing models seem to perform better in different circumstances. For example, for short distance rides, the combination of Krauss car following model and SL (2015) lane changing model seems to perform better than Wiedemann-SL. On the other hand, traffic build-up (as per a specific query) seems to happen slower for Weidemann (for both lane-changing models) when compared to Krauss (for both lane-changing models).

While we focus our attention in this paper on car-following and lane-changing models, we believe that the integrated tool will be useful in in-depth analyses of other models and questions in traffic management and policy design.

We present the prerequisite background and the tools in the next section. Section 3 briefly discusses the tool integration details. In Sect. 4, we discuss queries that illustrate the utility of the tool chain, along with results and discussions. We conclude the paper with a discussion on future directions.

2   Background

2.1   SMC and MultiVeStA

The "quantitative" variant of statistical model checking seeks to estimate the probability that a system (say, a stochastic discrete event simulator) satisfies a property stated formally (say, as a formula in a temporal logic). The SMC algorithm answers this through a Monte Carlo sampling based evaluation. Consequently, the running time depends on the desired level of confidence. Variants that answer qualitative queries – does the system satisfy the specification formula with probability at least θ have also been studied. For such applications, typically statistical techniques like hypothesis testing are employed.

MultiVeStA is a statistical model checking tool from the VeSta family. The first in the series, VeSta, is a tool that allows a variety of model specification formalisms like (discrete and continuous) Markov chains, and the executable specification language PMaude for probabilistic read-write theories [1, 19]. Property specification languages like the PCTL and CTL are supported, but importantly, Vesta supports the QUAntitative Temporal EXpressions language (QuaTEx). PVesTa improves the performance by distributing the simulations on difference processing units [6]. The tools in the VeSTa family work as long as discrete event simulations can be performed on the models and the probability measures are well defined on the paths of the model.

MultiVeStA builds on these tools and facilitates direct integration with discrete event simulators [17]. Additionally, it offers more sophisticated analysis capabilities like counter-factual analysis, and an enhanced interface [17]. The integrated tool chain has been made available for the interested reader at https:// github.com/ThamilselvamB/Multivesta-With-SUMO.git.

In the interest of space, we will not discuss details like the syntax and semantics of Quatex and Multiquatex. Instead, we will explain the semantics of the queries that we will use in the paper.

2.2   SUMO - Simulation of Urban MObility

Simulation of Urban MObility (SUMO) is an open source tool for microscopic road traffic simulation. SUMO supports various traffic demand modeling and measurement of road network parameters like vehicle types, emission etc. We use the TRAffic Control Interface (Traci) to control the SUMO simulator. Traci is a Python package which interacts in an online manner and retrieves all objects involved in SUMO. SUMO also supports measurement and monitoring of a large number of traffic parameters including pollutant emissions of vehicles, and details of each vehicle's journey. Additionally, it allows simulation of various detectors and detector outputs–the lane area detector and loop detectors. SUMO supports several car-following models and lane changing models.

2.3   Car-Following and Lane Changing Models

Two of the most important dynamics of a vehicle on a road are movement along the longitudinal direction and lateral movement. Car-following models attempt to capture how a given vehicle follows the vehicle immediately ahead of it [5,10,16]. Similarly, lateral movement between lanes and sub-lanes are modelled by Lane-changing models [8,9]. We briefly discuss the models that are used in this work. These models are also supported by SUMO.

Car Following Models. In modeling the car-following logic, various *motion parameters* like the accelerations, velocities and relative positions of the leading and the following car are relevant. Indeed, many models employ these heavily.

1. The **Krauss** [11] model calculates a vehicle's speed in relation to the vehicle in front of it. The primary objective in this model is to calculate a safe speed V_{safe} for a vehicle in relation to the vehicle ahead:

$$V_{safe} = V_l(t) + \frac{g(t) - V_l(t)t_r}{\frac{V_l(t)+V_f(t)}{2b} + t_r},$$

   where $V_l(t)$ is speed of the leading vehicle at time t, $g(t)$ is gap to the vehicle ahead, t_r is driver's reaction time and b is maximum deceleration of the vehicle. By adhering to this speed, the vehicle remains "safe", and provides one car-following model.

2. The **Wiedemann** [22] model is a very popular psycho-physical car-following model. Based on the instantaneous values of the motion parameters, a car is in one of several regimes–for example, *following, cruising, approaching* or *emergency*. The driver is believed to behave differently in these regimes and the behavior, in terms of acceleration, deceleration or steady speed, is modeled accordingly.

3. The **Intelligent Driver Model (IDM)** [21] is a simple model that calculates the speed of the following vehicle based on the basic motion parameters:

$$\frac{dv}{dt} = a \left[1 - \left(\frac{v}{v_0} \right)^\delta - \left(\frac{s^*(v, \Delta v)}{s} \right)^2 \right]$$

   where

$$s^*(v, \Delta v) = s_0 + vT + \frac{v\Delta v}{2\sqrt{ab}}.$$

   Here, v is the current speed of the vehicle, v_0 is the desired speed, $\frac{dv}{dt}$ is the proposed acceleration, a and b are the maximum acceleration and deceleration respectively, Δv difference in the speed of the current vehicle with the vehicle ahead, s_0 is the required minimum net distance desired between the vehicles, T a headway considered safe in terms of time and δ, is an acceleration exponent.

Lane Changing Models. Lateral movement of vehicles between lanes are captured by the so-called lane-changing models. Modeling a vehicle's behaviour in its current lane is somewhat simpler because the only factors that matter are the preceding vehicle's speed and location. Lane changing, on the other hand, is more difficult because the decision to change lanes is based on several conflicting objectives. There are no analytic correlations that cover the complete lane switching procedure. Instead, it is usually depicted as a series of decision-making phases such as: (i) Wishing to switch lanes (ii) Choosing the target lane (iii) Ensuring that lane change is feasible and (iv) Finally, the execution of lane change based on availability of gaps in the destination lane. We discuss two important lane-changing models that are supported by SUMO.

1. **LC2013:** This model [13] considers three main reasons for a lane change: (i) Strategic: in order to avoid dead-ends, (ii) Cooperative: to allow a nearby vehicle to perform a lane change, and (iii) Tactical: to gain speed.
2. **SL2015:** This model [9] supports sub-lanes when more than one vehicle could be present in the same lane side-by-side (provided their dimensions permit). This model builds on LC2013 and includes parameters like lateral alignment, which determines the preference of staying in the middle of lane or any one of its side.

3   Integration of MultiVeStA and SUMO Simulator

As mentioned earlier, we use the MultiVesStA model checker. Therefore, we directly integrate the model checker with the traffic simulator SUMO instead of modeling using formalisms like Markov Chains or (probabilistic) rewrite theories. We now describe briefly the process of integration.

3.1   Initial Step

In order to integrate MultiVeStA with SUMO, one needs to extend the New-State class in MultiVeStA and create instances of SUMO simulator in the same class. Had SUMO been developed in Java, then extending the NewState class in MultiVeStA would have been easier since MultiVeStA is developed in Java. Since SUMO is developed in C++, one needs to create a wrapping method to have an interface between SUMO and MultiVeStA. This interface is provided by Traci (TRAffic Control Interface) which provides the necessary package for cross platform and cross language integration. The two ways to accomplish the integration are socket communication using Traci or Traci API which is provided as a C++ library. The Traci socket communication results in communication overhead because of the protocol and server communication. We use the Traci API which can be linked with the client code, in our case MultiVeStA.

The SUMO source code is available from the SUMO website [2]. SUMO needs to be built with SWIG (Simplified Wrapper and Interface Generator). The Traci API Library will be available as the libsumo-version-SNAPSHOT.jar file in the bin folder. As mentioned before, we use this library as an interface between SUMO and MultiVeStA. After installing MultiVeStA, we have to load the SUMO library file and MultiVeStA NewState in the same class.

3.2   Integration

The class sumoState extends the NewState of MultiVeStA and is used to act as an interface between MultiVeStA and SUMO. In the constructor part, we pass the parameters to NewState of MultiVeStA (multivesta.jar) and load the SUMO library (libsumo-version-SNAPSHOT.jar) using JNI (Java Native Interface). After completing the initial steps, we override some of the methods in NewState class. The overrides are described below.

setSimulatorForNewSimulation(randomSeed): Since SUMO does not support reset simulation directly, we create generateRouteRandom(seed) function to fulfill the requirement of MultiVeStA. A python generated uniform random seed is used to generate the route files. In each run, one of the route files is picked uniformly at random. This is equivalent to resetting the simulation with the initial state.

performOneStepOfSimulation(): We call the function Simulation.step() to advance the simulation one step further.

performWholeSimulation(): To run the simulation until it reaches the state in which there is no vehicle in the simulation.

rval(int): This function is used to link observable quantities of SUMO to Multi-VeStA. For example, the speed of the vehicle, number of vehicles loaded into the simulation, number of vehicles reached the destination etc. The rval() functions that are used in this work are listed here. The value returned by the function is given against the corresponding rval() entry.

```
rval(0)   - the current time
rval(3)   - the number of cars waiting
rval(4)   - the time loss of vehicle
rval(6)   - number of vehicles that reach their
            destination
rval(7)   - the CO2 emission
rval(10)  - traffic volume at Intersection-1
rval(11)  - traffic volume at Intersection-2
rval(12)  - time at which emergency vehicle
            reaches its destination
rval(15)  - current traffic load
rval(17)  - time at which "normal" vehicle reaches the
            destination. In the experiment, this vehicle
            is started at same time and same location to
            emergency vehicle
rval(21)  - returns  traffic load at the previous step
            of the simulation
```

Listing 1.1. rval() Method.

4   Simulation Experiments and Results

In all our experiments, we consider a topology of three intersections in a line (Fig. 1) and compare combinations of car-following and lane-changing models.

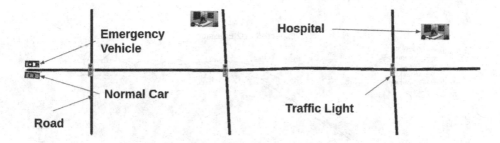

Fig. 1. Road network with hospital and emergency vehicle

For the SUMO simulations, we use a heterogenic vehicles with different physical properties [20]. For emergency vehicles, which are central to Query 1 in Sect. 4.2, we set the speedFactor as "1.9", jmDriveAfterRedTime as "300" and jmDriveAfterRedSpeed as "5.56". These configurations are available at the github repository for the tool. We mention here that the vehicles are introduced into the road network based on the Poisson distribution with different rates.

Listing 1.2 shows some of the important parameter values that we set for all our experiments.

```
-m data / cross.sumocfg
-l serversLists / oneLocalServer
-f quatex / exper1 . quatex
-bs 30 -a 0.1 -d1 x
//x = 2 for queries in sections 4.1 and 4.4. All other
//queries involve a probabilistic operator. Hence
//x = 0.1 for these queries
-vp TRUE
-osws ONESTEP -sots 0 -sd sumoState
```

Listing 1.2. Parameters of MultiVeStA Client

Of particular note are the parameters 'a' and 'd1', representing the α and δ values for confidence interval computation: The actual value in question lies within the interval $\pm\delta/2$ of the estimate with probability at least $1 - \alpha$. While we use $\alpha = 0.1$ for all the experiments, we use different values of δ for queries that involve probabilistic operators. The parameter 'bs' stands for block size, and determines number of simulations after which inclusion in the confidence interval is checked.

4.1 Simple Queries

We begin by running some simple but useful Multiquatex queries that estimate vehicular CO_2 emissions and throughput (the number of vehicles that have
reached their destination in the simulation). The queries are given respectively
in Listing 1.3 and Listing 1.4.

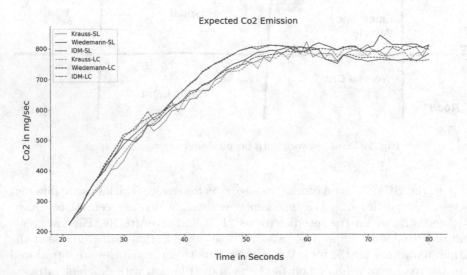

Fig. 2. Expected CO_2 emissions.

```
expCo2Emission(x) = if ( s.rval(0) >= x )
                       then  (s.rval(7))
                       else #expCo2Emission((x)) fi ;
eval parametric(E[ expCo2Emission((k)) ],
k,1.0,1.0 ,100.0) ;
```

Listing 1.3. Expected CO2 emissions within simulation time.

```
expThroughput(x) = if ( s.rval(0) >= x )
                      then  (s.rval(6))
                      else #expThroughput((x)) fi ;
eval parametric(E[ expThroughput((k)) ],
k,1.0,1.0 ,160.0) ;
```

Listing 1.4. Expected throughput within simulation time.

The results of queries are shown in Fig. 2 and Fig. 3. As one would expect, the
CO_2 increases steadily among all the car-following/lane-changing combinations
at first, before plateauing. The throughput also increases with time, but the
IDM-LC combination performs better.

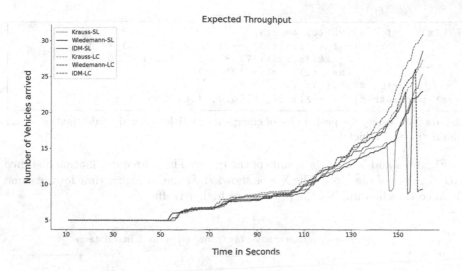

Fig. 3. Expected throughput

Next we look at some queries which illustrate the usefulness of statistical model checking for analysing traffic models. The queries that we use are motivated by interesting real-life questions.

We work with changing traffic loads. To do so, we incorporate different *regimes* of traffic injection rates. For the first three queries, we use two regimes of Poisson arrivals of the vehicles onto the road network. The first regime (at the rate of 20 vehicles per hour) is valid for the first 50 s, and the second one (200 vehicles per hour) is valid subsequently. For the last query (Query 4), we use four regimes (50, 20, 200, 50 vehicles per hour for 0–50, 50–150, 150–200 and 200–400 s respectively), to simulate fluctuating traffic conditions.

4.2 Query 1: Behaviour on Emergency Vehicles

The first query that we ask is a natural question that arises in emergency situations.

Suppose an "emergency vehicle" (say, an ambulance) and a "normal" vehicle of similar type, start at the same time from the same point. An emergency vehicle differs from "normal" vehicles in their movement dynamics–such vehicles are not obligated to strictly adhere to normal traffic rules. Which lane changing and car following model combination results in the emergency vehicle reaching the destination faster?

More precisely, what is the probability that the difference in the arrival times of the emergency vehicle and the normal vehicle is more that 20? Listing 1.5 provides the MultiQuatex formulation that we use.

```
EVR(x) = if ( s.rval(0) >= x )
          then ( if (s.rval(13) == 1 && s.rval(16) == 1
                 && (s.rval(17) - s.rval(12)) < 20 )
                 then (1)   else (0) fi)
          else #EVR((x)) fi ;
eval parametric( E[ EVR(k) ], k, 0.0, 1.0, 200.0) ;
```

Listing 1.5. Query for probability of emergency vehicle reached its destination faster than a "normal vehicle"

Figures 4 and 5 show the results of the query. The source-destination distance fixed for each of the plots. The X-axis shows the time. A higher time for the same distance travelled implies the presence of higher traffic.

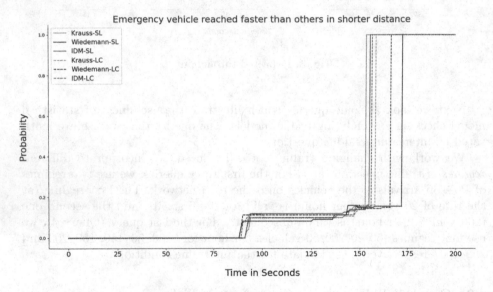

Fig. 4. Probability that emergency vehicle (ambulance) will reach its destination faster than others - shorter distance

As one would expect, when the distance between the source and destination is small, the probability that the emergency vehicle reaches significantly ahead of the normal vehicle is small. However, for scenarios of heavy traffic, (for higher time instances in Fig. 4), the probability that the emergency vehicle reaches much ahead is higher, given the relaxation in driving rules for such vehicles. Indeed, regardless of the car-following and lane-changing model, after a certain threshold traffic, the emergency vehicle reaches the destination earlier almost certainly. It is interesting to note that the Wiedemann car following model, for both lane changing models, reaches this stage somewhat later. The effect of regime change in the traffic injection rate that happens after 50 time units, is visible after a lag.

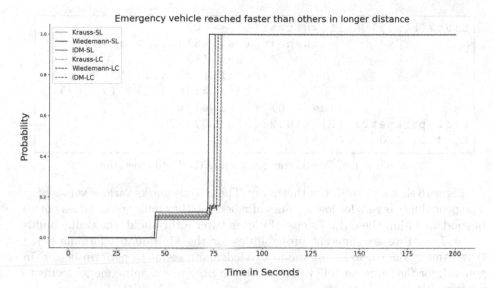

Fig. 5. Probability that emergency vehicle (ambulance) will reach its destination faster than others - longer distance

This probability increases with an increase in the distance from source to destination. This is observed in all the lane changing and car-following models. In fact, for longer distances, the probability that the emergency vehicle reaches much ahead of the normal vehicle approaches one for lighter traffic scenarios, see Fig. 5. In this case, the jump in probability occurs even before the higher traffic injection regime kicks in. The consequence of the regime change at 50 time units is apparent earlier than the previous short distance experiment.

4.3 Query 2: Traffic Load Comparison

Through this query, we demonstrate the use of the *Until* operator of temporal logic systems like PCTL and CSL, for analyzing traffic problems. The query that we show is merely illustrative, several other queries that enable insightful what-if analysis are possible.

Consider two intersections I_1 and I_2. Define "instantaneous traffic volume" at an intersection to be the instantaneous number of vehicles within 500 m of the intersection in all four directions put together. Suppose we wish to ascertain that the traffic volume at intersection I_1 is less (denote it by the propositional formula ϕ_1), until the point the traffic volume is high at the intersection I_2 (denote it by the propositional formula ϕ_2). The temporal logic formula, involving the *Until* fragment, would be $\phi_1 U^{\leq \tau} \phi_2$, for different values of τ. The motivation behind such a query would be to ensure that both intersections are not heavily loaded at the same time. Following is the MultiQuatex formulation of the query:

```
t1Ut2(k,x,y) = if ( s.rval(0) <= k)
                  then if ( s.rval(11) > x )
                        then (1)
                        else if ( s.rval(10) <= y )
                        then #t1Ut2((k),(x),(y))
                  else   (0) fi fi else (0) fi ;
eval parametric(E[ t1Ut2((k),(20),(15)) ],
k, 1.0, 1.0, 200.0);
```

Listing 1.6. Parametric query using the Until Operator

Figure 6 shows the result of this query. The x−axis marks various values of τ. The probability is zero for lower values of τ because the traffic volume does not go beyond 15 within these time-steps. However, after a threshold, the traffic builds up at I_2 and we see different probabilities for the Multiquatex formula being true. Among the car following models, Wiedemann seems to perform better. In general, for the same car-following model, the SL lane-changing model seems to perform better.

For higher values of τ, the probability for the Krauss car-following model remains low for both lane-changing models. As the simulation proceeds, the traffic at intersection I_2 does increase beyond 20. However, the traffic load at I_1 also increases beyond 15, thus evaluating the formula to *false*.

Interestingly, when the traffic stabilizes after the change of the traffic injection rate regime, the probability-estimate stabilizes for all car-following and lane-changing models.

4.4 Query 3: Load Conditions for Traffic Jams

Car-following and lane-changing models can differ in their ability of handling traffic loads without causing traffic jams.

Our next query analyzes this ability: What is the minimum traffic load that causes the number vehicles waiting at an intersection go above a threshold?

```
minJam(x,th) = if ( s.rval(0) >= x)
                  then if ( s.rval(3) > th )
                        then (s.rval(15))
                        else (0) fi
                  else #minJam((x),(th)) fi;
  wVeh(x) = if(s.rval(0)>= x)
               then (s.rval(3))
            else #wVeh((x)) fi;
eval parametric(E[ minJam((k,5))],
E[wVeh(k)], k, 1.0, 1.0, 200.0);
```

Listing 1.7. Minimum traffic load to jam traffic flow

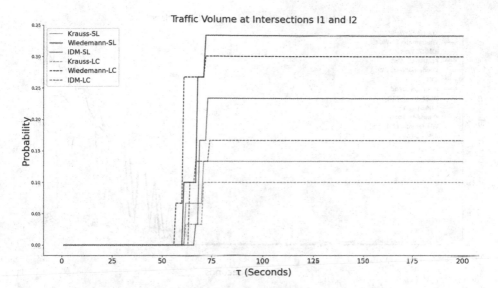

Fig. 6. Probability that the "traffic volume" at I_1 is less than 15 *Until* the traffic volume at I_2 is greater than 20.

Figure 7 shows the results of this query. As before, the x-axis marks time, but we have two sets of curves for each car-following/lane-changing combination. The dashed curves indicate the number of vehicles waiting at the intersections, while the solid curves indicate the total number of vehicles on the road network. For this query, IDM-LC2013 and IDM-SL2015 perform better–the number of vehicles on the road network is higher for the same approximately the same number of vehicles waiting at the intersections. We see dips in the number of vehicles occasionally as vehicles reach their destinations. Since these dips occur earlier, it also indicates that the IDM-SL2015 combination has higher throughput under the regimes in consideration.

4.5   Query 4: Impending Drop in Traffic

The *neXt* operator of various temporal logics allows to query about the state of the system in the "next" step.

In the context of traffic modeling and prediction, a natural question would be about the state of the traffic at the next step. We therefore ask the following query in Multiquatex: what is the probability that the traffic volume falls to 95% of the current volume in the next step? Such a drop is possible if the rate of vehicle injection into the traffic is low. If there is an increasing (or even constant, but high) traffic load, then probability of the volume dropping significantly would be expected to be low.

Listing 1.8 details the formal query.

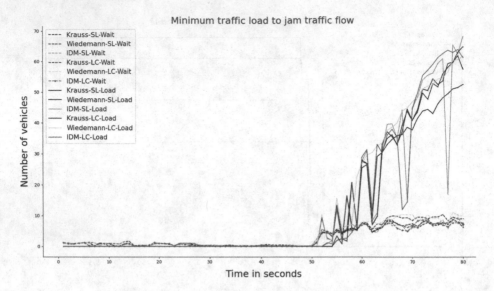

Fig. 7. Minimum traffic load to cause traffic jams

```
TL_DropTo(x,p) = if ( s.rval(0) >= x )
                    then (if(( s.rval(21) - s.rval(15))/
                              s.rval(21) >= p)
                         then (1)
                         else (0) fi)
                    else #TL_DropTo((x),(p)) fi ;
eval parametric( E[ TL_DropTo((x),(0.05)) ],
  x, 0.0, 10.0, 400.0);
```

Listing 1.8. Query for probability that the traffic volume drops to 95 percentage in the "next step"

For illustration, we fluctuate the traffic in SUMO to the effect. The results are shown in Fig. 8. Recall that for this experiment, we use four regimes of Poisson arrival of vehicles into the road network. Initially, since the rate of arrival of the vehicles is very small (50 vehicles per hour), and several of the vehicles reach their destinations, the traffic load dips with a high probability for all car-following/lane-changing combinations. Subsequently, a steadily increasing traffic volume results in a reduction in the probability that the volume drops to 95%. However, when the rate of injection of traffic drops down to 20 vehicles per hour in the next regime, this probability rises. It turns out that this drop in traffic injection rate is not sufficient to sustain the higher probability and it dips again. Since the subsequent regimes are of higher traffic injection rate, it continues to stay at 0.

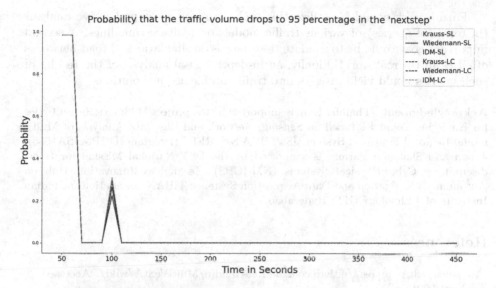

Fig. 8. Probability that the traffic volume drops to 95% in the "next step"

4.0 Running Times

We ran all our experiments on a system with the following configuration: RAM 16 GB, Intel Core i5-8250U processor at 1.60 GHz × 8, and 64-bit Ubuntu 20.04 operating system.

With this configuration, the running times are shown in Table 1. These running times include the simulation overhead as well as the query evaluation time. As one would expect, for a narrow confidence interval ±δ, the required number of simulations is higher. Consequently, the running time is also higher.

Table 1. Running times in minutes

Parameters	Query 1 (Mins)		Query 2 (Mins)	Query 4 (Mins)
	Shorter	Longer		
a = 0.1, d1 = 0.1	4.31	6.68	5.83	3.81
a = 0.1, d1 = 0.5	0.47	0.48	0.29	0.42

5 Conclusion and Future Work

In this paper, we introduce the technique of statistical model checking to traffic modeling and simulation. We demonstrate its potential by comparing combinations of various car-following and lane-changing models that are supported by SUMO. We believe that the tool chain described in the paper will help traffic engineers in analyzing micro-simulation models and performing what-if analyses.

Future work would be utilize this tool chain for a comprehensive analysis (in terms of queries) of various traffic models on realistic time-lines. A second important goal would be to validate the analysis on simulations of road-networks of cities in the real-world. Finally, an in-depth causal analysis of the results of such queries would yield insights into traffic problems and solutions.

Acknowledgment. Thamilselvam is supported by the project M2Smart: Smart Cities for Emerging Countries based on Sensing, Network and Big Data Analysis of Multimodal Regional Transport System, JST/JICA SATREPS (Program ID JPMJSA1606), Japan and Shubham Parmar is supported by the DST National Mission for Interdisciplinary Cyber-Physical Systems (NM-ICPS), Technology Innovation Hub on Autonomous Navigation and Data Acquisition Systems: TiHAN Foundations at Indian Institute of Technology (IIT) Hyderabad.

References

1. MultiVeStA. https://github.com/andrea-vandin/MultiVeStA/wiki/. Accessed 28 Sept 2021
2. Simulation of Urban MObility. https://www.eclipse.org/sumo/. Accessed 06 Aug 2021
3. Agha, G., Palmskog, K.: A survey of statistical model checking. ACM Trans. Model. Comput. Simul. (TOMACS) **28**(1), 6 (2018)
4. Agha, G.A., Meseguer, J., Sen, K.: PMaude: rewrite-based specification language for probabilistic object systems. Electron. Notes Theor. Comput. Sci. **153**(2), 213–239 (2006)
5. Ahmed, H.U., Huang, Y., Lu, P.: A review of car-following models and modeling tools for human and autonomous-ready driving behaviors in micro-simulation. Smart Cities **4**(1), 314–335 (2021)
6. AlTurki, M., Meseguer, J.: PVESTA: a parallel statistical model checking and quantitative analysis tool. In: Corradini, A., Klin, B., Cîrstea, C. (eds.) CALCO 2011. LNCS, vol. 6859, pp. 386–392. Springer, Heidelberg (2011). https://doi.org/10.1007/978-3-642-22944-2_28
7. Baier, C., Katoen, J.P.: Principles of Model Checking (Representation and Mind Series). The MIT Press, Boston (2008)
8. Erdmann, J.: Lane-changing model in SUMO. In: Proceedings of the SUMO 2014 Modeling Mobility with Open Data, vol. 24, May 2014
9. Erdmann, J.: SUMO's lane-changing model. In: Behrisch, M., Weber, M. (eds.) Modeling Mobility with Open Data. LNM, pp. 105–123. Springer, Cham (2015). https://doi.org/10.1007/978-3-319-15024-6_7
10. Kanagaraj, V., Asaithambi, G., Kumar, C.N., Srinivasan, K.K., Sivanandan, R.: Evaluation of different vehicle following models under mixed traffic conditions. Proc. Soc. Behav. Sci. **104**, 390–401 (2013). 2nd Conference of Transportation Research Group of India (2nd CTRG)
11. Krauß, S., Wagner, P., Gawron, C.: Metastable states in a microscopic model of traffic flow. Phys. Rev. E **55**(5), 5597 (1997)
12. Lopez, P.A., et al.: Microscopic traffic simulation using sumo. In: The 21st IEEE International Conference on Intelligent Transportation Systems. IEEE, November 2018

13. Mintsis, E., et al.: TransAID deliverable 3.1 - modelling, simulation and assessment of vehicle automations and automated vehicles' driver behaviour in mixed traffic, September 2019
14. Nimal, V.: Statistical approaches for probabilistic model checking. Ph.D. thesis, University of Oxford (2010)
15. Olstam, J., Tapani, A.: Comparison of car-following models. In: VTI meddelande 960A (2004)
16. Pourabdollah, M., Bjärkvik, E., Fürer, F., Lindenberg, B., Burgdorf, K.: Calibration and evaluation of car following models using real-world driving data. In: 2017 IEEE 20th International Conference on Intelligent Transportation Systems (ITSC), pp. 1–6 (2017)
17. Sebastio, S., Vandin, A.: Multivesta: statistical model checking for discrete event simulators. In: Horváth, A., Buchholz, P., Cortellessa, V., Muscariello, L., Squillante, M.S. (eds.) 7th International Conference on Performance Evaluation Methodologies and Tools, ValueTools 2013, pp. 310–315. ICST/ACM (2013)
18. Sen, K., Viswanathan, M., Agha, G.: Statistical model checking of black-box probabilistic systems. In: Alur, R., Peled, D.A. (eds.) CAV 2004. LNCS, vol. 3114, pp. 202–215. Springer, Heidelberg (2004). https://doi.org/10.1007/978-3-540-27813-9_16
19. Sen, K., Viswanathan, M., Agha, G.A.: VESTA: a statistical model-checker and analyzer for probabilistic systems. In: Second International Conference on the Quantitative Evaluaiton of Systems (QEST 2005), 19-22 September 2005, Torino, Italy, pp. 251–252. IEEE Computer Society (2005)
20. Thamilselvam, B., Kalyanasundaram, S., Rao, M.V.P.: Scalable coordinated intelligent traffic light controller for heterogeneous traffic scenarios using UPPAAL STRATEGO. In: 2021 International Conference on COMmunication Systems NETworkS (COMSNETS), pp. 404–412 (2021)
21. Treiber, M., Hennecke, A., Helbing, D.: Congested traffic states in empirical observations and microscopic simulations. Phys. Rev. E **62**(2), 1805 (2000)
22. Wiedemann, R.: Simulation des strassenverkehrsflusses. Institut fur Verkehrswesen der Universitat Karlsruhe (1994)
23. Younes, H.L.S., Kwiatkowska, M., Norman, G., Parker, D.: Numerical vs. statistical probabilistic model checking: an empirical study. In: Jensen, K., Podelski, A. (eds.) TACAS 2004. LNCS, vol. 2988, pp. 46–60. Springer, Heidelberg (2004). https://doi.org/10.1007/978-3-540-24730-2_4
24. Younes, H.L.S., Simmons, R.G.: Probabilistic verification of discrete event systems using acceptance sampling. In: Brinksma, E., Larsen, K.G. (eds.) CAV 2002. LNCS, vol. 2404, pp. 223–235. Springer, Heidelberg (2002). https://doi.org/10.1007/3-540-45657-0_17

Visual Specification of Properties for Robotic Designs

Waldeck Lindoso Jr.$^{(\boxtimes)}$, Sidney C. Nogueira, Renato Domingues, and Lucas Lima

Departamento de Computação, Universidade Federal Rural de Pernambuco, Recife, PE, Brazil
{waldeck.lindoso,sidney.nogueira,renato.domingues,lucas.albertins}@ufrpe.br

Abstract. RoboChart is a diagrammatic notation based on UML designed for modelling robotic software that has well-defined semantics in the notation of CSP process algebra, enabling the automatic proof of process refinements using the FDR tool. Although RoboChart allows the specification of the robot software, the definition of application-specific properties of RoboChart models must be specified using the CSP notation. Thus, the designer must be familiar with CSP to define and verify properties. This work proposes an approach for the automatic verification of properties using a diagrammatic notation that expresses the behaviour of RoboChart models. The approach proposes a diagrammatic notation based on UML activity diagrams that support the specification of behaviour mixing standard elements of the activity diagram with elements of RoboChart as events and operations. The diagram behaviour is formalised as a CSP process used to verify the properties of a RoboChart component. A plug-in for the Astah modelling tool has been developed to translate the diagram to CSP and call the FDR refinement checker, which verifies whether the RoboChart model refines the property specified with the proposed notation. Our proposed approach allows the designer to specify and verify properties of RoboChart models using diagrammatic notations with no knowledge of the underlying formal semantics.

Keywords: RoboChart properties · Activity diagram · Astah · CSP · FDR

1 Introduction

In the context of critical systems, where failures can result in serious problems, such as the loss of human lives or financial loss, it is crucial to ensure that robot software satisfies the expected properties.

Due to the high complexity of robots controller software, several DSL (Specific Domain Languages) for modelling and simulation [1, 4, 14] for robots have been proposed to support the validation and verification of robotic controllers. Test and simulation are often used to verify robots. However, they can not ensure

S. Campos and M. Minea (Eds.): SBMF 2021, LNCS 13130, pp. 34–52, 2021.
https://doi.org/10.1007/978-3-030-92137-0_0

that the system has the properties expected. Thus, formal verification techniques become fundamental to ensure the properties.

RoboChart [11] is a DSL that uses a diagrammatic notation based on state machines notation from UML (Unified Modelling Language) to describe robot behaviour. The properties of RoboChart models are verified through formal verification; this contrasts with DSLs for robotics designed for simulation. RoboTool[1] provides a graphic editor for RoboChart and automatically generates the CSP (Communicating Sequential Processes) [15] specification for RoboChart models. This tool is integrated with the FDR refinement checker [5] that proves classical properties (for instance, deadlock freedom), as well as application-specific properties that are stated as process refinement assertions. A property is defined as a set of behaviours that the behaviour of the RoboChart model must refine.

A current limitation of RoboTool is that the specification of application properties is defined in the notation of CSP; properties are defined as CSP processes whose alphabet follows the encoding for RoboChart. The property designer must be familiar with CSP operators and the CSP alphabet representing the RoboChart elements relevant to the property. As reported in [12], unfamiliarity with formal notations can result in challenges for RoboTool users during the verification process. Since RoboChart is a diagrammatic notation, it would be more convenient to express properties using some diagrammatic notation that hides details of the CSP semantics and is similar to some well-accepted modelling language.

Activity diagrams have been used for a variety of purposes. Business and system analysts use them to specify business processes, use cases and document the implementation of system processes. Moreover, they can be used to model algorithms given the expressivity of their constructors that allows the modelling of condition, loop and concurrent behaviours. These features make such notation suitable for specifying system properties that must be refined by valid models, which is the goal of the current work.

This work defines a language based on the notation of activity diagrams of UML that allows the specification of application-specific properties for RoboChart. The language abstracts the internal structure of the components and aims at expressing the expected order for inputs, outputs and operations calls of RoboChart components. The proposed notation mix nodes of an activity diagram with nodes that are specialised for expressing RoboChart events and operations. In addition, the language introduces stereotypes that express two common patterns of behaviour that ease the specification of properties. The language has well-defined semantics in the notation of CSP that has the same encoding of RoboChart semantics; this enables the automatic verification of properties using FDR. Properties can be authored using the Astah UML tool[2]. Moreover, a plug-in for Astah has been developed to translate the property diagram to CSP and call FDR to verify the property in the target RoboChart element. A preliminary validation consisted of expressing CSP properties for RoboChart models

---

[1] https://robostar.cs.york.ac.uk/robotool/.
[2] https://astah.net/products/astah-uml/.

with the proposed notation and checking whether the semantics of the original property matches the semantics of the property in the proposed language.

The next section overviews the background for this work. Section 3 presents syntax and semantics for the language for specifying properties. Section 4 details the tool support developed to automatise the translation of the property to CSP and its verification. Section 5 discusses related work. Finally, Sect. 6 concludes and presents future works.

2 Background

In this section, we present the RoboChart language. We also discuss UML activity diagrams and the CSP notation.

2.1 RoboChart

RoboChart models specify the behaviour of a software that controls and interacts with a robotic platform (hardware). A module is the RoboChart component that specifies the flow of events between software controllers and a robotic platform. Controller behaviour is specified by state machines. Input and outputs events, as well as operation calls, are possible observations for a module, controller and state machine. Naturally, properties for a RoboChart consider the expected order of such observations. Due to space restrictions, we focus on the notation for a state machine that is used to illustrate the property language proposed by this work. Further details on the notation of RoboChart refer to [11].

Figure 1 presents the state machine model for a simple mobile robot that changes directions when an obstacle is detected. This state machine defines the behaviour of a controller that interacts with the robotic platform. It is an adaptation of the model that can be found in the RoboCalc website[3].

A robotic platform abstracts the hardware that is controlled by software. Hardware is abstracted through variables, constants, operations and events. In our example, the platform specifies an operation move that receives two parameters: lv and av. They represent linear and angular movements of the robot. Such an operation is part of the interface MovementI provided by the platform. Events represent atomic communications. In our example, the event obstacle is an input event coming from the platform; it represents the robot encounters a obstacle and needs to dodge, thus avoiding a collision. This event is part of the interface ObstacleI that is defined by the platform.

The state machine SMovement requires the interface MovimentI and uses the interface ObstacleI. Moreover, it defines the constants lv and av. The value for the constants is defined at the time the CSP specification is generated by RoboTool.

Each state machine is composed of states, junctions and transitions. States can have actions: entry, during and exit. In the SMovement state machine, the initial node leads to the state Moving, which has an entry action that calls

---

[3] https://www.cs.york.ac.uk/circus/RoboCalc/other_examples/SimFW/index.html.

the operation move(lv,0) that makes the robot to perform a linear movement (av equals zero). When an obstacle is detected, the event obstacle triggers a transition that leads to the Turning state. The Turning state has an entry action that executes an angular movement move(0,av), causing the robot to rotate, dodging the obstacle. In sequence, a transition to the Moving state is triggered.

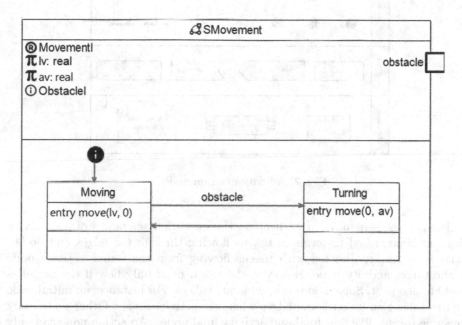

Fig. 1. SimFW robot state machine

2.2   UML Activity Diagram

A UML activity diagram is a graph of activity nodes interconnected by activity edges [13]. An activity node can be either an action node, an object node or a control node. Activity edges are directed connections between two activity nodes. They can be either a control flow used to sequence the execution of activity nodes explicitly or an object flow, which can communicate data between two nodes. Action nodes execute the desired behaviour when ready, including sending or receiving signals or invoking another activity. Object nodes explicitly hold objects that arrive in their incoming edges and offers them to the outgoing edges. Control nodes organise the order flows are traversed. They act as "traffic switches" across the activity edges. Nodes and edges can be grouped in swimlanes (or partitions), used to organise parts of flows. They can be vertical or horizontal, and their primary purpose is to delimit boundaries of responsibility for each group of behaviour. Figure 2 shows all types of control nodes, some of the main types of action nodes and object nodes grouped by their swimlanes.

The descriptive semantics for each constructor can be seen in the UML specification [13].

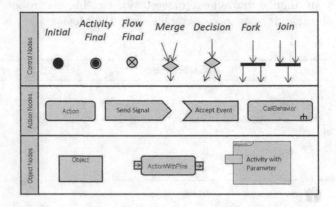

Fig. 2. Activity diagram nodes.

Besides the semantics of each node, the execution semantics of an activity diagram is described in terms of tokens flowing through the edges and nodes. Activity edges are directed with tokens flowing from the source activity node to the target activity node. However, the token must only flow if the target is ready to accept it. Some nodes may generate tokens. For instance, an initial node creates tokens on its outgoing edges when the activity starts. Other nodes only consume tokens, like flow final and activity final nodes. An action node can only be executed once all incoming edges are offering tokens, and when it terminates, it must offer tokens in its outgoing edges.

Finally, an activity diagram can only terminate in two scenarios: if no active tokens are flowing through the activity after it has been started, or if an activity final node has consumed a token. In the latter case, all current flows are halted.

2.3 CSP Notation, Templates and Tools Used in the Work

The CSP process algebra is very expressive to specify systems composed of interacting components. In CSP, a process is the basic unit for describing behaviour. It is defined in terms of events and other processes. The function $\alpha(P)$ yields the alphabet of a process P, that is, the events that the process P may communicate. The primitive process *SKIP* represents successful termination. The process $a \rightarrow P$ offers the event a to the environment and then behaves as the process P. CSP channels abstract a set of events with a common prefix. The syntax $c?x$ represents the channel c inputs a value x, such that $x \in A$, which is the type for the channel c. The value for x is chosen by the environment. The syntax $c.e$ $(c!e)$ represents an expression $e \in A$ is communicated through the channel c. The sequential composition $P1; P2$ behaves like the process $P1$ and, provided it terminates successfully, $P2$ takes over. The CSP notation has no explicit operator for recursion, but it allows one to use the name of the process in its definition. For instance, the process $P = a \rightarrow P$ communicates the event a and then behaves as P.

The external choice $P1 \square P2$ initially offers events of both processes $P1$ and $P2$. The communication of the first event resolves the choice in favour of the process that performs it. The parallel composition $P1 \,[\![\, cs \,]\!]\, P2$ synchronise $P1$ and $P2$ on the events in the set cs; events not in cs occur independently. Processes composed in interleaving $P1 \,|||\, P2$ progress in parallel without synchronisation. The event hiding operator $P \backslash cs$ internalises the events that belong to the set cs, which become no longer visible to the environment. The interruption operator ($\triangle$) allows a process to be interrupted by another. The process $P \triangle Q$ behaves as P until Q communicates an event. When this happens, we say that P has been interrupted by Q.

The traces of a process P, say $traces(P)$, is the set of possible sequences of events performed by P. We can compare the traces of two processes using a refinement assertion denoted by $P \sqsubseteq_\tau Q$. Such an assertion holds if, and only if, $traces(Q) \subseteq traces(P)$. The FDR tool [5] verifies process refinement as well as classical properties like deadlock and nondeterminism.

3   Diagrammatic Language for Properties

The visual language to specify properties of RoboChart models allows the definition of the expected order for inputs, outputs and operation calls of RoboChart components. Properties defined with this language are used to define the possible behaviours a component can perform. A property is valid if the behaviour of the component is a subset of the behaviour of the property. Consider P_Prop is the CSP process that represents the semantics of a visual property Prop. The property Prop holds in a RoboChart component named CName if, and only if, the traces for a component is a subset of the traces of the property. Formally.

$$P\_Prop \sqsubseteq_\tau P\_CName$$

The remaining of this section presents the syntax and the semantics of the language.

3.1   Language Syntax

The language for properties is based on the notation of UML activity diagrams. Standard activity diagram nodes (Fig. 2) can mixed with specialised nodes and stereotypes to specify the expected flow of observations for a RoboChart component. Table 1 shows the notation of the proposed language.

First row in Table 1 shows the diagram that represents a RoboChart property has a unique swimlane with the same of the RoboChart component (state

Table 1. Property notation

N°	Notation	Description
1	CName	Swimlane with the nodes of the property
2	op(p1, ..., pn)	Operation **op** with parameters **p1,...,pn**
3	i	Simple input i
4	o	Simple output o
5	i(v)	Input i with value v
6	o(v)	Output o with value v
7	v : S / i	Input i with value v within S
8	v : S / o	Output o with value v within S
9	<<UNTIL>>	Edge with <<UNTIL>> stereotype
10	<<ANY>> Don't care	Call behaviour with <<ANY>> stereotype

machine, controller or module). Inside the swimlane are the nodes that specify
the property. A call to a RoboChart operation *op* with parameters *p1, ..., pn*
is represented as an action in the property language (Row 2). Furthermore, a
RoboChart input (output) event *i* (*o*) that does not communicate values is represented in the property language as an accept event (send signal)—Rows 3 and
4. If the input (output) communicates a value *v*, such a value is put between
parenthesis—Rows 5 and 6. The property language allows the specification of the
range of input (output) values using an output (input) pin. Consider S is a set
of values that is a subset of the values for the input (output) event *i* (*o*) defined
in the RoboChart model. Rows 7 and 8 of Table 1 show how to specify a range
of values for input (and outputs). The stereotype ≪UNTIL≫ labels edges that
target a send signal, an accept event or an operation—Row 9. This stereotype

specifies that the diagram performs any possible observation in the RoboChart component, between the source node and the target node (except the target node event/operation). If the diagram executes the target node event/operation, the diagram follows the outgoing edge of the target node. The stereotype ≪ANY≫ labels call behaviours—Row 10. When the diagram executes a call behaviour with this stereotype, any sequence of observation in the context of the component can be performed by the diagram.

There is an important difference in the meaning of a signal sending and receipt in the property language and the original meaning in the activity diagram. The original meaning is that a send signal synchronises with an accept event. In the proposed property language nodes do not synchronise. This will more explicit in the next section that presents the semantics for the language.

Considering the combination of the standard nodes for activity diagram and the introduced abstraction patterns, it is possible to define a range of properties using the proposed notation. We illustrate the usage of the notation with examples.

Figure 3 illustrates a property, say Angular, for the SMovement state machine. This property specifies that whenever the robot receives an obstacle event, it turns to avoid a collision with a constant angular speed. We explain how this property is expressed using the proposed notation. The diagram starts with a merge node with a control edge with the stereotype ≪UNTIL≫. This edge targets a signal receipt node that represents the reception of the obstacle event. As explained, this stereotype specifies that any observation can happen in the RoboChart model before the obstacle event. After the obstacle, the move operation must happen with the parameters 0 and 2, and the pattern repeats. If the designer wants to specify that the move operation eventually happens, then the edge between the obstacle event and the move operation should have the UNTIL stereotype.

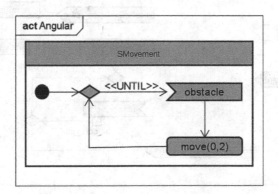

Fig. 3. Property for SimFW.

To validate the proposed language, we modelled properties for RoboChart models found in the literature. For instance, we could specify some of the properties verified in [3] for the Solar Panel Vacuum Cleaner (SPVC) RoboChart model. Figure 4 is a sample property (ReturnToCharge) for the State Machine PathPlanningSM of the SPVC RoboChart model. This model and its properties encoded in CSP, including the one we modelled in Fig. 4, are available on the RoboTool website[4]. Due to space restrictions, we do not present the complete diagram for ReturnToCharge; the omitted part has been replaced by a call behaviour with the ≪ANY≫ stereotype. Such a property specifies the robot returns to the docking station and begins charging if the battery level is low. The initial behaviour of the diagram is to communicate all possible inputs, outputs and operations in PathPlanningSM, except the input battery_level. Whenever the value b associated with the battery level is less or equal to zero, the robot will turn left two times, move forward and disable the clean mode (set as false). At this point, the property enters a loop that repeats while the value u from the input ultrasonic is less than one. The loop exits if the value is greater than or equal to one. The behaviour after the loop is to get the left direction, move forward, charge the battery and repeat the behaviour after the first merge node. If the battery level is greater than zero, the robot turns left. From this point on, the robot can perform any possible input, output or operation.

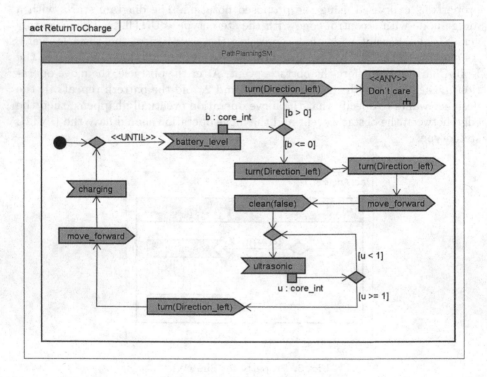

Fig. 4. Property for PathPlanningSM

[4] https://robostar.cs.york.ac.uk/case_studies/RoboVacuum/index.html.

3.2   Language Semantics

We adapt the compositional semantics in [6] for activities to represent properties. Let $ACTIVITY$ be the a process that represents an activity, and α_C the set of control events of this process. The process $PROP$ formalises the semantics for a property; it is defined as the parallel composition of the processes $ACTIVITY$, and the interleaving of auxiliary processes used in the semantics of stereotypes $\ll$UNTIL$\gg$ and $\ll$ANY$\gg$. This interleaving is interrupted by the process $endDiagram \rightarrow SKIP$. This last event is communicated by the process $ACTIVITY$ to indicate the conclusion of the diagram. The composition synchronises on control events that belong to the channels $begin$, end, $chaos$ and $endDiagram$. The first three channels are used to specify the behaviour of the stereotypes, the last channel belongs to α_C. The channels $begin$ and end are in the synchronisation set if the stereotype $\ll$UNTIL$\gg$ is used in the definition of the property. The channel $chaos$ is in the synchronisation set if the stereotype $\ll$ANY$\gg$ is used.

$$
\begin{aligned}
PROP = (\ &ACTIVITY \\
&[|\ |\ begin, end, chaos, endDiagram\ |\ |] \\
&(|||\ P : AUXILIARY \bullet P \vartriangle endDiagram \rightarrow SKIP) \\
)\ &\backslash\ \alpha_C \cup \{|\ begin, end, chaos\ |\}
\end{aligned}
$$

The process $ACTIVITY$ represents the behaviour of an activity adapted to represent RoboChart observations as inputs, outputs and operation calls.

$$
\begin{aligned}
ACTIVITY = (\ &startActivity \rightarrow SKIP;\ Nodes;\ endDiagram \rightarrow SKIP) \\
&|[|\ update, clear, endDiagram\ |]| \\
&TokenManager
\end{aligned}
$$

The behaviour of $ACTIVITY$ is the parallel composition of the nodes and the $TokenManager$ process. An activity starts when the $startActivity$ event is communicated, then it behaves as the process $Nodes$. The $startActivity$ event may receive input data required by the activity parameter nodes. As soon as an activity terminates, it communicates the $endActivity$ event with the data available in its output parameter nodes. The underlying semantics of activity diagrams is described by the flow of tokens from a node to another. The process $TokenManager$ tracks the number of active tokens (flows) of the diagram and controls termination of the activity. We omit the definition of such a process since it has the same specification presented in [6].

According to UML semantics, an activity is described in terms of nodes and edges between the nodes. In our CSP semantics, these elements are represented by processes and events, respectively. The process $Nodes$ is the parallel composition of the processes that represent each node. Node processes synchronise on the events that represent edges. The outgoing edge of a node is the incoming edge of another node. Control edges are represented by events in the form $ce.id$ and object edges by events in the form $oe.id$, such that id is the edge identifier.

For instance, if there is a control edge $ce.1$ between two nodes $N1$ and $N2$, the event $ce.1$ is part of the synchronisation alphabet of both processes. Events in the form $ce.id$ and $oe.id$ belong to α_C, and are not visible because events in α_C are hidden in the process $PROP$.

We present the semantics for the nodes whose semantics are particular to property language in what follows. Nodes that are not presented here keep the semantics presented in [6].

We start showing the semantics for a node named Node that represents an operation call, a input or an output (Rows 2–6 in Table 1). The process P_Node represents the formal semantics for such nodes. Let $\{m..n\}$ be the range of indices for the incoming edges of the node, and $\{u..t\}$ the range of indices for the outgoing edges. The semantics of these nodes is to wait for the communication of the incoming edges, then to communicate an event in the form $CName :: event$. After communicating the event, the behaviour is to wait for the communication of the outgoing edges and to behave as P_Node. The wait for the incoming (outgoing) edges is specified as the interleaving of the communication of the events for the edges followed by a successful termination. In CSP, the parallel composition only terminates if all the processes in the composition do terminate.

$$
\begin{aligned}
P\_Node = \ & (ce.m \rightarrow SKIP \ ||| \ \dots \ ||| \ ce.n \rightarrow SKIP); \\
& CName :: event \rightarrow SKIP; \\
& (ce.u \rightarrow SKIP \ ||| \ \dots \ ||| \ ce.t \rightarrow SKIP); \\
& P\_Node
\end{aligned}
$$

The value for $event$ has a particular format for each kind of node. The string for $event$ equals $op.p1...pn$ if Node represents an operation op with parameters p1,...,pn. It equals $i.in.v$ ($o.out.v$) if the node represents an input (output) named i (o) with value v. And, equals $i.in$ ($o.out$) if the node represents a simple input (output) named i (o). For instance, $obstacle.in$ is the event for the signal receipt node and $move.0.2$ is the event for the action node in Fig. 3.

Nodes that specify a range of input (output) have a similar semantics. The difference to P_Node is that the CSP event $i.in.v$ ($o.out.v$) is replaced by $i.in?v$ ($o.out?v$). Moreover, the outgoing control edges $ce.i$, such that $u \le i \le t$, are replaced by object edges $oe.i!v$.

Next, we discuss the semantics for nodes reached by an edge with the stereotype ≪UNTIL≫ and for a call behaviour node with the stereotype ≪ANY≫. These two kinds of nodes synchronise with the process $AUXILIARY$ (recall the definition of $PROP$) in the events of the channels $begin$, end and $chaos$. Nodes reached by an edge with the stereotype ≪UNTIL≫ communicate events $begin.id$ and $end.id$, and call behaviour nodes with the stereotype ≪ANY≫ communicate $chaos.id$ events. The value for id is unique for each usage of ≪UNTIL≫ and ≪ANY≫. Let $A\_PROCESSES$ be the set of auxiliary processes. Moreover, let the expression $||| \ P : S \bullet P$ be equivalent to the process $P_1 \ ||| \ \dots \ ||| \ P_n$, for $S = \{P_1, \dots, P_n\}$. The semantics for $AUXILIARY$ is the interleaving of the processes in $A\_PROCESSES$ interrupted by the event $endDiagram$.

$$AUXILIARY = (\left|\right|\left|\right| A : A\_PROCESSES \bullet A) \triangle endDiagram \rightarrow SKIP$$

The definition for an auxiliary process depends on the stereotype. We show the semantics for auxiliary processes in what follows.

The process *CallBehaviour* formalises the semantics for a call behaviour node with the ≪ANY≫ stereotype (Row 10 in Table 1). Such a process waits for the communication of the incoming edges, then communicates *chaos.id* and behave as *CallBehaviour*.

$$\begin{aligned}CallBehaviour = &(ce.m \rightarrow SKIP \left|\right|\left|\right| \ldots \left|\right|\left|\right| ce.n \rightarrow SKIP);\\ &chaos.id \rightarrow SKIP;\\ &CallBehaviour\end{aligned}$$

Consider $\square\ ev : S \bullet ev \rightarrow P$ is equivalent to the choice $ev_1 \rightarrow P$ $\square$ $\ldots \square\ ev_k \rightarrow P$, for $S = \{ev_1, \ldots, ev_k\}$. The process $RUN(S) = \square\ ev : S \bullet cv \rightarrow RUN(S)$ is the CSP process that produces the traces in S^*. Moreover, let P_CName be the CSP process that formalises the untimed semantics of RoboChart component CName. The process $AUX1 = chaos.1 \rightarrow RUN(\alpha(P\_CName))$ represents the auxiliary process for a node with the ≪ANY≫ stereotype. This process synchronises with the process *CallBehaviour* in the *chaos.id* event and behaves as the process $RUN(\alpha(P\_CName))$.

The semantics for a node that is reached by an edge with the ≪UNTIL≫ stereotype (Row 9 in Table 1) is formalised by the process $Until\_Node^5$. Only three kinds of nodes can be reached by an edge with ≪UNTIL≫: send signal (output), an accept event (input) or an action (operation). The semantics for such a node is to wait for the communication of the event for the incoming edge, to communicate *begin.id* and *end.id* events, wait for the communication of the outgoing edges, and to behave as *Until_Node*.

$$\begin{aligned}Until\_Node = &(ce.m \rightarrow SKIP);\\ &begin.id \rightarrow end.id \rightarrow SKIP;\\ &(ce.u \rightarrow SKIP \left|\right|\left|\right| \ldots \left|\right|\left|\right| ce.t \rightarrow SKIP);\ Until\_Node\end{aligned}$$

The process $WAIT$ is used in the definition of the auxiliary process for *Until_Node*. Consider the CSP process $Recurse(S, P) = \square\ evt : S \bullet evt \rightarrow P$ that offers a choice of all events in the set S; after the process communicates the event in the choice it behaves as P. The process $WAIT$ is parametrised by the event ev. The behaviour of this process is to communicate the events of the

---

[5] The semantics for the ≪UNTIL≫ stereotype is not equivalent to the until operator used in temporal logics. The expressiveness of CSP refinement and its relation to temporal logics is reported in [7, 16].

alphabet of P_CName except ev, and to behave as $WAIT(ev)$. If the event ev is communicated, the process terminates.

$$WAIT(ev) = Recurse(\alpha(P\_CName)\backslash\{ev\}), WAIT(ev))$$
$$\square$$
$$ev \rightarrow SKIP$$

The process $AUX2$ formalises the auxiliary process for $Until\_Node$. The events of this process synchronise with the same events in the $Until\_Node$. In between these events, it behaves as $WAIT(CName :: event)$.

$$AUX2 = begin.id \rightarrow WAIT(CName :: event); \ end.id \rightarrow AUX1$$

The semantics for a node of any kind has an implicit interruption with the $endDiagram$. The effect of this interruption is that the behaviour of all nodes are interrupted by such an event, whenever the $TokenManager$ process communicates this event. This is kept implicit to simplify the presentation of the semantics.

Consider the function $compose$ that follows. This function is used to specify the composition of a sequence of nodes. The first function parameter is a sequence of process identifiers, and the second is the set of events that have already been used in the synchronisation of the parallel composition. Let α_{id} be the alphabet of control events of a node identified by id. Such a function uses generalised parallel composition to compose the nodes of a property. Synchronisation set of the parallel composition contains the control alphabet of the node to be composed, and the $endDiagram$ event that allows the nodes to terminate together. The synchronisation set excludes the events already used in the composition of previous nodes of the network of processes formed by the already composed nodes.

$$compose(\langle id \rangle, \_) \qquad = Node_{id}$$
$$compose(\langle id \rangle \frown tail, past) = Node_{id}$$
$$\| [(\alpha_{id} \backslash past) \cup \{endDiagram\})] \|$$
$$compose(tail, \alpha_{id} \cup past)$$

The formal definition for the process $Nodes$ is

$$Nodes = compose(seq(Nodes\_IDs), \{\})$$

In such a definition $Nodes\_IDs$ represents the set of identifiers for processes that formalise nodes and seq is a function that converts a set into a sequence.

The order of nodes returned by the function seq is arbitrary; however, the order does not change the semantics of the composition. This holds since the generalised parallel composition operator is associative with different synchronisation alphabets if the synchronisation set between the processes contain the intersection of the alphabets of the processes (refer to [15] for the laws of parallel composition operators).

To illustrate our semantics, we show the process *P_Angular* that captures the semantics of the property Angular in Fig. 3. For conciseness, instead of presenting the syntax of the process obtained by the compositional semantics, we present an equivalent process that has a shorter representation. Let *P_SMovement* be the CSP process that formalises the behaviour of the *SMovement* state machine. The behaviour of *P_Angular* is to recurse if an event different from obstacle is communicated. When an obstacle event happens, then it communicates *SMovement* :: *moveCall*.0.2. In the sequence it behaves as *P_Angular*.

$$P\_Angular = Recurse(\alpha(P\_SMovement) - \{SMovement :: obstacle.in\},$$
$$P\_Angular)$$
$$\square$$
$$SMovement :: obstacle.in \rightarrow SMovement :: moveCall.0.2 \rightarrow$$
$$P\_Angular$$

The property Angular in SMovement holds iff. the following refinement holds.

$$P\_Angular \sqsubseteq_\tau P\_SMovement$$

As explained in Sect. 2.1, the state Turning of the machine *SMovement* performs the call move(0,av). The value for the constants lv and av are defined when the CSP model for the machine *SMovement* is generated by RoboTool. If we consider the values for these constants are 1 and 1, and check the following refinement using the FDR tool, we have that the refinement does not hold and FDR yields the counterexample trace.

$$\langle SMovement :: move(1, 0), SMovement :: obstacle.in, SMovement :: move(0, 1)\rangle$$

However, if the value for the constants is 1 and 2 the refinement does hold, since the CSP untimed semantics for the state machine calls move(0,2) whenever an obstacle is detected.

We used FDR to verify whether the semantics of properties using the proposed language equals the semantics of the original property specified as CSP processes. For instance, we could verify the visual specification for the Return-ToCharge property presented in Sect. 3 is equivalent to the original property written in CSP.

4 Tool Support

Our framework has been implemented as a plug-in for the Astah UML modelling environment, which can be extended by the integration of plug-ins to add new features. Our tool has been built based on another plug-in that verifies properties on activity diagrams [6]. We use the Astah Java API to programmatically read activity diagrams as properties, translate them to CSP and verify properties on RoboChart models using the integration built with FDR.

The developed plug-in is divided into modules, which are: UI, Controller, Parser, FDR Bridge and Traceability. The UI module is responsible for making the connection between the user and the controller through the plug-in menu. The Controller module is responsible for receiving information (commands and diagrams) from the UI module, managing the entire plug-in operation, and returning a response (messages and/or diagrams) to the UI module.

The Parser module is responsible for receiving a diagram from the Controller module, translating it according to the semantics described in Sect. 3.2, and returning a CSP file to the Controller module. In order to analyse this CSP, the user must provide the path to the RoboChart file whose property is being verified.

The FDR Bridge module is responsible for communicating with FDR, using the Java Reflection technique, which allows us to load the FDR API dynamically. It invokes the assertions specified in the CSP file generated by the parser. When the assertion does not hold, it is also responsible for collecting the counterexample returned by FDR (list of events) and returning it to the Controller. In order to make this integration possible, the user has to inform the path to the FDR installation folder. This can be performed by accessing the plug-in UI menu `Tools -> Properties Plug-in Configuration -> FDR Location`.

After modelling the activity diagram as a property and providing the path to the RoboChart file, the user can start the verification process in the menu we

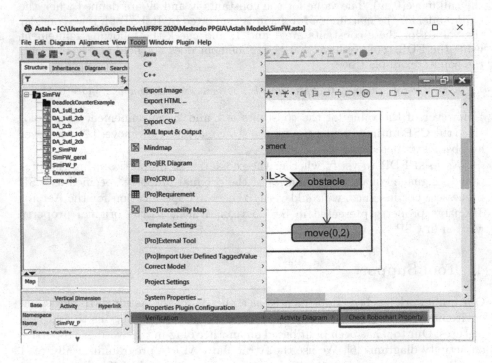

Fig. 5. Checking a RoboChart property in Astah.

have created in Astah as can be seen in Fig. 5. This action triggers the following tasks: the tool generates the corresponding CSP specification (Parser module), loads it in FDR and invokes the assertion that checks if the property is valid in the RoboChart model (FDR Bridge module). If the property does not hold, FDR returns a counterexample trace displaying the sequence of events that led to the violation.

The Traceability module is responsible for receiving an event list (trace) of the Controller module and providing a diagrammatic view of it. It is currently under development and we plan to create a sequence diagram that shows the path traversed by the trace.

5   Related Work

This work focuses on the verification of properties for RoboChart that are expressed in the form of process refinements. This is the first language for the specification of diagrammatic properties for RoboChart models.

Miyazawa et al [10] propose a tool that checks both classical and application-specific properties for RoboChart models that use time constraints. The proposed tool deals with properties with time constraints that are specified as CSP process refinement expressions.

The authors in [3] use RoboChart to model the behaviour of a robotic system and CSP processes to express application-specific properties. Informal requirements are formalised as CSP process refinements expressions that are verified using FDR. Processes that abstract behavioural patterns have been proposed to help the specification of properties. One of these patterns have directly influenced the ≪UNTIL≫ stereotype proposed by our work.

The work [8] surveys notations and verification techniques based on formal methods in the context of autonomous robotic systems. Most of the works propose verification methods that input the specification as a logic formula (for instance, temporal logic [2]). As the semantic domain of RoboChart is CSP, we do not use temporal logic to specify properties but behaviours in terms of processes that the model must refine.

Visual notations have been used previously for the specification of properties [9,12]. Activity diagrams have been used in [9] to specify requirements for logic controllers. Requirements are manually mapped into temporal logic formulas that are used for model checking the system model. The work [12] uses block diagrams to formalise logical properties that are automatically verified using Simulink Design Verifier.

6   Conclusion

We have presented a diagrammatic language based on activity diagrams for reasoning on application-specific properties of RoboChart models. Several diagram elements like swimlanes, actions, pins have been adapted to specify RoboChart observations as events and calls to operations. Furthermore, we have extended activity diagrams with the ≪*UNTIL*≫ and ≪*ANY*≫ stereotypes to increase the expressiveness of the notation. The presented language has compositional semantics in terms of CSP processes, which uses the same encoding for CSP events used in the underlying semantics of RoboChart models. This allows us to verify the specified properties against RoboChart models using FDR. Finally, we have implemented a plug-in for the Astah UML tool to specify these properties using extended activity diagrams and verify them against the specifications of RoboChart models in an automated manner.

The mechanisation of the approach is relevant because the users of RoboTool must specify application-specific properties directly in CSP and check them using FDR. The current work enables RoboChart designers to specify both the system and the properties at the same level of abstraction, given that models and properties use diagrammatic notations. We hope that hiding the formal notation of CSP can facilitate and increase the adoption of RoboChart by the robotics community.

The proposed notation is based on activity diagrams that are very popular and have a repertoire of constructs that allow the specification of a wide range of behaviours. Nonetheless, it is not expressive as the CSP notation that has a richer language. Comparing the expressiveness of the proposed language with the expressiveness of CSP is left as future work.

Application-specific properties over RoboChart models are formulated as process refinement assertions. Different CSP models can be used to verify safety (traces model) and liveness properties (failures-divergence and refusal traces). The properties specified by the proposed language can be verified using any of the existing CSP models; however, this work considered only safety properties. A future plan is to consider other kinds of properties.

Although the properties can be specified using diagrammatic models and analysed in our plug-in, the counterexample is not given at the diagrammatic level when a property does not hold. However, we are implementing a mechanism to provide the counterexample returned by FDR is presented as a sequence diagram. In this approach, instead of reading a sequence of CSP events that may be difficult to map back to the RoboChart model, the user can analyse the trace according to the order of RoboChart events exchanged between the controller being verified and its environment. Moreover, this notation will be similar to the one used to specify the RoboChart model. Another point of improvement is to allow the specification of visual properties in the RoboTool platform instead of using a different tool to model and verify the properties.

Although the CSP specifications generated from our diagrammatic properties are usually larger than those specified directly in CSP, we verified that they have equivalent semantics whenever the corresponding property is available in CSP. Using FDR compression functions, the complexity of CSP specifications is significantly reduced, and this allowed us to perform the analysis at similar times compared to properties specified in CSP. Nevertheless, we plan to perform a more concrete study on scalability in the future.

Our tool supports a considerable number of activity diagram constructors, which allows the designing of potentially elaborated properties. However, we plan to increase this number to augment expressiveness. For instance, we do not cover timing aspects of the properties in the current version of our semantics. At last, we plan to develop more case studies to explore the proposed language and the reasoning strategy.

Acknowledgement. We thank CAPES – Finance Code 001 for partially supporting the authors. We are grateful to Augusto Sampaio and Ana Cavalcanti for discussions and feedbacks. Finally, we thank Madiel Conserva for the support with RoboTool.

References

1. Alexandrova, S., Tatlock, Z., Cakmak, M.: RoboFlow: a flow-based visual programming language for mobile manipulation tasks. In: 2015 IEEE International Conference on Robotics and Automation (ICRA), pp. 5537–5544. IEEE (2015)
2. Clarke, E.M., Emerson, E.A., Sistla, A.P.: Automatic verification of finite-state concurrent systems using temporal logic specifications. ACM Trans. Program. Lang. Syst. **8**(2), 244–263 (1986). https://doi.org/10.1145/5397.5399
3. Darolți, B.: Software engineering for robotics: an autonomous robotic vacuum cleaner for solar panels. Master's thesis, University of York (2019)
4. Dhouib, S., Kchir, S., Stinckwich, S., Ziadi, T., Ziane, M.: RobotML, a domain-specific language to design, simulate and deploy robotic applications. In: Noda, I., Ando, N., Brugali, D., Kuffner, J.J. (eds.) SIMPAR 2012. LNCS (LNAI), vol. 7628, pp. 149–160. Springer, Heidelberg (2012). https://doi.org/10.1007/978-3-642-34327-8_16
5. Gibson-Robinson, T., Armstrong, P., Boulgakov, A., Roscoe, A.W.: FDR3—a modern refinement checker for CSP. In: Ábrahám, E., Havelund, K. (eds.) TACAS 2014. LNCS, vol. 8413, pp. 187–201. Springer, Heidelberg (2014). https://doi.org/10.1007/978-3-642-54862-8_13
6. Lima, L., Tavares, A., Nogueira, S.C.: A framework for verifying deadlock and nondeterminism in UML activity diagrams based on CSP. Sci. Comput. Program. **197**, 102497 (2020). https://doi.org/10.1016/j.scico.2020.102497
7. Lowe, G.: Specification of communicating processes: temporal logic versus refusals-based refinement. Form. Asp. Comput. **20**(3), 277–294 (2008). https://doi.org/10.1007/s00165-007-0065-0
8. Luckcuck, M., Farrell, M., Dennis, L.A., Dixon, C., Fisher, M.: Formal specification and verification of autonomous robotic systems: a survey. ACM Comput. Surv. 52(5) (2019). https://doi.org/10.1145/3342355
9. Menghi, C., Tsigkanos, C., Berger, T., Pelliccione, P.: PsALM: specification of dependable robotic missions. In: 2019 IEEE/ACM 41st International Conference on Software Engineering: Companion Proceedings (ICSE-Companion), pp. 99–102 (2019). https://doi.org/10.1109/ICSE-Companion.2019.00048
10. Miyazawa, A., Ribeiro, P., Li, W., Cavalcanti, A., Timmis, J.: Automatic property checking of robotic applications. In: 2017 IEEE/RSJ International Conference on Intelligent Robots and Systems (IROS), pp. 3869–3876. IEEE (2017)
11. Miyazawa, A., Ribeiro, P., Li, W., Cavalcanti, A., Timmis, J., Woodcock, J.: RoboChart: modelling and verification of the functional behaviour of robotic applications. Softw. Syst. Model. **18**(5), 3097–3149 (2019)

52   W. Lindoso et al.

12. Murray, Y., Anisi, D.A., Sirevåg, M., Ribeiro, P., Hagag, R.S.: Safety assurance of a high voltage controller for an industrial robotic system. In: Carvalho, G., Stolz, V. (eds.) SBMF 2020. LNCS, vol. 12475, pp. 45–63. Springer, Cham (2020). https://doi.org/10.1007/978-3-030-63882-5_4
13. OMG: OMG unified modeling language (OMG UML), version 2.5.1. Technical report, Object Management Group, December 2017. https://www.omg.org/spec/UML/About-UML/
14. Pembeci, I., Nilsson, H., Hager, G.: Functional reactive robotics: an exercise in principled integration of domain-specific languages. In: Proceedings of the 4th ACM SIGPLAN International Conference on Principles and Practice of Declarative Programming, pp. 168–179 (2002)
15. Roscoe, A.W.: The Theory and Practice of Concurrency. Prentice Hall PTR, Hoboken (1998)
16. Roscoe, A.W.: On the expressive power of CSP refinement. Form. Asp. Comput. **17**(2), 93–112 (2005). https://doi.org/10.1007/s00165-005-0065-x

Model Checking and Strategy Synthesis for Multi-agent Systems for Resource Allocation

Nils Timm[✉] and Josua Botha

Department of Computer Science, University of Pretoria, Pretoria, South Africa
ntimm@cs.up.ac.za

Abstract. We present a technique for verifying strategic abilities of multi-agent systems via SAT-based bounded model checking. In our approach we focus on systems of agents that pursue goals with regard to the allocation of shared resources. The problem to be solved is to determine whether a coalition of agents has a joint strategy that guarantees the achievement of all resource goals, irrespective of how the opposing agents in the system act. Our approach does not only decide whether such a strategy exists, but also synthesises the strategy. The technique is based on a propositional logic encoding of the model checking problem. The encoding is satisfiable if and only if some specified coalition of agents has a strategy to reach a resource allocation goal. Each satisfying truth assignment of the encoding characterises a successful strategy.

1 Introduction

Multi-agent systems for resource allocation (MRAs) have been introduced in [8] as a concept for modelling competitive resource allocation problems in distributed computing. An MRA is composed of a set of agents and a set of resources. Agents have access to a subset of the overall set of resources. Moreover, each agent has a goal in terms of the amount of resources to accumulate. Particular resources can be allocated by means of *request* actions. Further types of actions are *release* and *idle*. MRAs run in discrete rounds. In each round each agent selects an action, and the tuple of selected actions gets executed in a simultaneous manner. Once an agent has achieved its goal, it releases all accumulated resources and starts to allocate them again. Hence, agents pursue to achieve their goals repetitively. Since resources are generally shared, the achievement of goals is a competition between agents. Several practically relevant scenarios of resource allocation can be modelled as an MRA.

For MRAs (or more specifically, for the scenarios that they model) it is typically of importance that they are designed in a way such that for certain group of agents the achievement of goals can be guaranteed, no matter how the remaining agents in the system may counter-act. We call such a group of agents a *coalition* and the remaining agents the *opposition*. Goal-achievability properties of a coalition A against an opposition B can be formalised in alternating-time logics

© Springer Nature Switzerland AG 2021
S. Campos and M. Minea (Eds.): SBMF 2021, LNCS 13130, pp. 53–69, 2021.
https://doi.org/10.1007/978-3-030-92137-8_4

such as ATL or ATL* [1], which extend classical temporal logics by strategic operators. An alternating-time formula $\langle\langle A \rangle\rangle\, \varphi$ expresses that the coalition A has a *strategy* to achieve φ, irrespective of how the opposition acts, where φ is a classical temporal logic formula. In this context, a strategy is a mapping between states of the underlying MRA and actions to be taken by the agents in A in these states. The corresponding strategic model checking problem is to determine whether such a succeeding strategy exists or not. Established tools for deciding the PTIME-complete ATL model checking problem of general multi-agent systems are based on binary decision diagrams (BDDs) and only offer limited support for synthesising a succeeding strategy [2,13]. Algorithms for the 2EXPTIME-complete ATL* model checking have been theoretically defined, but due to the high complexity no practically relevant implementation exists.

In this paper we present a SAT-based bounded model checking technique for verifying goal-achievability properties of multi-agent systems for resource allocation. Our technique does not only decide the model checking problem, it also synthesises a corresponding strategy if existent. The properties that we consider in our approach are not expressible in ATL but in ATL*. Our approach encodes the bounded model checking problem in propositional logic. Thus, model checking can be performed via SAT solving. From a satisfying truth assignment of the encoded problem a succeeding strategy can be immediately derived. For our bounded model checking problems linear completeness thresholds exist, which also makes unbounded model checking feasible.

A distinct feature of our technique is our iterative strategy synthesis algorithm. Instead of directly checking whether the coalition A has a strategy for achieving the goals against *all* possible strategies of the opposition B, the algorithm approaches the problem as follows: 1. It initialises a set Σ containing a small number of strategies of the opposition. 2. It checks whether A has a strategy α for achieving the goals against the opposition's strategies in Σ. If not, then no succeeding strategy for A exists. 3. It checks whether B has a strategy β for preventing A from reaching the goals against the strategy α, generated in Step 2. If not, then α is a universally succeeding strategy for A. Otherwise, the algorithm adds the strategy β to Σ and repeats the Steps 2 and 3 until a definite result is obtained. The dual principle of the algorithm allows to avoid the exhaustive consideration of all possible strategies for many practical instances.

We have implemented our model checking and strategy synthesis technique on top of the solver PicoSAT [4]. First experiments show promising performance results. To the best of our knowledge our approach is the first SAT-based bounded model checking technique for verifying alternating-time properties and the first SAT-based strategy synthesis technique.

2   Multi-agent Systems for Resource Allocation

In our approach we focus on model checking *multi-agent systems for resource allocation* (MRAs), originally introduced in [8].

Definition 1 (Multi-agent System for Resource Allocation). *A multi-agent system for resource allocation is a tuple* $M = (Agt, Res, d, Acc)$ *where*

- *$Agt = \{a_1, \ldots, a_n\}$ is a finite set of agents,*
- *$Res = \{r_1, \ldots, r_m\}$ is a finite set of resources,*
- *$d : Agt \rightarrow \mathbb{N}$ is a demand function that defines the number of resources that each agent needs to allocate in order to achieve its individual goal,*
- *$Acc : Agt \rightarrow 2^{Res}$ is an accessibility function that defines the subset of resources that each agent can access.*

Example. The graph describes the agents a_1, a_2, a_3, the resources r_1, r_2, r_3, r_4, and the accessibility function of the MRA. The MRA is fully specified once the demand function is defined, e.g. $d(a_1) = 2, d(a_2) = 2, d(a_3) = 1$.

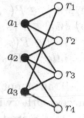

Each agent has the goal to gradually allocate a number of resources such that its demand is finally satisfied. The actions that can be performed for this are:

Definition 2 (Actions). *Given an MRA M, the set of actions Act is the union of the following types of actions:*

- *request actions: $\{req_r^a \mid a \in Agt, r \in Acc(a)\}$*
- *release actions: $\{rel_r^a \mid a \in Agt, r \in Acc(a)\}$*
- *release-all actions: $\{rel_{all}^a \mid a \in Agt\}$*
- *idle actions: $\{idle^a \mid a \in Agt\}$*

Hence, an agent can request a particular resource, release a particular resource that it currently holds, release all resources that it currently holds, or just idle. An MRA runs in discrete rounds where in each round each agent chooses its next action. In a round the tuple of chosen actions, one per agent, gets executed simultaneously. The execution of actions leads to an evolution of the system between different states over time.

Definition 3 (States). *A state of an MRA M is a function $s : Res \rightarrow Agt^+$ where $Agt^+ = Agt \cup \{a_0\}$ and a_0 is a dummy agent. If $s(r) = a_0$ then resource r is unallocated in state s. If $s(r) = a_i$ and $i > 0$ then r is allocated by agent a_i in s. We denote by s_0 the initial state of M, where $s(r) = a_0$ for each $r \in Res$, i.e. initially all resources are unallocated. We denote by S the set of all possible states of M. If we want to express that resource r is currently allocated by agent a_i but the current state is not further specified, then we simply write $r = a_i$.*

Hence, states describe the current allocation of resources by agents. An agent may not be able to observe the entire state of the MRA. We assume that agents can only observe the (state of the) resources they have access to.

Definition 4 (State Observations). *Let M be an MRA, let $a_i \in Agt$ and let $s \in S$. Then the observation of agent a_i in state s is a function $s_{a_i} : Acc(a_i) \rightarrow Agt^+$ such that $s_{a_i}(r) = s(r)$ for all $r \in Acc(a_i)$. We denote by S_{a_i} the set of all possible state observations of a_i.*

In our example, agent a_1 cannot access resource r_4. Hence, the state observation of this agent in a state where all resources are available and in a state where r_4 is the only allocated resource would be the same. In each state only a subset of actions may be available for execution by an agent, which we call the protocol:

Definition 5 (Action Availability Protocol). *The action availability protocol is a function $P : S \times Agt \to 2^{Act}$ defined for each $s \in S$ and $a \in Agt$:*

1. *if $|s^{-1}(a)| = d(a)$ then $P(s, a) = \{rel_{all}^a\}$;*
2. *otherwise:*
   (a) $rel_{all}^a \notin P(s, a)$;
   (b) $req_r^a \in P(s, a)$ iff $s(r) = a_0$;
   (c) $rel_r^a \in P(s, a)$ iff $s(r) = a$;
   (d) $idle^a \in P(s, a)$ iff $\forall r \in Acc(a) : s(r) \neq a_0$.

Thus, if an agent has reached its goal, it has to release all of its allocated resources. Otherwise, an agent can request an accessible resource that is currently unallocated, an agent can release a resource that it currently holds, and an agent can idle only if none of its accessible resources are currently available.

Definition 6 (Action Profiles). *An action profile in an MRA M is a mapping $ap : Agt \to Act$. AP denotes the set of all action profiles. We say that a profile ap is executable in a state $s \in S$ if for each $a \in Agt$ we have that $ap(a) \in P(s, a)$.*

Based on action profiles we can formally define the evolution of an MRA.

Definition 7 (Evolution). *The evolution of an MRA is a relation $\delta \subseteq S \times AP \times S$ where $(s, ap, s') \in \delta$ iff ap is executable in s and for each $r \in Res$:*

1. *if $s(r) = a_0$ then:*
   (a) if $\exists a : ap(a) = req_r^a \wedge \forall a' \neq a : ap(a') \neq req_r^{a'}$ then $s'(r) = a$;
   (b) otherwise $s'(r) = a_0$;
2. *if $s(r) = a$ for some $a \in Agt$ then:*
   (a) if $ap(a) = rel_r^a \vee rel_{all}^a$ then $s'(r) = a_0$;
   (b) otherwise $s'(r) = a$.

If an action profile is executed in a state of an MRA M, this leads to a transition of M into a corresponding successor state, i.e. a change in the allocation of resources according to the actions chosen by the agents. According to the evolution, the request of a resource r by an agent a will be only successful if a is the only agent that requests r in the current round. If multiple agents request the same resource at the same time, then none of the agents will obtain it.

We are interested in solving strategic model checking problems with regard to MRAs: Given a coalition of agents $A \subseteq Agt$, does this coalition has a *uniform strategy* that guarantees that all agents in A will eventually achieve their goal, irrespective of how the opposition of agents $Agt \backslash A$ acts?

Definition 8 (Uniform Strategy). *A uniform strategy of an agent $a \in Agt$ in an MRA is an injective function $\alpha_a : S_a \to Act$. A strategy can be also denoted by a relation $\alpha_a \subseteq S_a \times Act$ where $\alpha_a(s_a, act^a) = true$ iff $\alpha_a(s_a) = act^a$. Given $A = \{a_1, \ldots, a_r\} \subseteq Agt$, a joint strategy for A is a tuple of strategies $\alpha_A(\alpha_{a_1}, \ldots, \alpha_{a_r})$, one for each $a \in A$.*

A strategy determines which action an agent will choose under which observation. A strategy is uniform if the following holds: Each time when an agent makes the same observation, it will perform the same action according to the strategy. If a coalition of agents follows a joint strategy, this can have *multiple* possible execution paths as outcomes because the remaining agents outside the coalition may act in an arbitrary way. In our approach, we assume that the remaining agents may follow an arbitrary strategy from a set Σ. The outcome of a strategy α_A in a state s for a set of opposition's strategies Σ is a set of paths.

Definition 9 (Outcome of a Strategy). *Let M be an MRA, s a state of M, $A \subseteq Agt$ and $B = Agt \backslash A$. Moreover, let α_A be a joint strategy for A and Σ a set of joint strategies for B. Then the outcome of α_A in state s, assuming that the agents in B follow an arbitrary strategy from Σ, is a set of paths*

$$\Pi(s, \alpha_A, \Sigma) = \{\; \pi = s_0 s_1 \ldots \mid s_0 = s \; \wedge$$
$$\forall \beta_B \in \Sigma : \forall t \in \mathbb{N} : \exists (act_t^{a_1}, \ldots, act_t^{a_n}) \forall a \in Agt :$$
$$(act_t^a \in P(s_t, a) \wedge (a \in A \to \alpha_a((s_t)_a) = act_t^a) \wedge$$
$$(a \in B \to \beta_a((s_t)_a) = act_t^a) \wedge$$
$$(s_t, (act_t^{a_1}, \ldots, act_t^{a_n}), s_{t+1}) \in \delta)\}$$

where $(s_t)_a$ denotes the observation of agent a in state s_t.

The logic that we introduce for specifying strategic goal-achievability properties of agents in MRAs we call 1-ATL*. 1-ATL* is based on a subset of the alternating-time temporal logic ATL* [1].

Definition 10 (1-ATL* Syntax). *Let M be an MRA, $A \subseteq Agt$, $B = Agt \backslash A$ and Σ a set of joint strategies for B. Then formulas $\langle\langle A, \Sigma \rangle\rangle \varphi \in$ 1-ATL* over M are defined as follows:*

$$\varphi := a.goal \mid \neg\varphi \mid \varphi \vee \varphi \mid \varphi \wedge \varphi \mid \mathbf{F}\varphi$$

where $a \in Agt$ and $a.goal$ is an atomic proposition that expresses that agent a has reached its goal, i.e. $s(a.goal) = true$ iff $|s^{-1}(a)| = d(a)$ for $s \in S$.

Here **F** refers to 'finally'. 1-ATL* formulas are restricted to a single strategic operator $\langle\langle A, \Sigma \rangle\rangle$ at the beginning of a formula. Since we follow a SAT-based bounded model checking approach [5] we define bounded semantics for 1-ATL*.

Definition 11 (Bounded 1-ATL* Semantics). *Let M be an MRA, let $s \in S$ be a state of M, let $k \in \mathbb{N}$. Moreover, let $A \subseteq Agt$, $a \in Agt$, $B = Agt \backslash A$ and Σ a set of joint strategies for B. Then the k-bounded evaluation of a 1-ATL* formula $\langle\langle A, \Sigma \rangle\rangle \varphi$ on the state s, written $[M, s \models_k \langle\langle A, \Sigma \rangle\rangle \varphi]$, is inductively defined as:*

$$[M, s \models_k \langle\langle A, \Sigma \rangle\rangle \varphi] \equiv \exists \alpha_A \forall \pi \in \Pi(s, \alpha_A, \Sigma) : [M, \pi \models_k \varphi]$$
$$[M, \pi \models_k a.goal] \equiv |\pi(0)^{-1}(a)| = d(a)$$
$$[M, \pi \models_k \mathbf{F}\varphi] \equiv \exists 0 \leq t \leq k : [M, \pi(t) \models_k \varphi]$$

where $\pi(t)$ denotes the t-th state of the path π. Moreover, Boolean operators $\neg, \vee, \wedge$ are interpreted with the usual semantics.

While ATL* uses strategic operators of the form $\langle\langle A \rangle\rangle$, we use extended strategic operators $\langle\langle A, \Sigma \rangle\rangle$. The semantic difference is as follows: A formula $\langle\langle A \rangle\rangle \varphi$ expresses that the coalition A has a universal strategy to achieve φ, irrespective of how the opposition $Agt \backslash A$ acts, whereas $\langle\langle A, \Sigma \rangle\rangle \varphi$ expresses that the coalition A has a strategy to achieve φ against all the opposition's strategies in the set Σ. If we include all possible strategies of the opposition in Σ, then $\langle\langle A \rangle\rangle \varphi$ and $\langle\langle A, \Sigma \rangle\rangle \varphi$ are semantically identical. In our SAT-based approach we focus on solving strategic bounded model checking problems of the following form:

$$[M, s_0 \models_k \langle\langle A, \Sigma \rangle\rangle (\bigwedge_{a \in A} (\mathbf{F} a.goal))]$$

Thus, we check whether the coalition A has a uniform strategy guaranteeing that each agent in A will finally reach its resource goal within at most k time steps, assuming that the opposition follows an arbitrary strategy in Σ. Our technique does not only yield the model checking result but also returns a succeeding strategy for A if such a strategy exists. We will also show how our approach can be used for solving the corresponding *universal* problem $[M, s_0 \models_k \langle\langle A \rangle\rangle (\bigwedge_{a \in A} (\mathbf{F} a.goal))]$ efficiently. Moreover, we discuss how unbounded model checking can be established.

3   Propositional Logic Encoding

We now present our propositional logic encoding of strategic bounded model checking problems $[M, s \models_k \langle\langle A, \Sigma \rangle\rangle \varphi]$. We construct a propositional formula $[M, \langle\langle A, \Sigma \rangle\rangle \varphi, k]$ over a set of Boolean variables *Vars* that is satisfiable if and only if the encoded model checking problem holds. If the formula is satisfiable for a truth assignment $\alpha : Vars \rightarrow \{0, 1\}$, then α describes a uniform strategy α_A for the coalition A that guarantees that the goal φ will be reached against all the opposition's strategies in Σ. Since we have the correspondence between truth assignments and strategies we denote both of them by α resp. α_A. In a top-down manner now we break down the overall encoding into sub encodings:

$$[M, \langle\langle A, \Sigma \rangle\rangle \varphi, k] = [\langle\langle A \rangle\rangle, k] \wedge \bigwedge_{\beta \in \Sigma} ([\beta, k] \wedge [M, k]^\beta \wedge [\varphi, k]^\beta)$$

The sub formula $[\langle\!\langle A \rangle\!\rangle, k]$ encodes the condition that the agents in A must follow a uniform strategy and adhere to the protocol at each time step up to k. $[\beta, k]$ encodes that the agents in $B = Agt \backslash A$ exactly follow the strategy β. $[M, k]^{\beta}$ encodes all k-bounded paths of M starting in the initial state, and $[\varphi, k]^{\beta}$ is a constraint that restricts the paths of M to those that satisfy φ. Since for each strategy $\beta \in \Sigma$ different paths may be taken and sub formulas of φ may be satisfied in different states, we have for each β a distinct copy of the encoding of M and φ, indicated by the superscript. This means, for some $\beta \neq \beta'$ the encodings $[M, k]^{\beta}$ and $[M, k]^{\beta'}$ are structurally identical, but they are defined over distinct sets of variables. Henceforth, we typically omit the superscript, unless we want to emphasise that the encoding refers to a particular strategy β.

3.1   Overall Encoding

Subsequently, we present the details of the overall encoding. The encoding makes use of a number of basic encodings: $[r = a]_t$ denoting that resource r is allocated by agent a in the state at time step t, $\lfloor act^a \rfloor_t$ denoting that agent a chooses action act in the state at time step t, and $[a.goal]_t$ denoting that a has reached its goal in the state at step t. If the SAT solver generates a satisfying truth assignment α of the overall encoding and $\alpha([r = a]_t) = 1$ holds, then α characterises a path where at the t-th state resource r is allocated by agent a. Similar properties hold for the remaining basic encodings. For now we will remain with these informal definitions of these basic encodings. The formal definitions will follow in the next sub section. We start with the encoding of paths and the temporal logic formula before we consider the strategic parts $[\langle\!\langle A \rangle\!\rangle, k]$ and $[\beta, k]$. The encoding of k-bounded paths $[M, k]$ is composed of the following sub encodings

$$[M, k] = [Init]_0 \wedge \bigwedge_{t=0}^{k-1} [Evolution]_{t, t+1}$$

where $[Init]_0$ encodes the initial state at time step 0 and $[Evolution]_{t, t+1}$ encodes the evolution (Definition 7) of M from time step t to step $t + 1$.

Definition 12 (Encoding of the Initial State). *The encoding of the initial state of an MRA M at time step 0 where all resources are unallocated is*

$$[Init]_0 = \bigwedge_{r \in Res} [r = a_0]_0$$

where $[r = a_0]_0$ is defined according to the encoding of resource states (Sect. 3.2).

The initial state at time step 0 is the only state that is fixed in our encoding. States that will be reached at time steps $1 \leq t \leq k$ follow from the truth assignment generated by the solver. The subsequent encoding ensures that generated sequences of states are conform with the evolution:

Definition 13 (Encoding of the Evolution). *The evolution of an MRA M from time step t to t+1 is encoded as* $[Evolution]_{t,t+1} = \bigwedge_{r \in R} [r.evolution]_{t,t+1}$ *where* $[r.evolution]_{t,t+1} =$

$$\bigvee_{a \in Acc^{-1}(r)} \Big(\quad ([r = a]_{t+1} \wedge [req_r^a]_t \wedge \bigwedge_{a' \neq a} \neg[req_r^{a'}]_t)$$
$$\vee ([r = a]_{t+1} \wedge [r = a]_t \wedge \neg[rel_r^a]_t \wedge \neg[rel_{all}^a]_t)$$
$$\vee ([r = a_0]_{t+1} \wedge [rel_r^a]_t)$$
$$\vee ([r = a_0]_{t+1} \wedge [r = a]_t \wedge [rel_{all}^a]_t)$$
$$\Big)$$
$$\vee ([r = a_0]_{t+1} \wedge [r = a_0]_t \wedge \bigwedge_{a \in Acc^{-1}(r)} \neg[req_r^a]_t)$$
$$\vee ([r = a_0]_{t+1} \wedge [r = a_0]_t \wedge \bigvee_{a,a' \in Acc^{-1}(r), a \neq a'} ([req_r^a]_t \wedge [req_r^{a'}]_t)$$

and the sub encodings are defined according to the encoding of resource states and actions (Sect. 3.2).

The encoding of the evolution has a sub formula for each resource r in M. It describes how the allocation state of r changes based on agent actions at particular time steps. The first line of the encoding expresses that in the state at the next time step $t + 1$ the resource r will be allocated by agent a if at the current time step t agent a requests r and no other agent requests r.

We are interested in goal-reachability properties: Do the agents in A have a strategy to achieve the goal φ within k steps? The strategic part of the property gets encoded separately. The temporal logic part gets encoded as follows:

Definition 14 (Encoding of Goal-Reachability Formulas). *Let M be an MRA,* $A \subseteq Agt$ *and* $k \in \mathbb{N}$. *Then the k-bounded goal-reachability property* $\varphi = \bigwedge_{a \in A} \mathbf{F}(a.goal)$ *is encoded in propositional logic as*

$$[\varphi, k] = \bigwedge_{a \in A} \left(\bigvee_{t=0}^{k} [a.goal]_t \right)$$

where $[a.goal]_t$ *is defined according to the encoding of goals (Sect. 3.2).*

If we conjunct the encoding $[M, k]$ with $[\varphi, k]$, this restricts the k-bounded paths of M to those where each agent in A reaches its goal at least once. What we have encoded so far corresponds to a classical linear temporal logic bounded model checking problem for MRAs. We now extend the encoding with the strategic aspects of 1-ATL*. The strategic encodings uses two additional basic encodings: $[uniform.act^a]_t$ denoting that agent a chooses action act in the state at time step t and also at all other time steps where the same state observation is present, and $[s_a]_t$ denoting that the observation of agent a at time step t is s_a.

Definition 15 (Encoding of the Protocol). *Let M be an MRA, let* $A \subseteq Agt$ *and let* $k \in \mathbb{N}$. *Then the protocol of A for all time steps up to k is encoded in propositional logic as* $[\langle\!\langle A \rangle\!\rangle, k] = \bigwedge_{t=0}^{k} \bigwedge_{a \in A} [a.protocol]_t$ *where* $[a.protocol]_t =$

$$\bigvee_{r \in Acc(a)} \Big(\quad ([uniform.req_r^a]_t \wedge \neg[a.goal]_t \wedge [r = a_0]_t)$$
$$\vee ([uniform.rel_r^a]_t \wedge \neg[a.goal]_t \wedge [r = a]_t)$$
$$\Big)$$
$$\vee ([uniform.rel_{all}^a]_t \wedge [a.goal]_t)$$
$$\vee ([uniform.idle^a]_t \wedge \neg[a.goal]_t \wedge \bigwedge_{r \in Acc(a)} \neg[r = a_0]_t)$$

and the sub encodings are defined according to the encoding of actions with uniformity constraints, goals, and resource states (Sect. 3.2).

The constraint $[\langle\!\langle A \rangle\!\rangle, k]$ forces the agents in A to follow the protocol at all time steps up to k. This means only actions that are available in the current state can be chosen. Moreover, the constraint enforces the uniformity of choices with regard to the state observation. The first line of the protocol encoding ensures that some agent a can only request some resource r if the agent has not reached its goal yet and r is unallocated in the state at the current time step. Furthermore, the sub constraint $[uniform.req_r^a]_t$ ensures that if the agent chooses the req_r^a action in the state at time step t, then it has to choose the same action at all time steps where the agent's state observation is the same as at t. The final part of the encoding concerns strategies. In our approach, we use this part to fix the strategy that the opposition of agents $B = Agt \backslash A$ is following.

Definition 16 (Encoding of Strategies). *Let $A = \{a_1, \ldots, a_r\} \subseteq Agt$, let $\alpha_A(\alpha_{a_1}, \ldots, \alpha_{a_r})$ be a joint strategy for A and let $k \in \mathbb{N}$. Then the prescription of the strategy α_A to A at all time steps up to k is encoded as*

$$[\alpha_A, k] = \bigwedge\nolimits_{t=0}^{k} \bigwedge\nolimits_{a \in A} \bigwedge\nolimits_{(s_a, act^a) \in \alpha_a} \left([s_a]_t \to [act^a]_t\right)$$

where $[s_a]_t$ is defined according to the encoding of state observations and $[act^a]_t$ is defined according to the encoding of actions (Sect. 3.2).

Each clause $([s_a]_t \to [act^a]_t)$ in this encoding ensures that if at some time step t the state observation s_a holds, then the agent a has to choose action act^a according to the strategy α_a. This completes the definition of the overall encoding $[M, \langle\!\langle A, \Sigma \rangle\!\rangle \varphi, k] = [\langle\!\langle A \rangle\!\rangle, k] \wedge \bigwedge_{\beta \in \Sigma} ([\beta, k] \wedge [M, k]^\beta \wedge [\varphi, k]^\beta)$. We continue with the definition of the basic encodings used within the overall encoding.

3.2 Basic Encodings

An essential basic encoding in our approach is that a particular resource is allocated by a particular agent in the state at time step t. In the encoding we make use of the fact that the agents in an MRA are indexed from 0 to n where the 0-index indicates the dummy agent a_0 holding unallocated resources. Each index can be represented by an m-digit binary number, and each binary number can be logically represented by a conjunction of m negated or non-negated Boolean variables. We introduce m Boolean variables for each resource $r_j \in Res$ and encode that r_j is allocated by some agent $a_i \in Agt$ by building a conjunction that corresponds to the binary representation of the agent's index i:

Definition 17 (Encoding of Resource States). *Let M be an MRA, let $r_j \in Res$, let $a_i \in Agt^+$ and let $t \in \mathbb{N}$. Let $m = \lceil \log_2 |Agt^+| \rceil$ and let $b_{m-1} \ldots b_0$ be the m-digit binary representation of the agent's index number i. Then the allocation of resource r_j by agent a_i in the state at time step t is encoded as*

$$[r_j = a_i]_t := \bigwedge\nolimits_{l=m-1}^{0} \left((b_l \wedge [r_j]_t^l) \vee (\neg b_l \wedge \neg [r_j]_t^l)\right)$$

where $[r_j]_t^l$ with $0 \le l < m$ are the Boolean variables introduced for the encoding.

Note that in this encoding each b_l is a Boolean value (**0** or **1**), which means that either the left-hand side or the right-hand side of the disjunction evaluates to **0**. Thus, the encoding can be immediately simplified to a pure conjunction. Since we get a pure conjunction, it is excluded that at some step t a resource is falsely allocated by multiple agents: For some r and $a \neq a'$ there exists no truth assignment α such that $\alpha([r = a]_t) = 1$ and $\alpha([r = a']_t) = 1$. The conjunction over digits is built from the left-most position $m - 1$ to the right-most position 0. By following the definition above, we can encode a state where some resource r_1 is unallocated, r_2 is allocated by some agent a_1, and r_3 is allocated by a_2:

$$\left(\neg[r_1]_t^1 \wedge \neg[r_1]_t^0\right) \wedge \left(\neg[r_2]_t^1 \wedge [r_2]_t^0\right) \wedge \left([r_3]_t^1 \wedge \neg[r_3]_t^0\right)$$

Since $Agt^+ = \{a_0, a_1, a_2\}$, we introduce two Boolean variables per resource to be able to encode the binary representations **00**, **01**, **10**. Based on the encoding of resource states, we can now also encode state observations and goals of agents.

Definition 18 (Encoding of State Observations). *Let M be an MRA, $a \in Agt$, $s_a \in S_a$ and $t \in \mathbb{N}$. Then the observation s_a by a at step t is encoded as*

$$[s_a]_t := \bigwedge\nolimits_{r_j \in Acc(a)} [r_j = s_a(r_j)]_t$$

where $[r_j = s_a(r_j)]_t$ is defined according to the encoding of resource states.

Hence, the encoding of the state observation s_a by agent a at time step t is a conjunction over the states of accessible resources which are conform with s_a.

Definition 19 (Encoding of Goals). *Let M be an MRA, let $a \in Agt$ and let $t \in \mathbb{N}$. Then the achievement of a's goal in the state at time step t is encoded as*

$$[a.goal]_t = \bigvee_{\substack{R \subseteq Acc(a) \\ |R| = d(a)}} \left(\bigwedge_{r \in R} [r = a]_t \right)$$

where $[r = a]_t$ is defined according to the encoding of resource states.

An agent a has achieved its goal at time step t if the number of resources allocated by a in the current state is equal to the demand $d(a)$ of this agent. Since the number of accessible resources may be higher than the demand, all possibilities for satisfying the demand need to be considered. In the example below, we assume that a has access to the resources r_1, r_2, r_3 and its demand is 2. As a corresponding goal encoding for time step t we get:

$$[a.goal]_t = \left([r_1 = a]_t \wedge [r_2 = a]_t\right) \vee \left([r_1 = a]_t \wedge [r_3 = a]_t\right) \vee \left([r_2 = a]_t \wedge [r_3 = a]_t\right)$$

If the solver generates an assignment α with $\alpha([a.goal]_t) = 1$, then on the path corresponding to α agent a has reach its goal in the state at time step t.

In the encoding of actions by agents we follow a similar concept as in the encoding of resource states. We assign a unique binary number to each possible action of an agent a_i and we represent each action by a logical conjunction over negated or non-negated Boolean variables associated with this agent.

Definition 20 (Encoding of Actions). *Let* $a_i \in Agt$, $act^{a_i} \in Act(a_i)$, $t \in \mathbb{N}$, $m = \lceil \log_2 |Act(a_i)| \rceil$ *and* $f_{a_i} : Act(a_i) \to \{0, \ldots, m-1\}$ *a bijection that assigns a unique number to each possible action of* a_i. *Let* $b_{m-1} \ldots b_0$ *be the m-digit binary representation of* $f_{a_i}(act)$. *Then the action* act^{a_i} *of* a_i *at step* t *is encoded as*

$$[act^{a_i}]_t := \bigwedge_{l=0}^{m-1} \left(b_l \wedge [ac_i]_t^l \right) \vee \left(\neg b_l \wedge \neg [ac_i]_t^l \right)$$

where $[ac_i]_t^l$ *with* $0 \leq l < m$ *are the Boolean variables introduced for the encoding.*

Assuming that some agent a_1 can perform 6 different actions, we need 3 Boolean variables for their encoding. Moreover, assuming that the number 0 is assigned to the action $idle^{a_1}$, the corresponding encoding is:

$$[idle^{a_1}]_t = \neg [ac_1]_t^2 \wedge \neg [ac_1]_t^1 \wedge \neg [ac_1]_t^0$$

In the remainder of this sub section, we show how we enforce uniform behaviour of the agents in A and how we include a logical mechanism that allows us to synthesise uniform strategies for reaching the goal. Since a strategy links a state observation s_a with an action act^a, we define strategic decision encodings $[s_a.act^a]$. We include these decision encodings in our overall encoding such that a truth assignment α satisfies $[s_a.act^a]$ if and only if the strategy characterised by α links s_a with act^a. Since strategic decisions are universal and not restricted to a particular time step, this encoding does not include t as a parameter.

Definition 21 (Encoding of Strategic Decisions). *Let* M *be an* MRA, *let* $u_i \in Agt$, *let* $act^{a_i} \in Act(a_i)$ *and let* $s_{a_i} \in S_{a_i}$. *Moreover, let* $m = \lceil \log_2 |Act(a_i)| \rceil$ *and let* $f_{a_i} : Act(a_i) \to \{0, \ldots, m-1\}$ *be a bijection that assigns a unique number to each possible action of agent* a_i. *Let* $b_{m-1} \ldots b_0$ *be the m-digit binary representation of* $f_{a_i}(act^{a_i})$. *Then the strategic decision of agent* a_i *to perform action* act^{a_i} *in state observation* s_{a_i} *is encoded as*

$$[s_{a_i}.act^{a_i}] := \bigwedge_{l=0}^{m-1} \left(b_l \wedge [sac_i]^l \right) \vee \left(\neg b_l \wedge \neg [sac_i]^l \right)$$

where $[sac_i]^l$ *with* $0 \leq l < m$ *are the Boolean variables for the encoding.*

Similarly to the encoding of actions, we assign a unique binary number to each possible action of an agent a_i and we represent each strategic decision by a logical conjunction over negated or non-negated Boolean variables associated with this agent. This ensures that for different actions $act^{a_i} \neq act'^{a_i}$ no truth assignment can satisfy $[s_{a_i}.act^{a_i}]$ and $[s_{a_i}.act'^{a_i}]$ at the same time. This results in a guaranteed uniformity of strategies synthesised from the decision encodings.

The final part of the basic encoding concerns the uniform choice of actions:

Definition 22 (Encoding of Actions with Uniformity Constraints). *Let* $a_i \in Agt$, *let* $act^{a_i} \in Act(a_i)$ *and let* $t \in \mathbb{N}$. *Then the uniformity constraint with regard to action* act^{a_i} *by agent* a_i *at time step* t *is encoded as*

$$[uniform.act^{a_i}]_t := [act^{a_i}]_t \wedge \left(\bigvee_{s_{a_i} \in S_{a_i}, act^{a_i} \in P(s_{a_i})} \left([s_{a_i}]_t \wedge [s_{a_i}.act^{a_i}] \right) \right)$$

where $[s_{a_i}]_t$ *and* $[s_{a_i}.act^{a_i}]$ *are defined according to the encoding of state observations and strategic decisions.*

Here the uniform choice of actions by agents is enforced as follows: At each step t when an agent a makes a choice to perform action act^a, we connect this choice with the strategic decision encoding $[s_a.act^a]$ corresponding to the current state observation s_a and to act^a. This ensures that the action can only be chosen if there has been no time step with the same observation where a different action has been chosen, or synonymously, the same action is also chosen at all steps where the observation is the same as at t. This completes our encoding of strategic bounded model checking problems $[M, s \models_k \langle\langle A, \Sigma \rangle\rangle \varphi]$ into a propositional formula $[M, \langle\langle A, \Sigma \rangle\rangle \varphi, k]$. Next, we summarise the properties of the encoding.

3.3 Properties of the Encoding

The major property of our encoding is that it allows to perform sound model checking of the encoded problem via satisfiability solving.

Theorem 1 (Model Checking). *Let $[M, s \models_k \langle\langle A, \Sigma \rangle\rangle \varphi]$ be a strategic bounded model checking problem and let $[M, \langle\langle A, \Sigma \rangle\rangle \varphi, k]$ be its encoding over Vars. Then:*

$$[M, s \models_k \langle\langle A, \Sigma \rangle\rangle \varphi] \equiv \mathbf{sat}([M, \langle\langle A, \Sigma \rangle\rangle \varphi, k])$$

Hence, the coalition A has a uniform strategy to achieve the goal φ within k time steps against all opposition's strategies in Σ if and only if the propositional logic encoding is satisfiable. Moreover, our approach also allows us to synthesise such a uniform strategy that guarantees the achievement of the goal φ:

Theorem 2 (Strategy Synthesis). *Let $[M, s \models_k \langle\langle A, \Sigma \rangle\rangle \varphi]$ be a strategic bounded model checking problem, let $[M, \langle\langle A, \Sigma \rangle\rangle \varphi, k]$ be its encoding over Vars and let $\alpha : Vars \rightarrow \{0, 1\}$ with $\alpha([M, \langle\langle A, \Sigma \rangle\rangle \varphi, k]) = 1$. Then for the strategy*

$$\alpha_A = \left(\{(s_a, act^a) \mid s_a \in S_a \wedge act^a \in Act \wedge \alpha([s_a.act^a]) = 1\}_{a \in A} \right)$$

the following holds: $\forall \pi \in \Pi(s, \alpha_A, \Sigma) : [M, \pi \models_k \varphi]$.

Thus, from a truth assignment α that satisfies the encoding we can directly derive a corresponding uniform strategy α_A that guarantees φ. The correctness of Theorem 1 and Theorem 2 is closely linked. Subsequently, we present a sketch of the proof of correctness. Proof details can be found at github.com/TuksModelChecking/Satmas/blob/main/Proofs.pdf.

Proof Sketch
It can be shown that every satisfying truth assignment of $[M, k]$ characterises a k-bounded path in the state space of M that is conform with the evolution. Yet, such a path may not be conform with the protocol. $[M, k] \wedge [\varphi, k]$ is satisfied for assignments that characterise paths of M for which the property φ holds. The conjunction of this encoding with $[M, \langle\langle A \rangle\rangle, k]$ adds the constraint that the agents in A must follow a uniform strategy that is conform with the protocol. Assuming that β is a protocol-conform strategy for the opposition $B = Agt \backslash A$

and by adding $[\beta, k]$ to the encoding we restrict the paths to those where the opposition adheres to β. This can be generalised to having a set Σ of possible strategies for B. We finally get that the overall propositional formula is satisfiable if and only if the encoded model checking problem holds. Moreover, the strategic decision encodings $[s_a.act^a]$ that evaluate to *true* for a satisfying assignment α are exactly those that characterise the winning strategy for the coalition A.   □

4   Algorithm

Our SAT-based approach allows to solve model checking problems of the form $[M, s \models_k \langle\langle A, \Sigma \rangle\rangle \varphi]$ where the coalition A attempts to reach its goal against the opposition's strategies in Σ. However, it is typically of interest to synthesise a strategy that *universally* succeeds, i.e. against *all* possible strategies of the opposition. The common notation for this is: $[M, s \models_k \langle\langle A \rangle\rangle \varphi]$. Universal goal-achievability can be naively checked by including all possible strategies in Σ. But this would involve an exorbitant increase of the size of the encoding. We approach this problem by defining the iterative Algorithm 1 on the subsequent page that successively extends the strategy set Σ. In each iteration, two strategic model checking problems are solved: We first check whether $[M, s \models_k \langle\langle A, \Sigma \rangle\rangle \varphi]$ holds, i.e. whether A has a strategy α that succeeds against all strategies in Σ. If not, then we can immediately terminate with the result that the model checking problem does not hold. Otherwise, our algorithm will synthesise a strategy α that succeeds against Σ. Secondly, we consider the so-called complementary model checking problem $[M, s \models_k \langle\langle B, \{\alpha\} \rangle\rangle \neg\varphi]$, i.e. we check whether the opposition B has a strategy β that succeeds against α in preventing the coalition A from reaching the goal φ. If the opposition does not have such a strategy β, then we can conclude that α is a universally succeeding strategy for φ and the algorithm terminates with this result. Otherwise, we synthesise β, add it to Σ and run the next iteration. In our algorithm, we initialise Σ with a simple greedy strategy for B: As long as its goal is not reached and accessible resources are available, each agent in B requests the accessible and available resource r_j with the smallest index j.

In the worst case, the number of iterations is equal to the number of possible strategies for B. However, the concept of checking the original problem *and* the complementary problem in each iteration allows for early termination in many cases: If the complementary problem does not hold, then we already know that the current α is a universally succeeding strategy – even if we have not considered all possible strategies for B yet. Since our approach is based on *bounded* model checking it is incomplete, i.e. only bounded goal-reachability can be checked. However, if we can synthesise a succeeding strategy for some bound k, then we can conclude that this strategy will also guarantee success for all larger bounds and therefore also in the unbounded case. Conversely, having no succeeding strategy for some k does not allow us to conclude that such a strategy does not exist in the unbounded case. General completeness of bounded model checking can be established by determining the completeness threshold of the problem

---

Algorithm 1: *Strategy-Synthesis*$(M, \langle\langle A \rangle\rangle \varphi, k)$

---

1 $B := Agt \backslash A, \quad \Sigma := \{\beta^{greedy}\}$

2 **loop forever do**

3   **if** $\mathbf{sat}\big([M, \langle\langle A, \Sigma \rangle\rangle \varphi, k]\big)$ for some assignment α **then**

4 | **skip** /*α *succeeds against all strategies in* Σ */

5   **else**

6 | **return** '$[M, s_0 \not\models_k \langle\langle A \rangle\rangle \varphi$'

7   **if** $\mathbf{sat}\big([M, \langle\langle B, \{\alpha\} \rangle\rangle \neg\varphi, k]\big)$ for some assignment β **then**

8 | $\Sigma := \Sigma \cup \{\beta\}$ /*β *succeeds against* α */

9   **else**

10 | **return** '$[M, s_0 \models_k \langle\langle A \rangle\rangle \varphi]$ and α is a universally succeeding strategy'

---

instance and by setting k to this threshold. For the reachability properties that we consider, completeness thresholds are linear in the size of the state space [11].

5 Implementation and Experiments

We developed the tool SATMAS (available at github.com/TuksModel Checking/SATMAS) that implements our approach in Python. SATMAS takes a specification of an MRA M (set of agents, set of resources, accessibility relation, demand function) and a coalition A within M as an input. The strategic property to be checked is $\langle\langle A \rangle\rangle \big(\bigwedge_{a \in A} (\mathbf{F} a.goal) \big)$. The tool iterates over the possible values of the bound. In each iteration the encodings of the corresponding model checking problem and of its complement are built, and the algorithm *Strategy-Synthesis* is executed. The encoding process includes optimisations such as logical simplifications and the Tseitin transformation into conjunctive normal form. SATMAS employs PicoSAT [4] for checking the satisfiability of the encodings and for determining satisfying truth assignments from which strategies can be derived. In experiments we verified goal-reachability properties of MRAs with up to eight agents and eight resources. We were able to either synthesise universally succeeding strategies, or to show that such strategies do not exist. A selection of the results where a succeeding strategy for A could be synthesised is shown in Table 1. The *Scenario* column indicates the sizes of the coalition A, the opposition B and the overall number of resources. Moreover, $\mathcal{D}$ is the interval from which the demand of each agent was randomly selected, and $\mathcal{ACC}$ is the interval from which number of accessible resources of each agent was randomly selected.

Table 1. Experimental results.

Scenario	Bound	Time
$|A| = 3, |B| = 3, |Res| = 6, \mathcal{D} = [2,3], \mathcal{ACC} = [4,5]$	36	7.1 s
$|A| = 3, |B| = 3, |Res| = 6, \mathcal{D} = [4,5], \mathcal{ACC} = [5,6]$	36	19.1 s
$|A| = 4, |B| = 4, |Res| = 8, \mathcal{D} = [3,4], \mathcal{ACC} = [5,6]$	64	162 s
$|A| = 4, |B| = 4, |Res| = 8, \mathcal{D} = [5,6], \mathcal{ACC} = [6,7]$	64	755 s

6   Related Work

Model checking has been originally introduced as a technique for verifying temporal logic properties of hardware and software designs [3]. Classical symbolic model checking approaches include BDD-based CTL model checking [6] and SAT-based bounded LTL model checking [5]. CTL model checking has been also extended to multi-agent systems [16]. While CTL and LTL do not consider strategic aspects, [1] introduced the alternating-time logics ATL and ATL*, which are logics for reasoning about strategies in multi-agent systems. The general ATL model checking problem is PTIME-complete whereas the ATL* model checking problem is 2EXPTIME-complete. Thus, while for ATL model checking efficient BDD tools like MCMAS [13] and MOCHA [2] exist, ATL* has been rather considered on a theoretical level [17]. SAT-based bounded model checking of multi-agent systems has been proposed in [12,14]. Similar to our technique, [12,14] unfold the transition relation k times by means of a propositional formula. However, their approaches are limited to the verification of epistemic properties and do not support strategic operators. These approaches have been only theoretically defined but not implemented. [10] presents a SAT-based unbounded ATL model checking technique. Although based on a reduction to SAT, this technique is very different from ours. In [10] a BDD-encoded model checking problem gets translated into a corresponding set of quantified Boolean formulas and fix-point equations, which can be further translated into a plain propositional encoding. [10] does not support strategy synthesis. An existing tool for synthesising ATL strategies is SMC [15]. SMC operates on a BDD model of the multi-agent system to be verified. It iteratively guesses a strategy, fixes the strategy in the model and checks whether it is a succeeding strategy, which reduces ATL model checking to CTL model checking in each iteration. To the best of our knowledge our approach is the first SAT-based bounded model checking technique for verifying alternating-time properties and the first SAT-based strategy synthesis technique.

7   Conclusion and Outlook

We presented a SAT-based technique for model checking strategic abilities of coalitions in MRAs. Our technique does not only allow to verify whether a coalition of agents has the strategic ability to achieve a resource allocation goal, it also synthesises a corresponding uniform strategy if existent. In contrast to existing synthesis techniques that explore BDDs, our approach is based on a logical encoding of the model checking problem. Hence, we can exploit the power of modern SAT solvers in our approach. SAT-based model checking is limited to the exploration of bounded paths. However, for our goal-reachability properties completeness thresholds linear in the size of the state space exist, which also makes unbounded model checking feasible. A distinct feature of our technique is the iterative strategy synthesis algorithm. In each iteration it checks whether the coalition A has a strategy α for achieving its goal against all opposition's strategies from a set Σ, and additionally, whether the opposition B has a strategy β for preventing A from achieving its goal when A follows α. This dual principle of the algorithm allows to avoid an exhaustive exploration of all possible strategies for many practical instances. We have implemented our technique on top of the solver PicoSAT. First experiments show promising performance results.

In future work, we want to extend our technique such that properties like repetitive goal-reachability of the form $\mathbf{GF}\varphi$ can be verified. We plan to develop variants of the algorithm where strategies from different iterations get heuristically merged, rather than extending the strategy set. The protocol of MRAs can be adjusted such that alternative scenarios of resource allocation problems can be modelled. Further plans are the integration of partial order reduction [9] and symmetry reduction [7] in order to reduce the model checking complexity.

References

1. Alur, R., Henzinger, T.A., Kupferman, O.: Alternating-time temporal logic. J. ACM (JACM) **49**(5), 672–713 (2002)
2. Alur, R., Henzinger, T.A., Mang, F.Y.C., Qadeer, S., Rajamani, S.K., Tasiran, S.: MOCHA: modularity in model checking. In: Hu, A.J., Vardi, M.Y. (eds.) CAV 1998. LNCS, vol. 1427, pp. 521–525. Springer, Heidelberg (1998). https://doi.org/10.1007/BFb0028774
3. Baier, C., Katoen, J.P.: Principles of Model Checking. MIT Press, Cambridge (2008)
4. Biere, A.: PicoSAT essentials. J. Satisf. Boolean Model. Comput. **4**(2–4), 75–97 (2008)
5. Biere, A., Cimatti, A., Clarke, E.M., Strichman, O., Zhu, Y.: Bounded model checking. In: Handbook of Satisfiability, vol. 185, no. 99, pp. 457–481 (2009)
6. Cimatti, A., Clarke, E., Giunchiglia, F., Roveri, M.: NUSMV: a new symbolic model checker. STTT **2**(4), 410–425 (2000). https://doi.org/10.1007/s100090050046
7. Cohen, M., Dam, M., Lomuscio, A., Qu, H.: A symmetry reduction technique for model checking temporal-epistemic logic. In: IJCAI (2009)
8. De Masellis, R., Goranko, V., Gruner, S., Timm, N.: Generalising the dining philosophers problem: competitive dynamic resource allocation in multi-agent systems. In: Slavkovik, M. (ed.) EUMAS 2018. LNCS (LNAI), vol. 11450, pp. 30–47. Springer, Cham (2019). https://doi.org/10.1007/978-3-030-14174-5_3
9. Jamroga, W., Penczek, W., Sidoruk, T., Dembiński, P., Mazurkiewicz, A.: Towards partial order reductions for strategic ability. JAIR **68**, 817–850 (2020)
10. Kacprzak, M., Penczek, W.: Unbounded model checking for alternating-time temporal logic. In: CAV, pp. 646–653. IEEE (2004)

11. Kroening, D., Ouaknine, J., Strichman, O., Wahl, T., Worrell, J.: Linear completeness thresholds for bounded model checking. In: Gopalakrishnan, G., Qadeer, S. (eds.) CAV 2011. LNCS, vol. 6806, pp. 557–572. Springer, Heidelberg (2011). https://doi.org/10.1007/978-3-642-22110-1_44
12. Lomuscio, A., Penczek, W., Woźna, B.: Bounded model checking for knowledge and real time. Artif. Intell. **171**(16–17), 1011–1038 (2007)
13. Lomuscio, A., Qu, H., Raimondi, F.: MCMAS: an open-source model checker for the verification of multi-agent systems. STTT **19**(1), 9–30 (2017). https://doi.org/10.1007/s10009-015-0378-x
14. Luo, X., Su, K., Sattar, A., Reynolds, M.: Verification of multi-agent systems via bounded model checking. In: Sattar, A., Kang, B. (eds.) AI 2006. LNCS (LNAI), vol. 4304, pp. 69–78. Springer, Heidelberg (2006). https://doi.org/10.1007/11941439_11
15. Pilecki, J., Bednarczyk, M.A., Jamroga, W.: SMC: synthesis of uniform strategies and verification of strategic ability for multi-agent systems. J. Log. Comput. **27**(7), 1871–1895 (2017)
16. Raimondi, F., Lomuscio, A.: Automatic verification of multi-agent systems by model checking via ordered binary decision diagrams. J. Appl. Log. **5**(2), 235–251 (2007)
17. Schewe, S.: ATL* satisfiability is 2EXPTIME-complete. In: Aceto, L., Damgård, I., Goldberg, L.A., Halldórsson, M.M., Ingólfsdóttir, A., Walukiewicz, I. (eds.) ICALP 2008. LNCS, vol. 5126, pp. 373–385. Springer, Heidelberg (2008). https://doi.org/10.1007/978-3-540-70583-3_31

Temporal Reasoning Through Automatic Translation of tock-CSP into Timed Automata

Abdulrazaq Abba[1,2](✉) ⓘ, Ana Cavalcanti[1], and Jeremy Jacob[1]

[1] University of York, York, UK
[2] University of East London, London, UK
a.abba@uel.ac.uk

Abstract. We present an approach for automatic translation of *tock-CSP* into Timed Automata (TA) to facilitate using UPPAAL in reasoning about temporal specifications of *tock-CSP* models. The process algebra *tock-CSP* provides textual notations for modelling discrete-time behaviours, with the support of tools for automatic verification. Automatic verification of TA with a graphical notation is supported by UPPAAL. The two approaches provide diverse facilities for automatic verification. For instance, liveness requirements are difficult to specify with the constructs of *tock-CSP*, but they are easy to specify and verify in UPPAAL. We have developed a translation technique based on rules and a tool for translating *tock-CSP* into a network of small TAs for capturing the compositional structure of *tock-CSP*. For validating the rules, we begin with an experimental approach based on finite approximations of trace sets. Then, we consider using structural induction to establish the correctness.

Keywords: Translation · *tock-CSP* · Timed-Automata

1 Introduction

Communicating Sequential Processes (CSP) is an established process algebra that provides a formal notation for both modelling and verifying concurrent systems [17,31,33]. The use of CSP for verification has been supported by several tools including powerful model-checkers [13,31,35].

Interest in using existing tools of CSP motivated [31] the introduction of support for modelling discrete timed systems: *tock-CSP* provides an additional event *tock* to record the progress of time. As a result, *tock-CSP* has been used to verify real-time systems, such as security protocols [11] and railway systems [19]. Also, recently *tock-CSP* has been used to capture the semantics of RoboChart, a domain-specific language for modelling robotics applications [25].

In this work, we present a technique for automatic translation of *tock-CSP* into Timed Automata (TA) to enable using UPPAAL[5] and temporal logic to verify *tock-CSP* models. UPPAAL is a tool suite for modelling and verification of

© Springer Nature Switzerland AG 2021
S. Campos and M. Minea (Eds.): SBMF 2021, LNCS 13130, pp. 70–86, 2021.
https://doi.org/10.1007/978-3-030-92137-8_5

hybrid systems using a network of TAs. We describe the translation rules and their implementation into a tool.

Both temporal logic and refinement are powerful approaches for model checking [23]. The refinement approach models both the system and its specifications with the same notation [31,33]. Temporal logic enables asking whether a system captures logical formulæ of the requirements specification in the form of *system* $\models$ *formula* [8].

Lowe has investigated the relationship between the refinement approach (in CSP) and the temporal logic approach [23]. The result shows that, in expressing temporal logic checks using refinement, it is necessary to use the infinite refusal testing model of CSP. The work highlights that capturing the expressive power of temporal logic to specify the availability of an event (liveness specification) is not possible in the trace refinement model. Also, due to the difficulty of capturing refusal testing, automatic support becomes problematic, and FDR stops supporting refusal testing in its recent version [13].

Additionally, Lowe's work [23] proves that simple trace refinement checks cannot match the expressive power of temporal logic, especially of the three operators: *eventually* ($\Diamond p$: p *will hold in a subsequent state*), *until* ($p \mathcal{U} q$: p *holds in every state until q holds*) and their *negations*: $(\neg(\Diamond p))$ and $(\neg(p \mathcal{U} q))$. These three operators express behaviour captured by infinite traces. Our contribution presented here facilitates an alternative way of checking such specifications.

Example 1. Consider an Automatic Door System (ADS) that opens a door, and after at least one-time unit, closes the door in synchronisation with a lighting controller, which turns off the light. In *tock-CSP*, this is expressed as:

```
1        ADS = Controller [|{close}|] Lighting
2  Controller = open -> tock -> close -> Controller
3    Lighting = close -> offLight -> Lighting
```

The process ADS has two components—Controller and Lighting—that synchronise on the event close[1], which enables Lighting to turn off the light after closing the door. In *tock-CSP*, there is no direct way of checking if the system eventually turns off the light. However, temporal logic provides a direct construct for specifying liveness requirements, supported in UPPAAL, as follows.

```
- A<> offLight     -- The system eventually turns off the light
```

UPPAAL uses a subset of Timed Computation Tree Logic (TCTL) based on the notions of path and state [5]. A path *formula* quantifies over paths (traces), whereas a state *formula* describes locations. There are different forms of path formulæ. Liveness is either A<>q *(q is eventually satisfied)* or p --> q *(a state satisfying p leads to a state satisfying q)*. A reachability *formula* in the form of

---

[1] Here, the event *close* is asynchronisation event using the CSP operator ([|*Event*|]) for synchronising multiple concurrent processes, such that all the processes have to synchronise on the all the elements of the set *Event* before they can proceed.

E<>q *(a state satisfying q is reachable from the initial state)*. Safety is expressed as either A[]q *(q holds in all reachable states)* or E[]q *(q holds in all states on at least one path)*.

To verify the correctness of the translation technique, first, we use the developed translation technique and its tool to translate the formulated processes into TA for UPPAAL. Next, we use another tool we have developed to generate and compare finite traces of the input *tock-CSP* models and the traces of the translated TA models.

We use Haskell [18], a functional programming language, to express, implement and evaluate the translation technique. The expressive power of Haskell helps us provide formal descriptions of the translation technique as a list of translation rules, which is also suitable for developing a mathematical proof.

The structure of this paper is as follows. Section 2 provides background material. Section 3 summarises the translation technique. We discuss an evaluation of the translation technique in Sect. 4. In Sect. 5, we highlight related works and present a brief comparison with this work. Finally, we highlight future extensions of this work and conclude. Additional details of this work including proofs, implementation and additional examples are available in [1,2].

2 Background

As an extension of CSP, *tock-CSP* provides notations for modelling processes and their interactions, such as the basic processes: SKIP and STOP, for successful termination and deadlock, respectively. Operators include prefix (->) for describing availability of an event. For example, the process move->SKIP represents a mechanism that moves once and then terminates.

There are binary operators such as sequential composition (;), which combines two processes serially. For instance, the process P3 = P1;P2 behaves as process P1, and after successful termination of P1, P2 takes over and P3 behaves as P2. There are other binary operators for concurrency, choice and interruption. Also, CSP has a special event *tau* (τ) for representing invisible actions that are internal to a system. The collection of these operators provides a rich set of constructs for modelling untimed systems [31,33].

For modelling time, *tock-CSP* has a special event tock [31], which specifies that the process waits for one time unit before it engages with its environment. For example, the following process Pt specifies behaviour that moves and then after at least two time units, turns and terminates.

$$Pt = move->tock->tock->turn->SKIP$$

Timed Automata for UPPAAL model hybrid systems as a network of TA. Mathematically, a TA is a tuple (L, l_0, C, A, E, I), where L is a set of locations such that l_0 is the initial location, C is a set of clocks, A is a set of actions, E is a set of edges that connects the locations L, and I is an invariant associated to a location $l \in L$ in the form of $I : L \longrightarrow B(C)$. So, edges $E \subseteq (L \times A \times B(C) \times 2^C \times L)$ from a location $l \in L$ triggered by an action $a \in A$, guarded with a guard $g \in B(C)$ where $B(C)$ is the set of guards, and associated clock $c \in C$ that is reset on following the edge to a location $l \in L$ [5,7].

A system is modelled as a network of TAs that communicate via either synchronous channel communication or shared variables. A sending channel is decorated with an exclamation mark ($c!$) while the corresponding receiving channel is decorated with a question mark $c?$. A TA performs an action $c!$ to communicate with another TA that performs the corresponding co-action $c?$. There are also broadcast channels for communication among multiple TAs, in the form of one-to-many communications (one sender with multiple receivers).

For expressing urgency, there are urgent channels and urgent locations that do not allow delay. There are also committed locations; urgent locations that must participate in the next transition, which is useful for expressing atomicity; a compound action spanning multiple transitions that must be executed as a unit. Invariants specify precise delay and enforce progress [5]. In UPPAAL, networks of TAs model system's components and an explicit operating environment. Additional details with examples are available in [5,6,22].

3   An Overview of the Translation Technique

In this section, we describe the translation of the main constructs of *tock-CSP* via examples. The formal rules are omitted due to space restrictions, but are available in [1,2]. Our translation technique takes an input *tock-CSP* model and produces a list of TAs. The occurrence of each *tock-CSP* event is captured in a small TA with an UPPAAL action, which records an occurrence of the translated event. The small TAs are composed into a network of TAs that capture the behaviour of the input *tock-CSP* model. The network of small TAs give us enough flexibility to capture the compositional structure of *tock-CSP*.

Example 2. A translation of the process ADS, from Example 1, produces a network of small TAs in Fig. 1. TA00 captures concurrency by starting the two automata for the processes `Controller` and `Lighting` in two possible orders—either `Controller` then `Lighting` or vice versa—depending on the operating environment. Here, we use the committed locations (s2, s3 and s4) to show that starting the concurrent automata is a compound action. Then TA00 waits on state s5 for the termination actions in the two possible orders, either `finishID1?` then `finishID2?` or vice versa. However, for the termination, we do not use committed locations because the processes can terminate at different times. TA00 synchronises the processes before terminating the system with the action `finishID0!`.

TA01, TA02 and TA03 capture the behaviour of the process `Controller`. TA01 captures the occurrence of the event `open`. TA02 captures the occurrence of `tock` to synchronise with the environment TA in recording the progress of time. TA03 captures the event `close` to synchronise with the controller TA04.

TA05 and TA06 capture the behaviour of the process `Lighting`. TA05 captures `close`, which also synchronises with TA04. Then, TA06 captures the event

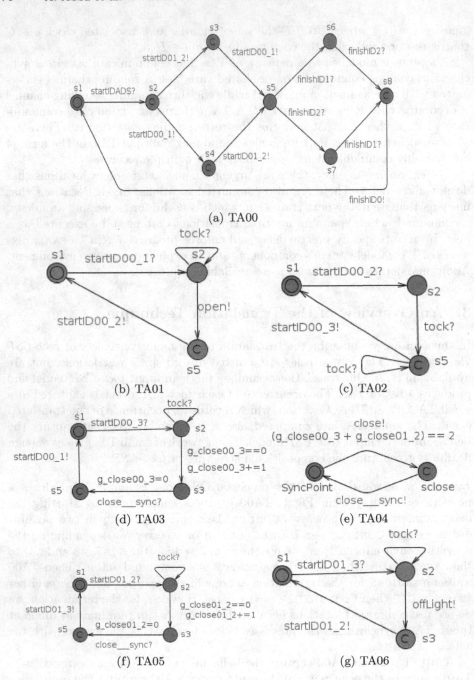

(a) TA00

(b) TA01

(c) TA02

(d) TA03

(e) TA04

(f) TA05

(g) TA06

Fig. 1. A list of networked TAs for the translation of the process ADS.

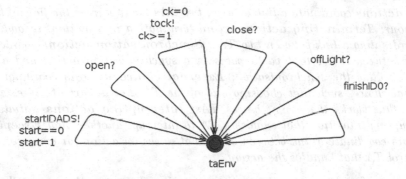

Fig. 2. An environment TA for the translated behaviour of the process ADS.

offLight. Finally, Fig. 2 shows the environment TA that has co-actions for all the translated events. The environment TA serves the purpose of 'closing' the overall system as required for the model checker. In the environment TA, we use the variable start to construct a guard start==0 that blocks the environment from restarting the system.

The main reason for using a list of small TAs is to capture the compositional structure of *tock-CSP*, which is not available in TA [9]. For instance, it can be argued that a linear process constructed with a series of prefix operators can be translated into a linear TA[2]. However, the compositional structure of *tock-CSP* is not suitable for this straightforward translation. For instance, consider a case where the linear process is composed with an interrupting process[3]: the behaviour is no longer linear because the process can be interrupted at any stable state, as illustrated in Example 4. This problem can be seen in translating a process P = (e1->SKIP) [] ((e2->SKIP) ||| (e3->SKIP)), which contains both external choice and concurrency. However, a network of small TAs provides enough flexibility for composing TA in various ways to capture the behaviour of the original *tock-CSP* process.

In constructing the networked TAs, we use additional **coordinating actions** to link the list of small TAs to establish the flow of the input *tock-CSP* model. For example, the channel startIDADS links the environment TA (Fig. 2) with TA00 (Fig. 1), on performing the action startIDADS! and its co-action startIDADS?. A precise definition of the coordinating action is as follows.

Definition 1. *A **Coordinating Action** is an* UPPAAL *action that does not correspond to a tock-CSP event. There are six types of coordinating actions:*

---

[2] A TA with linear transitions only, no branches.

[3] Also, *tock-CSP* inherits the operator interrupt (/\) from CSP, which allows a process to shut down another and takes over the control. For instance, initially the process (P/\Q) behaves as P but at any time before its termination if the process Q performs a visible action, the process P hands over the control to the process Q. Therefore, the process P terminates and the whole process (P/\Q) behaves as Q.

Flow actions coordinate a link between two TAs for capturing the flow of their behaviour; **Terminating actions** record termination information, in addition to coordinating a link between two TAs; **Synchronisation actions** coordinate a link between a TA that participates in a synchronisation action and a TA for controlling the synchronisation; **External choice actions** coordinate an external choice, such that choosing one of the TA that is part of the external choice thus blocks the other choices TAs; **Interrupting actions** initiate an interrupting transition that enables a TA to interrupt another; and **Exception actions** coordinate a link between a TA that raises an action for exception and a control TA that handles the action.

The names of each coordinating action are unique to ensure the correct flow of the translated TAs[4]. In our tool, the names of the flow actions are generated in the form `startIDx`, where x is either a natural number or the name of the input *tock-CSP* process. For instance in Fig. 1, `startID00_1` is the flow action that connects TA00 and TA01.

Likewise, the names of the remaining coordinating actions follow similar pattern: `keywordIDx`, where `keyword` is a designated word for each of the coordinating actions; `finish` for a terminating action, `ext` for an external choice action, `intrp` for an interrupting action, and `excp` for an exception action. Similarly, we provide a special name for a synchronising action in the form `eventName___sync`: an event name appended with the keyword `___sync` to differentiate a synchronising action from other actions. This is particularly important for analysis and are in the reserved keywords for the supporting tool.

For each translated *tock-CSP* specification, we provide an environment TA, like the TA in Fig. 2, which has corresponding co-actions for all the translated events of the input *tock-CSP* model, plus three coordinating actions that link the environment TA with the networked TAs. The first flow action links the environment with the first TA in the list of the translated TA (as illustrated in Fig. 2, the action `startIDADS` links the environment TA with TA00 in Fig. 1). This first flow action activates the behaviour of the translated TA. Second, a terminating action links back the terminating TA to the environment TA to capture a successful termination of a process (as shown in Fig. 2 with the action `FinishID0`). Third, a flow action `tock` records the progress of time. A precise definition of the structure of the environment TA is as follows.

Definition 2. An environment TA *models operating environments for* UPPAAL. *The environment TA has one state and transitions for each co-action of all the events in the input tock-CSP process, in addition to three transitions: the first starting flow action, the final terminating co-action and the action* `tock` *for recording the progress of time.*

In translating multi-synchronisation, we adopt a centralised approach developed in [28] and implemented using Java in [12], which uses a separate cen-

---

[4] We use terminating actions where a TA needs to communicate a successful termination for another TA to proceed. For instance, in translating sequential composition P1;P2, the process P2 begins only after successful termination of the process P1.

tralised controller for handling synchronisation. Here, we use a separate TA with an UPPAAL broadcast channel to communicate synchronising information. In Fig. 1, we illustrate the translation of synchronisation in translating the event close, which synchronises TA03 and TA05 using the broadcasting channel close___sync.

Each synchronising TA has a guard to ensure synchronisation with the correct number of TAs. The guard requires that the sum of special synchronisation variables from all the TAs that synchronise on the synchronisation action equals the number of such actions. Each TA updates its synchronisation variable from 0 to 1 to show its readiness for the synchronisation and waits for the synchronisation action. For instance, in Fig. 1, the synchronising TA (TA04) has a guard expression (g_close00_3 + g_close01_2)==2, which becomes true only when TA03 and TA05 update their synchronisation variables: g_close00_3 and g_close01_2, from 0 to 1. Then, TA04 notifies the occurrence of the action close and broadcasts the synchronising action close___sync!. After the synchronisation, each TA resets its variable to zero and performs its remaining behaviour. A precise definition of the synchronisation TA is as follows.

Definition 3. *A **synchronisation TA** coordinates synchronisation actions. The synchronisation TA has an initial state, and a committed state for each synchronisation action, such that each committed state is connected to the initial state with two transitions. The first transition from the initial state has a guard and an action. The guard is enabled only when all the processes are ready for synchronisation, which also enables the synchronising TA to perform the associated action that notifies the environment of its occurrence. In the second transition, the TA broadcasts the synchronisation action to all the processes that synchronise, which enables them to synchronise and proceed.*

In translating external choice, we provide additional transitions to capture the behaviour of the chosen process in blocking the behaviour of the other processes. Initially, in the translated TA, all the initials[5] of the translated processes are available such that choosing one process blocks all the other choices.

Example 3. A translation of external choice is illustrated in Fig. 3 for the process Pe = (left->STOP)[](right->STOP), which composes two processes left->STOP and right->STOP using the external choice operator ([]).

In Fig. 3, TA00 captures the operator external choice. TA01 and TA03 capture the LHS process (left->STOP). TA02 and TA04 capture the RHS process (right->STOP). TA00 has three transitions labelled with the actions: startIDpExtChoice?, startID00_1! and startId01_2!. TA00 begins with the first flow action startIDpExtChoice? and then starts both TA01 and TA02, using the actions startID00_1! and startId01_2!, available for choice.

Initially, TA01 synchronises on startID00_1 and moves to location s2 that has three transitions labelled: left_exch?, right_exch! and tock?.

---

[5] The term initials describe the first visible events of a process.

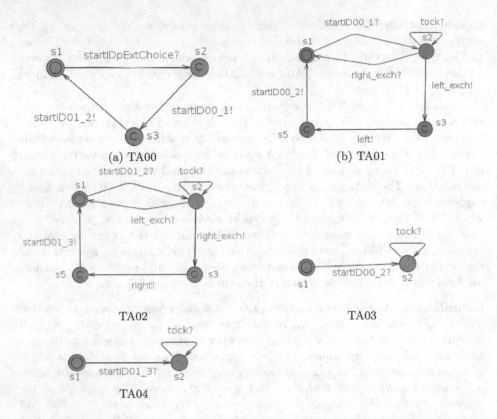

Fig. 3. A list of TAs for the translated behaviour of the process Pe

With the co-action `tock?`, the TA records the progress of time and remains on the same location s2. With the co-action `right_exch?`, the TA performs an external choice co-action for blocking the LHS process when the environment chooses the RHS process, and TA01 returns to initial location s1.

Alternatively, TA01 performs the action `left_exch!` when the environment chooses the LHS process, and TA01 proceeds to location s3 to perform the chosen action `left!` that leads to location s5 and performs the flow action `startID00_2!`, which activates TA03 for the subsequent process `STOP`. For the RHS process, TA02 captures the similar translation of the event `right`. The omitted environment TA is similar to that in Fig. 2.

In *tock-CSP*, a process can be interrupted by another process when composed using an operator interrupt (/\). Thus, we provide additional transitions to capture the interrupting behaviour.

Example 4. An example of translating interrupt is in Fig. 4, for the translation of the process Pi = (open->STOP)/(fire->close->STOP).

In Pi, the RHS process `fire->close->STOP` can interrupt the LHS process `open->STOP` at any stable state. So, in the translated behaviour of the LHS

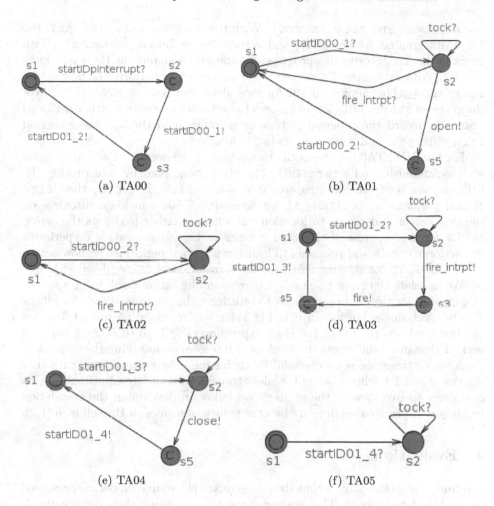

Fig. 4. A list of TAs for the translated behaviour of the process Pi.

process, we provide interrupting actions (like `fire_intrpt`) that enable the translated behaviour of the RHS process to interrupt that of the LHS process. The corresponding co-action of the interrupting actions are provided only for the initials of the RHS process (`fire`) because it can only interrupt with its initials.

In Fig. 4, TA00 is a translation of the operator interrupt. TA01 and TA02 capture the translation of the LHS process `open->STOP`, while TA03, TA04 and TA05 capture the translation of the RHS process `fire->close->STOP`. The environment TA is again similar to the TA in Fig. 2.

First, TA00 performs the actions `startID00_1!` and `startID01_2!` to activate TA01 and TA03. TA01 synchronises on `startID00_1` and moves to location s2 where there are three possible transitions for the actions:

tock?, open! and fire_intrpt?. With the co-action fire_intrpt?, the TA is interrupted by the RHS, and returns to its initial location s1. With tock?, the TA records the progress of time and remains on the same location s2. With open, the TA proceeds to location s5 to perform the flow action startID00_2! to activate TA02 for the subsequent process STOP. TA02 synchronises on startID00_2? and moves to location s2, where it either performs tock? to record the progress of time or is interrupted through the co-action fire_intrpt?, and returns to its initial location s1.

For the RHS, TA03 captures the translation of the event fire. TA03 begins with synchronising on startID01_2?, which progresses by interrupting the LHS process using the interruptive flow action fire_intrpt!, then fire !, and performs startID01_3! for activating TA04 which synchronises on the flow action and moves to location s2, where it either performs the action tock? for the progress of time and remains in the same location or performs the action close! and proceeds to location s5, then performs the flow action startID01_4! for starting TA05 for the translation of STOP (deadlock).

We translate the event tock into a corresponding action tock using a broadcast channel for the environment TA to broadcast the progress of time for all the TAs to synchronise. For instance, in Fig. 1, the environment TA has a transition labelled tock guarded with the clock expression $ck \geq 1$, so that tock happens every 1 time unit, and resets the clock $ck = 0$ to zero on following the transition.

Also, we translate non-deterministic choice into silent transitions, such that the translated TA follows one of the silent transitions non-deterministically. This completes an overview of the strategy we follow in developing the translation technique. A precise description of all the translation rules in Haskell is in [1,2].

4   Evaluation

A sound translation ensures that the properties of the source model are preserved in the translated model. This is determined by comparing their behaviours [4, 20,24,26]. We compare the behaviour of the input *tock-CSP* and the output TA in two phases: experimental evaluation and mathematical proof.

4.1   Experimental Evaluation

We use trace semantics to evaluate the equivalence of the traces. In carrying out the experiment, we have developed an evaluation tool, which uses our translation tool and both FDR and UPPAAL as black boxes for generating finite traces, as shown in Fig. 5, which shows the structure of the evaluation tool, available at [1].

In generating traces, like most model checkers, FDR produces only one trace (counterexample) at a time. So, based on the testing technique in [27], we have developed a trace-generation technique that repeatedly invokes FDR until we get all the required trace sets of the input process. Similarly, based on another

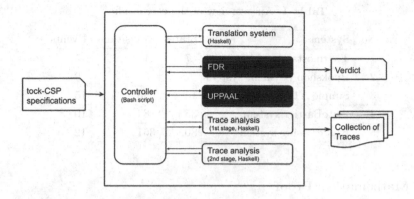

Fig. 5. Structure of the trace analysis system

testing technique with temporal logic [22], we have developed a trace-generation technique that uses UPPAAL to generate traces of the translated TA models.

These two trace-generation techniques form components of our evaluation tool (Fig. 5), which has two stages. In the first stage, we generate traces of the input *tock-CSP* and its corresponding translated TA, using both FDR and UPPAAL. Then, we compare the generated traces; if they do not match, it may be because FDR distinguishes different permutations of events (traces). In contrast, UPPAAL uses a logical formula to generate traces [5, 22] which do not distinguishes traces with different permutations. So, we move to a second stage, where we use FDR to complement UPPAAL in generating traces.

Essentially, UPPAAL checks if a system satisfies its requirement specifications (logical formula), irrespective of the behaviour of the system. For example, UPPAAL does not distinguish between the two traces $\langle e1, e2, e3 \rangle$ and $\langle e1, e3 \rangle$, if both traces satisfy the requirement specification formula, such as a system performs the event $e3$, either through $e2$ or before $e2$. However, FDR is capable of generating both traces. Thus, in the second stage, we use UPPAAL to check if all the traces of FDR are acceptable traces of the translated TA.

For evaluation, we have used a list of systematically formulated *tock-CSP* processes that pair the constructs of *tock-CSP*. The list contains 111 processes. Archives of the processes and their traces are available in a repository [1].

In addition, we test the translation technique with larger examples from the literature, such as an automated barrier to a car park [33], a thermostat machine for monitoring ambient temperature [33], an Automated Teller Machine (ATM) [32], a bookshop payment system [33], and a railway crossing system [31]. An overview of these case studies is in Table 1, while the details, including the traces, are also available in the repository of this work [1].

Considering that the experimental approach with trace analysis is an approximation for establishing correctness with a finite set of traces, covering infinite sets of traces in proving correctness has to use mathematical proof.

Table 1. An overview of the case studies

No.	System	States	Transitions	Events
1	Thermostat machine	7	16	5
2	Bookshop payment system	7	32	9
3	Simple ATM	15	33	15
4	AutoBarrier system	35	84	10
5	Rail crossing system	80	361	12

4.2   Mathematical Proof

Here, we illustrate part of the proof using one of the base cases of the structural induction. A more detailed account of our proof can be found in [1,2]. A TA is defined as the tuple[6] (Sect. 2). Consider TA1 as the translation of the process STOP (TA05 from Fig. 4), then mathematically TA1 is expressed as follows.

$$TA1 = (\{s1, s2\}, s1, \{ck\}, \{startID01\_4, tock\},$$
$$\{(s1, startID01\_4, \emptyset, \emptyset, s2), (s2, tock, ck \leq 1, ck, s2)\}, \{\}) \quad (1)$$

In the language of TA, a path [3,7] is a sequence of consecutive transitions that begins from the initial state. A trace [3,7] (or word): is a sequence of actions in each path. In TA1, there is only one infinite path, the first transition from location $s1$ to location $s2$ and the second transition from location $s2$ back to location $s2$, repeated infinitely. The traces on the path are as follows.

$$traces'_{TA}(TA1) = \{\langle\rangle\} \cup \{\langle startID01\_4\rangle^\frown \langle tock\rangle^n \mid n \in \mathbb{N}\} \quad (2)$$

The function $trace'_{TA}(TA)$ computes the traces of the translated TAs generated by our translation technique. It takes a list of networked TAs and returns a set of traces. For instance, in Eq. 2, the first empty trace is for the initial state of the TA, before the first transition; the action $startID01\_4$ happens on the first transition; the action $tock$ happens on the second transition, which is repeated infinitely for the infinite traces $\langle tock\rangle^n$.

Another function $trace_{TA}(TA)$ is similar to $traces'_{TA}(TA)$ but removes all the coordinating actions (Definition 1) from the traces.

$$traces_{TA}(TA) = \{t \setminus CoordinatingActions \mid t \in traces'_{TA}(TA)\} \quad (3)$$

Therefore, without coordinating actions, the traces of TA1 become:

$$traces_{TA}(TA1) = \{\langle tock\rangle^n \mid n \in \mathbb{N}\} \quad (4)$$

---

[6] TA $= (L, l_0, C, A, E, I)$ where L is a set of locations, l_0 is the initial location, C is a set of clocks, A is a set of actions, E is a set of edges and I is an invariant.

Our goal is to establish that the traces of *tock-CSP* models are the same as those of the translated TA models. Here, transTA is the translation function we have formalised for translating *tock-CSP* models into TA models. Thus, for each valid *tock-CSP* process P, within the scope of this work, we need to establish the following theorem.

Theorem 1.

$$traces_{tock-CSP}(P) = traces_{TA}(transTA(P)) \tag{5}$$

Proof. For each translation rule, we have to prove that the translated TAs capture the behaviour of the corresponding input *tock-CSP* model P.

Starting with the basic process STOP, Eq. 5 becomes

$$traces_{tock-CSP}(STOP) = traces_{TA}(transTA(STOP)) \tag{6}$$

Using structural induction in Haskell, we show that:

```
1  (traces_tockCSP n STOP = traces_TA n (transTA STOP))
2  => (traces_tockCSP (n+1) STOP = traces_TA (n+1) (transTA
        STOP))
```

Each step is evaluated automatically. The detailed steps of the proof are available in the extended reports [1,2].

5   Related Work and Conclusions

Timed-CSP [33] is another popular extension of CSP for capturing temporal specifications. Unlike *tock-CSP*, Timed-CSP records the progress of time with a series of positive real numbers. However, the approach of Timed-CSP cannot specify deadline nor urgency. Also, traces of Timed-CSP are infinite, which is problematic for automatic analysis and verification [31]. Thus, there is no proper tool support for verifying Timed-CSP models. Therefore, researchers have explored various approaches, such as model transformations in translating Timed-CSP into *tock-CSP* for using FDR in automatic verification [29]; translation of Timed-CSP into UPPAAL, initially reported in [9] and then subsequently improved in [14]; and translation of Timed-CSP into Constraint Logic Programming (CLP) for reasoning with the constraint solver CLP(R) [10]. Additionally, using PAT for verifying Stateful Timed CSP (a variation of Timed-CSP) [34] and using FDR for verfiying a variation of Timed-CSP [30].

However, there is less focus on applying the same transformation techniques for *tock-CSP*. Although, an attempt to transform TA into *tock-CSP* was proposed in [21], in this work, we consider the opposite direction.

Apart from CSP and TA, model transformations have been used for improving various formal modelling notations. For instance, Circus has been translated into CSP||B for using the tool ProB for automatic verification [36]. Additionally, the language B has been translated into TLA+ for automatic validation with

TLC [16]. Also, translating TLA+ to B has been investigated for automated validation of TLA+ with ProB [15], such that both B and TLA+ benefit from the resources of each other, and their supporting tools ProB and TLC, respectively.

In conclusion, we have presented a technique for translating *tock-CSP* into TA for UPPAAL to facilitate using temporal logic and facilities of UPPAAL in verifying *tock-CSP* models. This work contributes an alternative way of using TCTL to specify liveness requirements and other related requirements that are difficult to verify in *tock-CSP* with refinement. Also, our work sheds light into the complex relationship between *tock-CSP* and TA (temporal logic model).

Currently, we have used trace analysis to justify the correctness of the translation work. Also, we translate the event `tock` into an action that is controlled by a timed clock in UPPAAL. A next step is to relate the notion of `tock` to the notion of time in TA and get rid of `tock` as an action. This additional extension will help us to explore additional interesting facilities of UPPAAL to verify temporal specifications. Also, in future work, a better understanding of relating *tock-CSP* to TA will help us to explore using a single TA instead of network TAs for more efficient verification.

Acknowledgements. Abba gratefully acknowledges the financial support of Petroleum Technology Development Fund (PTDF). Cavalcanti is funded by the Royal Academy of Engineering grant CiET1718/45 and the UK EPSRC grants EP/M025756/1 and EP/R025479/1.

References

1. A repository of this work. https://github.com/ahagmj/TemporalReasoning.git
2. Abba, A.: Temporal reasoning about robotics applications: refinement and temporal logic. Ph.D. thesis, The University of York (2021)
3. Alur, R., Dill, D.: A theory of timed automata. Theor. Comput, Sci. **126**, 183–235 (1994)
4. Back, R.: On correct refinement of programs. J. Comput. Syst. Sci. **23**(1), 49–68 (1981)
5. Behrmann, G., David, A., Larsen, K.G., Håkansson, J., Petterson, P., Wang, Y., Hendriks, M.: UPPAAL 4.0. Third Int. Conf. Quant. Eval. Syst. QEST 2006 pp. 125–126 (2006). https://doi.org/10.1109/QEST.2006.59
6. Bouyer, P.: Model-checking timed temporal logics. Electr. Notes Theor. Comput. Sci. **231**, 323–341 (2009)
7. Bouyer, P.: An introduction to timed automata. In: Seatzu, C., Silva M., van Schuppen J. (eds) Control of Discrete-Event Systems. Lecture Notes in Control and Information Sciences, vol. 433, pp. 79–94. Springer, London (2011). https://doi.org/10.1007/978-1-4471-4276-8_9
8. Clarke, E.M., Emerson, E.A., Sistla, A.P.: Automatic verification of finite-state concurrent systems using temporal logic specifications. ACM Trans. Program. Lang. Syst. (TOPLAS) **8**(2), 244–263 (1986)
9. Dong, J.S., Hao, P., Qin, S., Sun, J., Yi, W.: Timed automata patterns. IEEE Trans. Softw. Eng. **34**(6), 844–859 (2008)

10. Dong, J.S., Hao, P., Sun, J., Zhang, X.: A Reasoning method for timed CSP based on constraint solving. In: Liu, Z., He, J. (eds.) ICFEM 2006. LNCS, vol. 4260, pp. 342–359. Springer, Heidelberg (2006). https://doi.org/10.1007/11901433_19

11. Evans, N., Schneider, S.: Analysing time dependent security properties in CSP using PVS. In: European Symposium on Research in Computer Security. pp. 222–237. Springer (2000)

12. de Freitas, A.F.: From Circus to Java: Implementation and verification of a translation strategy. Master's thesis, University of York (2005)

13. Gibson-Robinson, T., Armstrong, P., Boulgakov, A., Roscoe, A.W.: FDR3: a parallel refinement checker for CSP. Int. J. Softw. Tools Technol, Transf. **18**, 149–167 (2016)

14. Göthel, T., Glesner, S.: Automatic validation of infinite real-time systems. In: 2013 1st FME Workshop on Formal Methods in Software Engineering (FormaliSE), pp. 57–63. IEEE (2013)

15. Hansen, D., Leuschel, M.: Translating TLA+ to B for validation with ProB. In: International Conference on Integrated Formal Methods, pp. 24–38. Springer (2012)

16. Hansen, D., Leuschel, M.: Translating B to TLA+ for validation with TLC. In: International Conference on Abstract State Machines, Alloy, B, TLA, VDM, and Z, pp. 40–55. Springer (2014)

17. Hoare, C.A.R.: Communicating sequential processes. Commun. ACM **21**(8), 666–677 (1978)

18. Hutton, G.: Programming in Haskell. Cambridge University Press, Cambridge (2016)

19. Isobe, Y., Moller, F., Nguyen, H.N., Roggenbach, M.: Safety and line capacity in railways – an approach in timed CSP. In: Derrick, J., Gnesi, S., Latella, D., Treharne, H. (eds.) IFM 2012. LNCS, vol. 7321, pp. 54–68. Springer, Heidelberg (2012). https://doi.org/10.1007/978-3-642-30729-4_5

20. Kahani, N., Bagherzadeh, M., Cordy, J.R., Dingel, J., Varró, D.: Survey and classification of model transformation tools. Softw. Syst. Model. **18**(4), 2361–2397 (2018). https://doi.org/10.1007/s10270-018-0665-6

21. Khattri, M.: Translating timed automata to tock-CSP. In: Proceedings of the 10th IASTED International Conference on Software Engineering, SE 2011 (2011)

22. Lindstrom, B., Pettersson, P., Offutt, J.: Generating trace-sets for model-based testing. In: The 18th IEEE International Symposium on Software Reliability (ISSRE'07), pp. 171–180. IEEE (2007)

23. Lowe, G.: Specification of communicating processes: temporal logic versus refusals-based refinement. Form Aspect. Comput. **20**(3), 277–294 (2008)

24. Mens, T., Van Gorp, P.: A taxonomy of model transformation. Electr. Rotes Theoret. Comput. Sci. **152**, 125–142 (2006)

25. Miyazawa, A., Ribeiro, P., Li, W., Cavalcanti, A., Timmis, J., Woodcock, J.: RoboChart: a State-Machine Notation for Modelling and Verification of Mobile and Autonomous Robots. Tech. Rep. pp. 1–18 (2016)

26. Nielson, H.R., Nielson, F.: Semantics with Applications: an Appetizer. Springer Science & Business Media, London (2007)

27. Nogueira, S., Sampaio, A., Mota, A.: Guided test generation from CSP models. In: International Colloquium on Theoretical Aspects of Computing. pp. 258–273. Springer, Cham (2008). https://doi.org/10.1007/978-3-030-85315-0

28. Oliveira, M.V.M.: Formal derivation of state-rich reactive programs using Circus. Ph.D. thesis, University of York (2005)

29. Ouaknine, J.: Discrete analysis of continuous behaviour in real-time concurrent systems. Ph.D. thesis, University of Oxford (2000)
30. Ouaknine, J., Worrell, J.: Timed-CSP = closed timed ε-automata. Nordic J. Comput. **10**(2), 99–133 (2003)
31. Roscoe, A.W.: Understanding Concurrent Systems. Springer Science & Business Media, London (2010)
32. Roscoe, A., Hoare, C., Bird, R.: The theory and practice of concurrency. 2005. Revised edition. Only available online (2005)
33. Schneider, S.: Concurrent and real time systems: the CSP approach. In: World Scientific Proceedings Series on Computer Engineering and Information Science (2010)
34. Sun, J., Liu, Y., Dong, J.S., Liu, Y., Shi, L., André, E.: Modeling and verifying hierarchical real-time systems using stateful Timed-CSP. ACM Trans. Softw. Eng. Methodol. **22**(1) (2013). https://doi.org/10.1145/2430536.2430537, https://doi.org/10.1145/2430536.2430537
35. Sun, J., Liu, Y., Dong, J.S., Pang, J.: PAT: towards flexible verification under fairness. In: Bouajjani, A., Maler, O. (eds.) CAV 2009. LNCS, vol. 5643, pp. 709–714. Springer, Heidelberg (2009). https://doi.org/10.1007/978-3-642-02658-4_59
36. Ye, K., Woodcock, J.: Model checking of state-rich formalism by linking to $CSP \parallel B$. Int. J. Softw. Tools Technol. Transf. **19**(1), 73–96 (2017)

Module Integration Using Graph Grammars (MIGRATE)

Diogo Raphael Cravo$^{(\boxtimes)}$ and Leila Ribeiro

Universidade Federal do Rio Grande do Sul (UFRGS), Porto Alegre, Brazil
diogo.raphael@inf.ufrgs.br

Abstract. Software, whether desktop, mobile or web, is becoming more
and more connected. Software development is also becoming more connected with ecosystems comprised of networks of millions of packages.
Engineering software today is writing code that weaves together libraries,
services and applications. Such fabrics are under constant changes due
to both internal requests, e.g. new features, or external demands, e.g.
dependency updates. Avoiding integration bugs in this scenario can be
a big challenge regardless of common strategies such as testing and versioning. We propose an approach, called Module Integration using Graph
Grammars (MIGRATE), to describe/analyze integration points among
software modules. We define module nets, a formalism to capture the
essential information regarding module integration, whose semantics is
defined in terms of graph transformations. This allows us to use the rich
theory of graph transformation, specially critical pair analysis, to analyze
the coupling among different modules and create warnings in case of possible integration problems. The approach is organized in three phases: (i)
transformation of code into module nets (model extraction), (ii) translation of module nets into graph grammars (semantics of integration) and
(iii) verification of module integration. We have built a prototype that
implements the MIGRATE approach.

Keywords: Graph grammar · Software integration · Verification tool

1 Introduction

Software is typically built on top of other software. Integration of components,
that can be classes, libraries or services, leads to dependencies that may com-
promise system behavior in case of careless updates.

There is a multitude of software ecosystems with all kinds of package managers. For example, Node Package Manager (NPM) for JavaScript/NodeJS has
over one million packages, and Maven for Java has more than six million indexed
artifacts. Studies about such ecosystems show that there are fundamental packages, which form a base to an entire ecosystem, and breaking changes to such
fundamental packages can have catastrophic effects [6]. A common example in
the NPM ecosystem is the left-pad incident in 2016, a trivial package that was
removed from the ecosystem causing thousands of others to break [6].

© Springer Nature Switzerland AG 2021
S. Campos and M. Minea (Eds.): SBMF 2021, LNCS 13130, pp. 87–103, 2021.
https://doi.org/10.1007/978-3-030-92137-8_6

A study with Java libraries released prior to 2011 has shown that roughly 35% of minor releases and 23% of patch releases contained breaking changes [21]. This is in contrast to semantic versioning principles, which restrict patch and minor updates to non-breaking changes. A more recent study in Java ecosystem has shown that roughly a quarter of changes were considered breaking, and the larger a library gets, the more breaking changes it introduces [25].

Integration issues are not restricted to libraries, services also suffer a great deal of compatibility problems. Aué *et al.* have studied millions of faults logged by a large scale web service in the payments business and came up with eleven categories for those faults [1]. While some errors can be attributed to end users, such as providing a maxed out credit card, others are due to the programming that integrates clients, service and third-parties. Even microservices, a relatively new architectural pattern known for achieving loosely coupled modules, are affected by compatibility problems, and API versioning and contracts are mentioned in 13 of 51 grey literature papers [23].

A common strategy adopted by users to avoid breaking compatibility is to keep dependencies to a minimum and select dependencies they trust [2]. For services, common advice is to relax the assumptions on data received, ignoring any extra information sent, which is a pattern known as the Tolerant Reader [10,17]. Versioning schemes signal to users the degree of changes and enable users to specify rules for automatic updates of their dependencies. Perhaps the most popular scheme in practice is Semantic Versioning (SemVer) [20]. Versioning is also used in services, where it can be found in addresses, HTTP headers or body [17].

Tests are yet another approach to ensure compatibility for both users and developers. There are all kinds of tests in the literature, but specifically integration tests address the problem of compatibility. In his blog, Fowler says that integration tests are meant to show whether software modules work as expected when brought together [11] and splits integration tests into two categories: "narrow integration tests" and "broad integration tests" [11]. While the former requires some kind of mock to replace the actual module integrated and thus isolate tested code to just a single module, the latter tests all modules working together.

We propose a new approach to describe/analyze integration points among software modules. We define module nets, a formalism to capture the essential information regarding module integration, whose semantics is defined in terms of graph transformations. This allows us to use the rich theory of graph transformation, specially critical pair analysis, to analyze the coupling among different modules and create warnings in case of possible integration problems. The approach is organized in three phases: (i) transformation of code into module nets (model extraction), (ii) translation of module nets into graph grammars (semantics of integration) and (iii) verification of module integration.

This article is organized as follows. Section 2 reviews the main concepts of graph grammars. Section 3 presents an overview of the proposed approach. Section 4 formalizes the concept of module nets, which is used in Sect. 5, where the MIGRATE approach is discussed. Finally, we present related work in Sect. 6 and final considerations in Sect. 7.

2 Graph Grammars

Graph-based formal description techniques are a friendly means of explaining complex situations in a compact and understandable way. Graph Grammars (or Graph Transformations) [8] are a generalization of Chomsky grammars from strings to graphs suitable for the specification of different kinds of systems. The basic notions of this formalism are: states are represented by graphs and possible state changes are modeled by rules, where the left- and right-hand sides are graphs. Graph rules are used to capture the dynamical aspects of the systems. That is, from the initial state of the system (the initial graph), the application of rules successively changes the system state.

In this section we review informally the main concepts of Graph Grammars. We follow the algebraic approach to graph grammars, for formal definitions, see e.g. [8]. Examples of graphs, rules and their analysis are presented in the following sections.

Graphs are structures that consist of a set of nodes and a set of edges. Each edge connects two nodes of the graph, one representing a source and another representing a target. A *total homomorphism* between graphs is a mapping of nodes and edges that is compatible with sources and targets of edges. Intuitively, a total homomorphism from a graph $G1$ to a graph $G2$ means that all items (nodes and edges) of $G1$ can be found in $G2$ (but distinct nodes/edges of $G1$ are not necessarily distinct in $G2$).

To be useful in practical applications, graphs may be extended by the notion of attributes [8], which are basically data values associated to vertices and/or edges of graphs. In the algebraic approach (followed here), data values are elements of algebras. The resulting notion of an attributed graph has thus two components: a structural (or graphical) part (a graph) and a data part (an algebra).

The use of algebras as data values allows putting variables and terms as attributes, which, in turn, makes constructing very general graph rules representing behavior possible.

When modeling a state as a graph, it is very convenient to distinguish different types of nodes and edges in a graph. This can be achieved by the notion of **typed graph** [8]. Let TG be a graph that represents all possible (graphical) types that are needed to describe a system. A homomorphism h from any graph G to TG associates a (graphical) type to each item of G. The triple $\langle G, h, TG \rangle$ is called *typed graph*, where TG is the *type graph* (nodes of TG denote all possible types of nodes of a system and edges of TG denote possible relationships between these types).

A **Graph Rule** describes how a system may change. It consists of: a *left-hand side (LHS)*, which describes items that must be present for this rule to be applied (required subgraph); a *right-hand side (RHS)*, describing items that will be present after the application of the rule; and a *mapping from LHS to RHS*, which describes items that will be preserved by the application of the rule. This mapping must be compatible with the structure of the graphs (i.e., a morphism between typed graphs) and may be partial. Items that are in the LHS and are not mapped to the RHS are *deleted*, whereas items that are in the RHS and are not in the image of the mapping from the LHS are *created*. We also assume that rules do not merge items, that is, they are injective.

Furthermore, it is usually very convenient to be able to define also a forbidden context that prevents rule application. This is done by equipping rules with a **negative application condition (NAC)**. A NAC is actually a collection of conditions representing situations that prevent the rule from being applied (NACs are described by mappings from LHS to the graph representing the forbidden context, these mapping must be homomorphisms).

A **Graph Grammar, short GG,** consists of a type graph, specifying the (graphical) types of the system, a (typed) graph representing the initial state of the system, and a set of rules over this type graph that define the system behavior. The application of a rule r to a graph G is possible if an image of the LHS of r is found in G (that is, there is a total typed-graph morphism from the LHS of r to G). The result of a rule application deletes from G all items that are not mapped in r and adds the ones created by r.

There are different techniques to perform analysis of graph grammars. In this paper we use critical pairs in the verification process, and the property of confluence in the translation grammar (to prove that translating a module net to a verification grammar is a deterministic process).

Conflicts and dependencies among rules can be detected by the use of **critical pairs**, that are pairs of rules such that the application of one may have an impact on the application of the other. For example, if a rule $r1$ deletes an item of type X and a rule $r2$ needs this item to be applied, it may be that applying $r1$ hinders the application of $r2$. Notice that this is a *potential* conflict: if there are in the state graph many items of type X, these two rules may be applied independently. There are essentially three kinds of conflicts that may arise in graph transformation systems containing rules with NACs [16]:

- **Preserve-delete (pd):** one of the rules preserves an element that is deleted by the other;
- **Delete-delete (dd):** both rules try to delete the same element;
- **Produce-forbid (pf):** one of the rules produces an element that triggers some NAC of the other rule.

The union of delete-delete and preserve-delete conflicts is referred as **use-delete**. A conflict of type **delete-delete** represents a mutual exclusion situation.

Analogously, dependency critical pairs can be defined, representing the possible dependencies between rules.

Conflict critical pairs denote points of choice in a system. As in term rewriting systems, proofs of termination of graph grammars can be done based on critical pairs (however, in the graph grammar setting these proofs are a bit more involved and require additional conditions, since graphs are more complex than strings [8]). Termination criteria for graph transformation systems are defined in [8] using the concept of **production (or rule) layers**. Intuitively, we classify the rules of a grammar in layers, such that elements of some type are only created by rules of the same layer, and may be deleted only by rules of subsequent layers. This ensures that if an element of a type is created by a transformation, some other transformation will delete it using rules of the same or subsequent layers only, when creation is no longer possible. To guarantee **termination** we additionally have to prove that each layer terminates before the grammar moves to the next layer of rules.

A graph transformation system is **confluent** if it is locally confluent and terminates. Confluence is relevant when we expect a system to exhibit a deterministc behavior, i.e. to produce unique final graph (up to isomorphism) for a given initial graph. Here we use graph grammars in two different ways: (i) verification grammar: to express the semantics of a module net, and (ii) translation grammar: to associate a semantics to a module net. A verification grammar is a grammar that describes the integration behavior of the underlying module net, whereas a translation grammar basically defines a model transformation, generating the verification grammar that corresponds to a module net. Verification grammars may be non-deterministic (since they express behavior of possibly non-deterministic systems), but the translation grammar must be confluent to associate a unique meaning (verification grammar) to each module net.

3   Illustration of the Proposed Approach

We illustrate our approach with Fig. 1. Our goal with this approach is to provide developers with useful information (warnings) concerning the integration of modules that compose their software. To produce such warnings, we start with software artifacts, such as source code like we have in Fig. 1(a), from which we extract a single module net (see next section for its definition), such as the one in Fig. 1(b). We use a confluent graph grammar, which we call the translation grammar, to translate this module net into another graph grammar, which we call verification grammar. The translation procedure is comprised of successive applications of rules to a host graph, generating new graphs. Figure 1(c) depicts this graph at the beginning of a translation, midway through, and after translation is completed. The verification grammar obtained after translation is depicted in Fig. 1(d), where we have omitted a few rules to save space. When verifying the verification grammar, we first generate critical pairs of rules, such as those in Fig. 1(e), and then analyse these pairs to produce warnings, Fig. 1(f), which are reported to users. We will explain each step in more detail in next sections.

Many integration bugs are related to how information is passed from a module to another. For example, if a service asks for more data than it uses, then we can suggest that excess attributes should be deprecated. On the other hand, if a client fails to provide information required by a service, then we can tell developers we have likely found a bug. In order to uncover such bugs, we have to analyse how information is used by each module and what are the actual dependencies that emerge from data.

Our verification procedure consists of interpreting the critical pairs of rules generated for a verification grammar. This verification grammar does not mirror

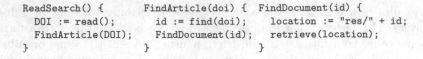

```
ReadSearch() {        FindArticle(doi) {  FindDocument(id) {
  DOI := read();        id := find(doi);    location := "res/" + id;
  FindArticle(DOI);     FindDocument(id);   retrieve(location);
}                     }                   }
```

(a) **Software artifacts** are taken as input

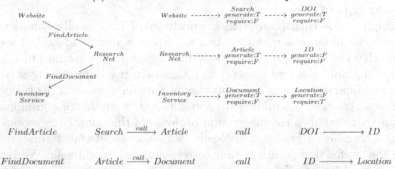

(b) **Extraction**: Module net is extracted from software artifacts

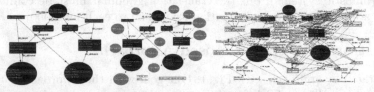

(c) **Translation**: Module net is translated into verification grammar using AGG

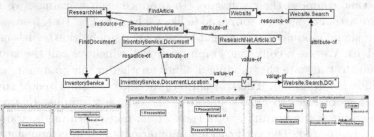

(d) **Verification grammar** resulting from translation

(e) **Verification**: Critical pairs of verification grammar generated using Verigraph
```
Website.Search.DOI can become outdated (generated and FindArticle)
The return of operation FindArticle is not used
The return of operation FindDocument is not used
```

(f) **Warnings** are generated based on critical pairs

Fig. 1. Overview of the proposed approach

the exact behavior of the software that originated it, but it rather reflects how information flows in this software (that is, the verification grammar describes a kind of software integration semantics).

4   Module Nets

MIGRATE aims to automatically produce warnings by interpreting the critical pairs generated for a graph grammar.

To enable this automation, MIGRATE requires that the graph grammar representing the integration aspects of the system to be created in a very specific way. Moreover, developers may want to make changes to extracted models either to experiment with changes of the system or to improve accuracy of model extraction. The notion of module nets serves as a more abstract level than graph grammars, so that developers can work on module nets and MIGRATE will automatically generate the graph grammar that will be analyzed. In the following, we present the definition of module nets.

A **directed graph**, is a tuple $G = (N, E, s, t)$ where N and E are sets of nodes and edges, respectively, and $s, t : E \rightarrow N$ are total functions assigning a source/target node to each edge. A **subgraph** of a graph G is a graph which contains subsets of the sets of nodes and edges of G, while preserving source and target functions. Quadripartite graphs are graphs in which the set of nodes is partitioned in two, and the set of edges in four. In this work, we will partition the set of nodes N in two sets, denoted N_l and N_r, representing the nodes in the left-hand side and right-hand side of a graph. This induces a partition of the set of edges E in sets E_{ll} (representing edges between nodes of N_l), E_{lr} (representing edges from N_l to N_r), E_{rl} (representing edges from N_r to N_l) and E_{rr} (representing edges between nodes of N_r). Considering these different kinds of edge partitions, we can build four different subgraphs of a graph.

Definition 1 (Quadripartite Directed Graph). *A **quadripartite graph** is a graph $Q = (N, E, s, t)$ such that*

- $N = N_l \cup N_r$ and $N_l \cap N_r = \emptyset$
- $E = \bigcup_{i \in \{ll, lr, rl, rr\}} E_i$ and $(E_i \cap E_j)_{i,j \in \{ll, lr, rl, rr\}, i \neq j} = \emptyset$ are pairwise disjoint
- $s = \bigcup_{i \in \{ll, lr, rl, rr\}} s_i$ with $(s_{ij} : E_{ij} \rightarrow N_i)_{i,j \in \{l, r\}}$
- $t = \bigcup_{i \in \{ll, lr, rl, rr\}} t_i$ with $(t_{ij} : E_{ij} \rightarrow N_j)_{i,j \in \{l, r\}}$

The graphs $(Q_{ij} = (N_i \cup N_j, E_{ij}, s_{ij}, t_{ij}))_{i,j \in \{l, r\}}$ are subgraphs of Q.

A **resource** is a unit of information, any kind of data a system may share between its modules, either structured data or not. Resources can be database entities, API models, HTTP tickets, instances of classes, files, any information at all. To further specify what kind of data a resource contains, we provide **attributes**, which are pieces of information that comprise a resource.

Definition 2 (Resource). *A **resource** is a pair composed by a resource name and a (finite) set of **attributes** (i.e., a set of names). Given a resource $r = (name, attr)$ we denote its name by $name^r$ and its attribute set by $attr^r$.*

Modules are the units of a system. Modules represent any kind of subsystem: a service, a library, a class, anything. Modules contain resources, which are the types of information a module of this kind may share with its peers. Modules contain functions **req** (for required) and **ger** (for generated) defined over its resources and their attributes. Required resources/attributes are necessary to perform some kind of unspecified but essential operation. These can be for example side effects such as data that is written to the screen, or data that is shared with a third-party module to which we have no access. Generated resources/attributes are generated by some unspecified operation within a module, such as data that is input by a person or data received from a third-party module to which we do not have access. Required and generated resources/attributes can also be used to omit modules obtaining smaller module networks, if we so wish.

Definition 3 (Module). *A **module** is a tuple* $\mathcal{M} = (name, R_{\mathcal{M}}, req^{\mathcal{M}}, ger^{\mathcal{M}})$ *where*

- *name is its name*
- $R_{\mathcal{M}}$ *is a finite set of resources with unique names,*
- $req^{\mathcal{M}}, ger^{\mathcal{M}} : R_{\mathcal{M}} \uplus A_{\mathcal{M}} \rightarrow \{T, F\}$ *are total functions, assigning to each attribute/resource a boolean value indicating whether they are required/generated in this module, where* $A_{\mathcal{M}} = \biguplus_{r \in R_{\mathcal{M}}} attr^r$.

We denote by $Resources^{\mathcal{M}}$ *the set of resource names of a module* $\mathcal{M}$.

Operations are the bindings between modules. Modules are containers of information, generating and requiring information, and operations define how information flows from a module to another. Even though it is not stated directly in the definition, operations range over two modules, a source or **caller** and a target or **callee**, just like an edge of a graph. Operations are quadripartite graphs augmented with an attribute relation. The nodes of an operation graph are resources of its caller and callee. The operation graph shows how the information flows from a resource of a module to a resource of another module. We will often refer to the subset of the edges from resources of caller as the **request** or **call**, and to the other subset with resource of callee as source, as the **response** or **return**.

Each edge of an operation graph (from a resource to another) is augmented with a relation from the attributes of the first resource to the attributes of the second. Edges of operation graphs represent the transfer of a value from attribute to attribute.

Definition 4 (Operation). *Given a set of resources* $\mathcal{R}$, *an **operation** op defines how the operation acts on resources/attributes, where* $op = (\mathcal{R}, E^{op}, s^{op}, t^{op}, rel^{op})$ *is a quadripartite graph and* $rel^{op} : E^{op} \rightarrow REL$ *is a total function that maps each edge* $e \in E^{op}$ *to a relation* $REL \subseteq attr^{s^{op}(e)} \times attr^{t^{op}(e)}$. *We write* $\mathcal{R} = \mathcal{R}_\rho \cup \mathcal{R}_\epsilon$ *the node partitioning of op and* $E^{op} = E^{op}_{\rho\epsilon} \cup E^{op}_{\epsilon\rho}$ *its edge partitioning, note that* $E^{op}_{\rho\rho} = E^{op}_{\epsilon\epsilon} = \emptyset$.

A **module network**, or short **module net**, is a graph whose nodes are modules and edges are operations. Additionally, modules of a module network do not share resources, i.e., resources are unique, and the set of all resources in a module network is the union of the resources in its modules. Essentially, operations of a module network carry information between modules.

To be well defined, a module network has to satisfy two properties. First, no two modules of a module network share resources, that is, the only way for modules to share data is through an operation. Second, operations have a caller $(s^{\mathcal{M}}(op))$ and a callee module $(t^{\mathcal{M}}(op))$ and that the resources of an operation (R^{op}) are subsets of the resources of caller $(R_{s^{\mathcal{M}}(op)})$ and callee modules $(R_{t^{\mathcal{M}}(op)})$ in the module net.

Definition 5 (Module network). *A **module network** is a tuple $MN = (\mathcal{M}, Op, s^{\mathcal{M}}, t^{\mathcal{M}})$ where*

- *$\mathcal{M}$ is a finite set of modules;*
- *Op is a finite set of operations over the resources $\mathcal{R} = \biguplus_{m \in \mathcal{M}} R_m$;*
- *resources are unique:*

$$\forall m1, m2 \in \mathcal{M}.Resources^{m1} \cap Resources^{m2} = \emptyset \qquad (1)$$

MN is a graph such that each operation edge is compatible with the modules of the module network:

$$\forall op \in Op.\mathcal{R}^{op} = \mathcal{R}_\rho^{op} \cup \mathcal{R}_\epsilon^{op} \rightarrow \mathcal{R}_\rho^{op} \subseteq R_{s^{\mathcal{M}}(op)} \text{ and } \mathcal{R}_\epsilon^{op} \subseteq R_{t^{\mathcal{M}}(op)} \qquad (2)$$

As an example, we will consider the module net in Fig. 1(b). In this figure we have following modules:

- $W = (Website, \{S\}, \{S \mapsto F, DOI \mapsto F\}, \{S \mapsto T, DOI \mapsto T\})$, where $S = (Search, \{DOI\})$
- $R = (ResearchNet, \{A\}, \{A \mapsto F, ID \mapsto F\}, \{A \mapsto T, ID \mapsto F\})$, where $A = (Article, \{ID\})$
- $I = (InventoryService, \{D\}, \{D \mapsto F, Location \mapsto T\}, \{D \mapsto T, Location \mapsto F\})$, where $D = (Document, \{Location\})$

In addition to modules, resources and attributes above, Fig. 1(b) also shows two operations:

- $FA = (\{S, A\}, \{call\}, \{call \mapsto S\}, \{call \mapsto A\}, \{call \mapsto \{(DOI, ID)\}\})$
- $FD = (\{A, D\}, \{call\}, \{call \mapsto A\}, \{call \mapsto D\}, \{call \mapsto \{(ID, Location)\}\})$

With all of the above we can finally define the module net as: $(\{W, R, I\}, \{FA, FD\}, \{FA \mapsto W, FD \mapsto R\}, \{FD \mapsto R, FD \mapsto I\})$.

5 MIGRATE Approach

Module Integration using Graph Grammars (MIGRATE) is an approach that aims to help developers in the process of integrating software modules. MIGRATE takes as input software artifacts, such as source code, and automatically produces a set of warnings informing developers what needs their attention. We refer to it as a **approach**, because it is not usable out of the box. In order to use this approach, each of its abstract procedures has to be instantiated with a concrete procedure. MIGRATE approach is comprised of following procedures:

- **Extraction**: receives software artifacts and produces a module net
- **Translation**: receives a module net and produces a graph grammar
- **Verification**: receives a graph grammar and produces a set of warnings

The approach is given as input a set of **software artifacts**. In theory, we believe these artifacts can be anything that is machine readable and provides insight into how information flows in a system. For services, these can be OpenAPI documents. For libraries and classes, the actual code and interfaces. Models (such as UML) can also be used as software artifacts for all kinds of modules. Further kinds of artifacts can be used such as dynamic data of real payload exchanges and logs for services, and execution traces and automated tests for libraries and classes.

The **extraction** procedure takes software artifacts and produces a module net. Extraction strategy can vary depending on what we choose as software artifacts.

Currently, this procedure is performed manually, but we intend to implement different extraction procedures in the future.

Module nets semantics is defined via a **translation** procedure that assigns a graph grammar, called verification grammar to each module net. Finally, the **verification** procedure builds upon existing graph grammar verification techniques to produce different kinds of **warnings** concerning the system under analysis. We now present in more details how these procedures were defined and implemented.

5.1 Translation

The **translation** takes a model in the source language (module net) and produces a model in the target language (graph grammar). We refer to the source model as just **module net** and to the target model as **verification grammar**. This translation was defined by a graph grammar called **translation grammar**. The translation grammar has an **initial graph**, which is a module net encoded as graph, and after the rule application process is carried out until termination we obtain a **final graph**, which is an encoded verification grammar. To summarize, the translation procedure is comprised of three steps:

- **Injection**: takes a module net and encodes it, producing an initial graph
- **Derivation**: applies translation grammar rules until termination
- **Extraction**: extracts a verification grammar from a final graph

The type graph used in the translation has three kinds of nodes, "MN" nodes are used to describe module net components, "TOKEN" nodes denote auxiliary items used in the translation process and "RAGRA" nodes describe components of the resulting verification. Before starting a translation, the initial graph is expected to have only nodes of "MN" types. During translation, nodes of "TOKEN" type will be created and deleted. At the end of the procedure, the final graph will contain only nodes of type "GRAGRA". The translation grammar has 35 rules and for that reason we omit these rules here. A few example rules are depicted in Fig. 2, with an example of a rule that creates tokens (TK1) in Fig. 2(a), a rule that consumes tokens (TR17) in Fig. 2(b), a rule that removes translated module net elements (CL29) in Fig. 2(c) and a rule that fixes duplicated edges created by the translation (AD34) in Fig. 2(d).

As stated before, this translation gives a semantics to module nets in terms of graph grammars. Thus, we have to guarantee that the translation procedure generates a well-defined graph grammar (**well-definedness**) and always terminates with an unique resulting grammar (**confluence**).

Generation of well-defined grammars and confluence are properties of the translation grammar. In the following we sketch how we have shown these properties.

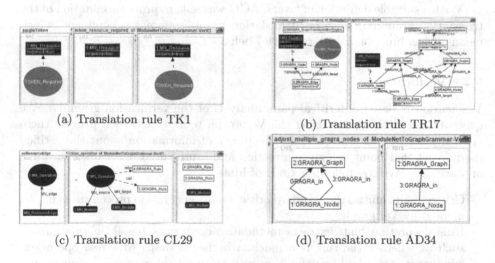

(a) Translation rule TK1   (b) Translation rule TR17

(c) Translation rule CL29   (d) Translation rule AD34

Fig. 2. Examples of translation rules

In order to show that the translation procedure produces well-defined grammars, we have argumented that each rule preserves a set of requirements that specify what is required for a grammar to be well-defined. In addition to that argumentation, we have also written atomic constraints and applied them to one example translation of a specific module net. Our constraints were basically of two kinds: graph grammar constraints check that edges have sources and targets and whether or not rules have left- and right-hand sides, and module net constraints that ensure no translated module net concept takes more than one role (for example, a graph grammar node that is the translation of a module cannot be at the same time the translation of other structures, such as resources, attributes, etc.). We have used the AGG tool [22] to check these constraints are satisfied by the final graph after translation. Details of this argumentation and the example translation verified by atomic constraints can be found in the dissertation [5].

Confluence is a combination of two properties, namely termination and local confluence. We used the tool AGG to show that both these properties are satisfied for the translation grammar. We start by showing local confluence. We must compute conflict critical pairs and show that, whenever there are different choices of rules to be made that are in conflict (i.e., are mutually exclusive) either choice will lead to the same final result.

Running this analysis in AGG for the translation grammar, generated no critical pairs of conflicts and therefore the translation grammar is locally confluent. To ensure that the translation grammar terminates, we first assign layers to rules. Roughly speaking, layers represent the phases of the translation process: if we can partition the set of rules in layers that satisfy some requirements, it is possible to prove termination.

With a suitable definition of layers, AGG was able to prove termination of the translation grammar. Thus our translation graph grammar is confluent, which means it has functional (deterministic) behavior.

5.2 Verification

Verification is based on critical pairs analysis of the verification grammar. We generate the critical pairs using the Verigraph tool [4] and then process these critical pairs to create hints. Hints are pieces of information about the verified module net that point in a given direction and can be used to create other hints or warnings. We have following kinds of hints:

- Critical pairs hint: is the standard critical pairs generation procedure as implemented by Verigraph;
- Rule decoration hint: extracts metadata about rules based on rule names, such as whether the rule is a mock, whether it maps to a real operation, whether it is required by default, as well as all sets of modules, resources and attributes contained in the graphs of this rule;
- Informational flow hint: analyses produce-use critical pairs of dependencies and finds subgraphs of overlapping graphs where we can tell that the information flows from a given attribute to another;
- Optional path hint: analyses the graph of produce-use critical pairs of dependencies, and finds rules which are not in a path to a rule considered required by default (by the rule decoration hint), modules, resources and attributes which are not found in any rules belonging to a path to a required rule are considered optional as well;

- Required path hint: analyses the graph of information flow produced by information flow hint and reports attributes and resources which are in a path to a required attribute or resource;
- Reachable rule hint: analyses produce-use (PU) critical pairs of dependencies and produce-forbid (PF) critical pairs of conflicts, and looks for dependencies such as $M \rightarrow_{PU} R$, where M is a mock (according to rule decoration hint), and then it tries to close a triangle with $M \rightarrow_{PF} P \rightarrow_{PU} R$, if it cannot find such a triangle for all such M, then R is considered unreachable;
- Critical pairs explanation hint: the critical objects of critical pairs of produce-use dependencies between rules of types operation, or between rules of types operation and generators, are considered outdated attributes.

With all hints provided so far, we can generate many different warnings:

- Optional attribute, resource, module or rule warning: is derived from optional path hints, creating optional attribute, resource, module or rule warnings;
- Strictly optional attributes warning: points out attributes which are in the path of required attributes, but do not contribute directly to the information flow, and are derived from required path hints;
- Unreachable operation warning: provides useful information for developers to detect issues in the information flow, which can be due to typos in resource or attribute names or even other kinds of failures in the specification, and this kind of warning is derived from reachable rule hints;
- Outdated attribute warning: highlights attributes copied from module X to module Y and then changed in module X, leaving the Y copy of that attribute with an outdated value, and are derived from critical pair explanation hints.

6   Related Work

Integration of Libraries: NOREGRETS+ [18] creates models of data flow between a library and its consumers. The models can then be used to check that each call to an updated library function still returns the same type and that the updated library still uses the same subset of arguments it used before the update. Veracode keeps track of inserted, deleted or changed methods [9], and APIDIFF [3] tracks types, methods and fields, to detect a series of breaking and non-breaking changes, such as adding final modifier to a type or removing a method or field. CLEVER [19] works by applying symbolic execution to both pairs of (client, previous lib version) and (client, new lib version) and determining whether code activated by client has been changed in the new lib version considering input constraints provided by the symbolic execution.

Approaches based on diffs determine whether or not a change was made to the implementation. Whereas diff checks cannot handle the behavior of functions, testing approaches are able to verify that the behavior is the same, but only for those cases covered by tests. In contrast, symbolic execution can cover every possible path by computing constraints on inputs imposed by client code. In comparison, our approach does not require automated tests and we suggest extracting module nets from source code directly. Unlike other approaches, we do not reason about the behavior of functions such as control flow, but rather we concentrate on data flow to find issues such as whether or not a module finds the data it needs in order to call an operation of another module.

Integration of Services: Perhaps the most similar work to ours is [14], which enables specification of requirements as graph grammar rules and match of such requirements to service specifications to check if a service does what clients want [14]. This work has many similarities to ours the main differences are: their work requires knowledge of graph grammars, while we want to provide tools to automate the verification process; they concentrate on services, while we created the notion of module nets, enabling verification of not only services but also libraries and anything else that can be considered a module; and their goals are to match specifications, whereas we focus on generating warnings.

"Differential Regression Testing" for REST services [12] compares the outputs of two tests with the same inputs looking for regressions. The authors suggest interacting with services through automatically generated clients and thus they test the (client, service) integration. Furthermore, they describe two kinds of tests, one which keeps the client version and varies the service version and one where client version varies.

Graph Grammar Applications: Our work can be divided into three phases: (i) model extraction, (ii) model transformation and (iii) verification using graph grammars. **(i)** is concerned with the extraction of models from source code, where the output models may be graph grammars. Extraction of graph grammars from a Java using traces has been studied in [7]. **(ii)** is concerned with the transformation of models from one language to another using graph grammars as the transformation engine. A desirable property for model transformation is functional behavior. Graph grammars can exhibit functional behavior as long as they are terminating and confluent, which is illustrated in [15] with the transformation from statecharts to Communicating Sequential Processes (CSP). The main disadvantage is the fact that matching a rule to a graph is a NP-complete problem [24]. **(iii)** is concerned with the verification of systems specified using graph grammars. We leverage existing methods to create our own verification algorithms. AGG 2.0 is a full graph grammar engine and graphical user interface one of the few supporting critical pair analysis [22] along with Verigraph [4].

7   Conclusion

In this work we addressed the problem of module integration using graph grammars. We have created a verification approach that allows us to generate warnings telling developers which integrations need their attention. We have provided implementations for the translation and verification procedures of MIGRATE approach.

MIGRATE approach imposes certain requirements on graph grammars it analyses, such as having specific rule names and rule patterns, as well as nodes and edges that can be interpreted back to operations, modules, resources, attributes and values. We needed a way to ensure graph grammars we analyse meet such requirements, while at the same time providing developers with the ability to make changes to models directly. For those reasons, we have created module nets, which are a formalism to express how modules integrate to each other. The semantics of module nets is given by a translation procedure that assigns a (verification) graph grammar to each module net. This enabled us to leverage existing critical pairs analysis theory, and also will enable us to leverage all different analysis techniques that have been developed for graph grammars in future work.

There are three major areas that will need our attention when building a verifier tool using the concepts of this paper: automatization of the extraction procedure, support of larger module nets, and interpretation of warnings. We are working already on automatization of the extraction procedure and have first prototypes that are under evaluation.

Larger module nets are specially difficult to handle during the derivation procedure applied in translation and the critical pairs computation. Since our translation grammar is confluent, we could improve by avoiding match randomization and always applying the first match we find. Critical pairs generatin could be improved if we restricted it to the generation of essential [16] or even initial [13] critical pairs, thus greatly reducing the amount of pairs generated (without loss of information).

In order to improve the warnings we support, we will have to improve each of the procedures we have presented, extending module nets to support more operation types and other procedures accordingly. Also we have concentrated in finding issues due to information flow, such as a attribute which is not necessary because it does not carry information to required attributes. However, we disregard completely control flow issues, which can lead to all sorts of bugs when changed, even if the flow of information is unchanged. Expanding types of warnings we support is left for future work.

References

1. Aué, J., Aniche, M., Lobbezoo, M., van Deursen, A.: An exploratory study on faults in web API integration in a large-scale payment company. In: Proceedings of the 40th International Conference on Software Engineering Software Engineering in Practice - ICSE-SEIP 2018, pp. 13–22. ACM Press, Gothenburg, Sweden (2018). https://doi.org/10.1145/3183519.3183537
2. Bogart, C., Kästner, C., Herbsleb, J., Thung, F.: How to break an API: cost negotiation and community values in three software ecosystems. In: Proceedings of the 2016 24th ACM SIGSOFT International Symposium on Foundations of Software Engineering - FSE 2016, pp. 109–120. ACM Press, Seattle, WA, USA (2016). https://doi.org/10.1145/2950290.2950325

3. Brito, A., Xavier, L., Hora, A., Valente, M.T.: APIDiff: Detecting API breaking changes. In: 2018 IEEE 25th International Conference on Software Analysis, Evolution and Reengineering (SANER). pp. 507–511. IEEE, Campobasso, March 2018. https://doi.org/10.1109/SANER.2018.8330249, http://ieeexplore.ieee.org/document/8330249/

4. Costa, A., et al.: Verigraph: a system for specification and analysis of graph grammars. In: Ribeiro, L., Lecomte, T. (eds.) Formal Methods: Foundations and Applications, LNCS, pp. 78–94. Springer, Cham (2016). https://doi.org/10.1007/978-3-319-49815-7_5

5. Cravo, D.R.: Module integration using graph grammars (MIGRATE) (2021). https://lume.ufrgs.br/handle/10183/226284. Accepted 8 2021-28T04:39:53Z

6. Decan, A., Mens, T., Grosjean, P.: An empirical comparison of dependency network evolution in seven software packaging ecosystems. Empir. Softw. Eng. **24**(1), 381–416 (2019). https://doi.org/10.1007/s10664-017-9589-y

7. Duarte, L.M., Ribeiro, L.: Graph grammar extraction from source code. In: Cavalheiro, S., Fiadeiro, J. (eds.) Formal Methods: Foundations and Applications, LNCS, vol. 10623, pp. 52–69. Springer, Cham (2017). https://doi.org/10.1007/978-3-319-70848-5_5

8. Ehrig, H. (ed.): Fundamentals of algebraic graph transformation. In: Monographs in Theoretical Computer Science, Springer, Berlin (2006). oCLC: ocm69242087

9. Foo, D., Chua, H., Yeo, J., Ang, M.Y., Sharma, A.: Efficient static checking of library updates. In: Proceedings of the 2018 26th ACM Joint Meeting on European Software Engineering Conference and Symposium on the Foundations of Software Engineering - ESEC/FSE 2018, pp. 791–796. ACM Press, Lake Buena Vista, FL, USA (2018). https://doi.org/10.1145/3236024.3275535

10. Fowler, M.: Tolerantreader (2011). https://martinfowler.com/bliki/TolerantReader.html

11. Fowler, M.: Integrationtest (2018). https://martinfowler.com/bliki/IntegrationTest.html

12. Godefroid, P., Lehmann, D., Polishchuk, M.: Differential regression testing for REST APIs. In: Proceedings of the 29th ACM SIGSOFT International Symposium on Software Testing and Analysis. pp. 312–323. ACM, Virtual Event USA, July 2020. https://doi.org/10.1145/3395363.3397374

13. Grochau Azzi, G., Corradini, A., Ribeiro, L.: On the essence and initiality of conflicts in M-adhesive transformation systems. J. Log. Algebr. Methods Program. **109**, 100482 (2019). https://doi.org/10.1016/j.jlamp.2019.100482, https://www.sciencedirect.com/science/article/pii/S2352220818301639

14. Hausmann, J.H., Heckel, R., Lohmann, M.: Model-based discovery of web services. In: Proceedings of the IEEE International Conference on Web Services, ICWS 2004, p. 324., IEEE Computer Society, USA, June 2004

15. Heckel, R., Küster, J.M., Taentzer, G.: Confluence of Typed Attributed Graph Transformation Systems. In: Corradini, A., Ehrig, H., Kreowski, H.J., Rozenberg, G. (eds.) Graph Transformation, LNCS, pp. 161–176. Springer, Berlin (2002). https://doi.org/10.1007/3-540-45832-8_14

16. Lambers, L., Ehrig, H., Orejas, F.: Efficient conflict detection in graph transformation systems by essential critical pairs. Electr. Notes Theor. Comput. Sci. **211**, 17–26 (2008). https://doi.org/10.1016/j.entcs.2008.04.026, https://www.sciencedirect.com/science/articleii/S1571066108002417

17. Lübke, D., Zimmermann, O., Pautasso, C., Zdun, U., Stocker, M.: Interface evolution patterns: balancing compatibility and extensibility across service life cycles. In: Proceedings of the 24th European Conference on Pattern Languages of Programs - EuroPLop 2019, pp. 1–24. ACM Press, Irsee, Germany (2019). https://doi.org/10.1145/3361149.3361164

18. Møller, A., Torp, M.T.: Model-based testing of breaking changes in Node.js libraries. In: Proceedings of the 2019 27th ACM Joint Meeting on European Software Engineering Conference and Symposium on the Foundations of Software Engineering - ESEC/FSE 2019, pp. 409–419. ACM Press, Tallinn, Estonia (2019). https://doi.org/10.1145/3338906.3338940

19. Mora, F., Li, Y., Rubin, J., Chechik, M.: Client-specific equivalence checking. In: Proceedings of the 33rd ACM/IEEE International Conference on Automated Software Engineering - ASE 2018, pp. 441–451. ACM Press, Montpellier, France (2018). https://doi.org/10.1145/3238147.3238178

20. Preston-Werner, T.: Semantic Versioning 2.0.0 (2020). https://semver.org/

21. Raemaekers, S., van Deursen, A., Visser, J.: Semantic Versioning versus breaking changes: a study of the maven repository. In: 2014 IEEE 14th International Working Conference on Source Code Analysis and Manipulation, pp. 215–224. IEEE, Victoria, BC, Canada, September 2014. https://doi.org/10.1109/SCAM.2014.30, http://ieeexplore.ieee.org/document/6975655/

22. Runge, O., Ermel, C., Taentzer, G.: AGG 2.0 – New features for specifying and analyzing algebraic graph transformations. In: Schürr, A., Varró, D., Varró, G. (eds.) Applications of Graph Transformations with Industrial Relevance, LNCS, pp. 81–88. Springer, Berlin (2012). https://doi.org/10.1007/978-3-642-34176-2_8

23. Soldani, J., Tamburri, D.A., Van Den Heuvel, W.J.: The pains and gains of microservices: a systematic grey literature review. J. Syst. Softw. 146, 215–232 (2018). https://doi.org/10.1016/j.jss.2018.09.082, https://linkinghub.elsevier.com/retrieve/pii/S0164121218302139

24. Taentzer, G., Toffetti Carughi, G.: A graph-based approach to transform XML documents. In: Baresi, L., Heckel, R. (eds.) Fundamental Approaches to Software Engineering, LNCS, pp. 48–62. Springer, Berlin (2006). https://doi.org/10.1007/11693017_6

25. Xavier, L., Brito, A., Hora, A., Valente, M.T.: Historical and impact analysis of API breaking changes: A large-scale study. In: 2017 IEEE 24th International Conference on Software Analysis, Evolution and Reengineering (SANER), pp. 138–147. IEEE, Klagenfurt, Austria, February 2017. https://doi.org/10.1109/SANER.2017.7884616, http://ieeexplore.ieee.org/document/7884616/

Cost Analysis for an Actor-Based Workflow Modelling Language

Muhammad Rizwan Ali$^{(\boxtimes)}$ and Violet Ka I Pun$^{(\boxtimes)}$

Western Norway University of Applied Sciences, Bergen, Norway
{mral,vpu}@hvl.no

Abstract. Workflow planning usually requires domain-specific knowledge from the planners, making it a relatively manual process. In addition, workflows are largely cross-organisational. As a result, minor modifications in the workflow of a collaborative partner may be propagated to other concurrently running workflows, which may result in significant adverse impacts. This paper presents a resource-sensitive formal modelling language, $\mathcal{R}$PL. The language has explicit notions for task dependencies, resource allocation and time advancement. The language allows the planners to estimate the effect of changes in collaborative workflows with respect to cost in terms of execution time. This paper proposes a static analysis for computing the worst execution time of a cross-organisational workflow modelled in $\mathcal{R}$PL by defining a compositional function that translates an $\mathcal{R}$PL program to a set cost equations.

Keywords: Cross-organisational workflows · Resource planning · Formal modelling · Static analysis

1 Introduction

Workflow management can be seen as an effective method of monitoring, managing, and improving business processes using IT assistance [1]. Workflow management systems (WMS) allow planners to create, manage, and execute workflows, as well as play a key role in collaborative business domains such as supply chain management and customer relationship management. As a result, WMS is regarded as among the most effective systems for facilitating cooperative business operations [12]. With the fast growth of e-commerce and virtual companies, corporations frequently work beyond organisational borders, engaging with others to meet competitive challenges. Moreover, the rapid growth of the Internet and digital technology encourages collaboration across widely distant businesses [26].

The adoption of cross-organisational workflow allows restructuring business processes beyond the limits of an organisation [2]. Cross-organisational workflows

Partially supported by *CroFlow: Enabling Highly Automated Cross-Organisational Workflow Planning, Pathology services in the Western Norwegian Health Region – a center for applied digitization* and *SIRIUS – Centre for Scalable Data Access* (www.sirius-labs.no).

© Springer Nature Switzerland AG 2021
S. Campos and M. Minea (Eds.): SBMF 2021, LNCS 13130, pp. 104–121, 2021.
https://doi.org/10.1007/978-3-030-92137-8_7

often comprise multiple concurrent workflows running in various departments within the same organisation or in different organisations. For example, the workflow of a retail company may involve a workflow of a supplier providing products and a workflow of a courier company delivering products to customers.

Furthermore, workflow planning often requires domain-specific knowledge to accomplish efficient resource allocation and task management, which makes planning cross-organisational workflow especially challenging. Additionally, modifying workflows is error-prone: one modification in a workflow may result in significant changes in other concurrently running workflows, and a minor mistake might have significant negative consequences.

Workflow planning has been significantly digitalised and automated, and tools such as Process-Aware Information Systems (PAIS) [13] and Enterprise Resource Planning (ERP) systems have been developed to facilitate workflow planning. However, cross-organisational workflow planning remains a rather manual process as the current techniques and tools often lack domain-specific knowledge to support automation in workflow planning and updates. Moreover, the planners may only have limited domain knowledge and do not have a common understanding of all the collaborative workflows, which can be catastrophic, especially in the healthcare domain. Therefore, there is a need for an analysis that over-approximates the cost before any changes in the workflows are implemented. With the cost analysis, the planners can first simulates the changes in the design of workflows, including the task dependencies and resource allocation, and see the effect of the changes in terms of execution time before the changes are implemented in the workflow in practice.

In this paper, we first present a formal modelling language $\mathcal{R}$PL. The language has explicit notions for task dependencies, resource usage and time consumption, which allows the cross-organisational planners to couple various workflows through resources and task dependencies. A preliminary idea of the language is presented in [8]. In addition, we present a technique based on the work in [21] to statically over-approximate the worst execution time of the workflows modelled as an $\mathcal{R}$PL program, by translating the program into a set of cost equations that can be fed to an off-the-shelf constraint solver (e.g., [5,14]). This enables planners to estimate the effects of the workflows (and its possible changes) in terms of execution time before the actual implementation. The language and the cost analysis can help facilitate planning cross-organisational workflows and may ultimately contribute to automated planning.

The rest of the paper is organised as follows: Sect. 2 introduces the syntax and semantics of the language. Section 3 shows a static analysis to over-approximate the execution time of an $\mathcal{R}$PL program. Section 4 shows the correctness of analysis. Section 5 briefly discusses the related work. Finally, we summarise the paper and discuss possible future work in Sect. 6.

$$P ::= R\ \overline{Cl}\ \{\overline{T\ x};\ s\} \qquad e ::= x\ \mid g\ \mid \textbf{this}$$
$$Cl ::= \textbf{class}\ C\ \{\overline{T\ x};\ \overline{M}\} \qquad g ::= b\ \mid f?\ \mid g \wedge g$$
$$M ::= Sg\ \{\overline{T\ x};\ s\} \qquad s ::= x = rhs\ \mid \textbf{skip}\ \mid \textbf{if}\ e\ \{s\}\ \mid \textbf{wait}(f)\ \mid \textbf{return}\ e$$
$$Sg ::= B\ m(\overline{T\ y}) \qquad\qquad \mid \textbf{hold}(r, e)\ \mid \textbf{release}(r, e)\ \mid \textbf{cost}(e)\ \mid s\ ;\ s$$
$$B ::= \texttt{Int}\ \mid \texttt{Bool}\ \mid \texttt{Unit} \quad rhs ::= e\ \mid \textbf{new}\ C\ \mid f.\textbf{get}$$
$$T ::= C\ \mid B\ \mid \textbf{Fut}\langle B\rangle \qquad\qquad \mid m(x, \overline{e})\ \textbf{after}\ \overline{f?}\ \mid\ !m(x, \overline{e})\ \textbf{after}\ \overline{f?}$$

Fig. 1. Syntax of $\mathcal{R}$PL

2 Formal Workflow Modelling Language $\mathcal{R}$PL

In this section, we present a formal modelling language $\mathcal{R}$PL. The language is inspired by an active object language, ABS [19], and has a Java-like syntax and actor-based concurrency model. In an actor-based concurrency model [4], actors are primitives of concurrent computation. They can send a finite number of messages to other actors, spawn a finite number of new actors or modify their private state. A primary feature of the actor-based model is that one message is being processed per actor, preserving the invariants of an actor without locks.

$\mathcal{R}$PL uses explicit notions to express time advancement and to indicate resources required for each task (expressed as a method) and dependencies between tasks. Using cooperative scheduling of method activations, $\mathcal{R}$PL controls the internal interleaving of processes inside an object with explicit scheduling points.

2.1 The Syntax of $\mathcal{R}$PL

The syntax of the language is given in Fig. 1. An overlined element represents a (possibly empty) finite sequence of such elements separated by commas, e.g., $\overline{T}$ implies a sequence $T_1, T_2, \ldots, T_n$.

An $\mathcal{R}$PL program P comprises resources R, a sequence of class declarations $\overline{Cl}$ and a main method body $\{\overline{T\ x};\ s\}$, where $\overline{T\ x}$; is the declaration of local variables and s is a statement. Types T in $\mathcal{R}$PL are basic types B, including integer, boolean and unit type, a class C and future types $\textbf{Fut}\langle B\rangle$, which types asynchronous method invocations (see below).

Resources $R : r \mapsto v$ maps resource identifiers r to integer values v, indicating the number of resources r is available. A class declaration $\textbf{class}\ C\ \{\overline{T\ x};\ \overline{M}\}$ has a class name C and a class body $\{\overline{T\ x};\ \overline{M}\}$ comprising state variables and methods of the class. Methods in $\mathcal{R}$PL have a method signature Sg followed by a method body $\{\overline{T\ x};\ s\}$. A method signature Sg consists of a return type B, method name m and a sequence of formal parameters $\overline{y}$. We assume each method name is unique. We further assume that the formal parameters $\overline{T\ y}$ is a non-empty set and has a fixed pattern $C\ o, \overline{C'\ o'}, \overline{T'\ x}$ where o is always the callee object identifier of the method of class C, $\overline{o'}$ are object identifiers of class $\overline{C'}$ and $\overline{x}$ are the remaining parameters. This assumption is the syntactic sugar that we use to realise the cost analysis introduced in Sect. 3. Expressions e include guards g, variables x and self-identifier **this**. A guard g allows a process to release control of an object. It can be boolean conditions b, return tests f? checking if the future variable f is resolved, or a conjunction of guards.

Statements include sequential composition, assignment, **if**, **skip**, and **return** are standard. Iterative loops are not included in the language, but can be implemented with recursion. $\mathcal{R}$PL uses **hold**(r, e) and **release**(r, e) to acquire and return e number of resources r. Statement **wait**(f) suspends the current process until future f is resolved, while other processes in the same object can be scheduled for execution. Statement **cost**(e), the only term in $\mathcal{R}$PL that consumes time, represents e units of time advancement.

The right-hand side rhs of an assignment includes expressions e, object creation **new** C, method invocations and synchronisation. Communication in $\mathcal{R}$PL is based on method calls, which can be either synchronous, written as $m(x, \bar{e})$ **after** $\overline{f?}$, or asynchronous, written as $!m(x, \bar{e})$ **after** $\overline{f?}$, where x is the callee object and $\overline{f?}$ is a sequence of futures that must be resolved prior to invoking method m. A synchronous method invocation blocks the caller object until the invoked method returns. Asynchronous method invocations, on the contrary, do not block the caller, allowing the caller and callee to run in parallel. An asynchronous method invocation is associated to a future variable of type **Fut**$\langle B \rangle$, where B is the return type of the invoked method. Moreover, the expression f.**get** blocks all execution in the object until future f is resolved.

One can see a future as a mailbox that is created by the time a method is asynchronously invoked, and the caller object continues its own execution after the invocation. When the invoked method has completed the execution, the return value will be placed into the mailbox, i.e., the future. The caller object will only be blocked if it uses a **get** statement to retrieve the value of a future that is not yet resolved.

Figure 2 shows a simple program in $\mathcal{R}$PL. The code snippet captures a simple collaboration between the workflows of a retail, a supplier and a courier company. Line 1 models the available resources. Lines 2–10 define a retail sale workflow. First, a request to the supplier for product supply is made asynchronously with associated future f_1 on Line 7. While waiting for the product (until f_1 is resolved), the retailer can continue with other tasks. After getting the product from the supplier (f_1 is resolved), it is sent to the customer by utilising the ser-

```
1   [Driver ↦ 5, Vehicle ↦ 3]
2   class Retail {
3     Unit sale(Retail o, Int ord) {
4       Fut<Bool> f₁;
5       Supplier sp = new Supplier;
6       Courier cr = new Courier;
7       f₁ = !supply(sp,ord) after;
8       Unit x = deliver(cr,ord,10) after f₁?;
9     }
10  }
11  class Courier {
12    Unit deliver(Courier o, Int ord, Int t) {
13      hold(Driver,1)(Vehicle,1);
14      cost(t);
15      release(Driver,1)(Vehicle,1);
16  }}
```

Fig. 2. A simple example.

vices of a courier company (Line 8). Lines 11–16 define the deliver workflow of the courier company. A driver and a vehicle (resources) are first acquired to deliver the product (Line 13). Line 14 depicts the time taken for delivery. Afterwards, the acquired resources are released (Line 15). For simplicity, we do not show the implementation of the supply workflow.

2.2   The Semantics of $\mathcal{R}$PL

To understand how time advances in $\mathcal{R}$PL and the cost analysis later, we briefly discuss the semantics of the language in this section. The semantics of $\mathcal{R}$PL is a transition system whose states are configurations cn with the runtime syntax defined in Fig. 3.

$$
\begin{aligned}
cn &::= \varepsilon \mid res \mid obj(o,a,p,q) \mid fut(f,val) & act &::= \varepsilon \mid o \\
&\quad \mid invoc(o,f,m,\overline{v}) \mid cn\ cn & val &::= v \mid \bot \\
p &::= \mathtt{idle} \mid \{l \mid s\} & res &::= [\, r \mapsto v\,] \\
q &::= \emptyset \mid \{l \mid s\} \mid q\ q & a &::= [\ldots, x \mapsto v, \ldots] \\
s &::= \mathbf{cont}(f) \mid \ldots & v &::= o \mid f \mid b \mid k
\end{aligned}
$$

Fig. 3. Runtime syntax of $\mathcal{R}$PL

A configuration cn includes futures, objects, message invocations, and resources. An empty configuration is ε, and whitespace denotes the associative and commutative union operator on configurations. A future $fut(f,val)$ holds a future identifier f and a return value val, where $\bot$ indicates that future has not been resolved.

An object is a term $obj(o,a,p,q)$ where o is the object identifier, a a substitution describing the object's attributes, p an active process, and q a pool of suspended processes. A process, written as $\{l \mid s\}$, has local variable bindings l and a statement s. A message invocation is a term $invoc(o,f,m,\overline{v})$, where o is a callee object, m a method name, f a future to which method m returns, and $\overline{v}$ the set of actual parameter values for m. Resources res is a mapping from resource identifier r to the number of resources. The statement $\mathbf{cont}(f)$ controls the scheduling when a synchronous call completes its execution, returning control to the caller. Values v include object, future identifier, and Boolean, Integer or constant values.

We discuss a selection of the semantics rules of $\mathcal{R}$PL (see Figs. 4 and 5) that are relevant to the analysis later. The rest of the semantics is standard, and can be found in the accompanying technical report [7]. In the semantics, we use the auxiliary functions $dom(l)$ and $dom(a)$ to return the domain of l and a, respectively. The evaluation function $[\![e]\!]_{(aol)}$ returns the value of e by computing the expressions and retrieving the value of identifiers stored either in a or l. Moreover, the function $\mathtt{atts}(C,o)$ is used to create an object of a class C, which binds this to o, and the function $\mathtt{bind}(o,f,m,\overline{v},C)$ returns a process that is going to execute method m with declaration $B\ m(\overline{T}\ y)\ \{T'\ x;\ s\}$, which is defined as:

$$
\mathtt{bind}(o,f,m,\overline{v},C) = \{[destiny \mapsto f, \overline{y} \mapsto \overline{v}, \overline{x} \mapsto \bot] \mid s[o/\mathtt{this}]\}
$$

The semantics in Figs. 4 and 5 includes object creation, communication, task dependencies, resource management and time advancement. For clarity, we use $\mathbb{F}$ to represent all the futures in the configuration in the semantics.

$$\frac{\begin{array}{c}(\textsc{New-Object})\\ o' = \mathtt{fresh}()\\ a' = \mathtt{atts}(C, o')\end{array}}{\begin{array}{c}obj(o, a, \{l \mid x = \mathbf{new}\ C; s\}, q)\\ \to obj(o, a, \{l \mid x = o'; s\}, q)\\ obj(o', a', \mathtt{idle}, \emptyset)\end{array}}$$

$$\frac{\begin{array}{c}(\textsc{Async-Call})\\ \forall f \in \overline{f}.fut(f, v) \in \mathbb{F} \wedge v \neq \bot\\ \overline{v} = [\![\overline{e'}]\!]_{(aol)} \quad o' = [\![e]\!]_{(aol)} \quad f' = \mathtt{fresh}()\end{array}}{\begin{array}{c}obj(o, a, \{l \mid x = !m(e, \overline{e'})\ \mathbf{after}\ \overline{f?}; s\}, q)\ \mathbb{F}\\ \to obj(o, a, \{l \mid x = f'; s\}, q)\\ invoc(o', f', m, \overline{v})\ fut(f', \bot)\ \mathbb{F}\end{array}}$$

$$\frac{\begin{array}{c}(\textsc{Get})\\ v \neq \bot\end{array}}{\begin{array}{c}obj(o, a, \{l \mid x = f.\mathbf{get}; s\}, q)\ fut(f, v)\\ \to obj(o, a, \{l \mid x = v; s\}, q)\ fut(f, v)\end{array}}$$

$$\frac{\begin{array}{c}(\textsc{Invoc})\\ \{l|s\} = \mathtt{bind}(o, f, m, \overline{v}, \mathtt{class}(o))\end{array}}{\begin{array}{c}obj(o, a, p, q)\ invoc(o, f, m, \overline{v})\\ \to obj(o, a, p, q \cup \{l \mid s\})\end{array}}$$

$$\frac{\begin{array}{c}(\textsc{Wait-True})\\ v \neq \bot\end{array}}{\begin{array}{c}obj(o, a, \{l \mid \mathbf{wait}(f); s\}, q)\ fut(f, v)\\ \to obj(o, a, \{l \mid s\}, q)\ fut(f, v)\end{array}}$$

$$\frac{\begin{array}{c}(\textsc{Wait-False})\\ v = \bot\end{array}}{\begin{array}{c}obj(o, a, \{l \mid \mathbf{wait}(f); s\}, q)\ fut(f, v)\\ \to obj(o, a, \mathtt{idle}, q \cup \{l \mid \mathbf{wait}(f); s\})\ fut(f, v)\end{array}}$$

$$\frac{\begin{array}{c}(\textsc{Sync-Call})\\ \forall f \in \overline{f}.fut(f, v) \in \mathbb{F} \wedge v \neq \bot \quad o' = [\![e]\!]_{(aol)} \quad o \neq o' \quad f' = \mathtt{fresh}()\end{array}}{\begin{array}{c}obj(o, a, \{l \mid x = m(e, \overline{c'})\ \mathbf{after}\ \overline{f?}; s\}, q)\ obj(o', a', p, q')\ \mathbb{F}\\ \to obj(o, a, \{l \mid f' = !m(e, e')\ \mathbf{after}\ \overline{f?}; x = f'.\mathbf{get}; s\}, q)\ obj(o', a', p, q')\ \mathbb{F}\end{array}}$$

$$\frac{\begin{array}{c}(\textsc{Self-Sync-Call})\\ \forall f \in \overline{f}.fut(f, v) \in \mathbb{F} \wedge v \neq \bot \quad o = [\![e]\!]_{(aol)} \quad \overline{v} = [\![\overline{e'}]\!]_{(aol)} \quad f'' = l(destiny)\\ f' = \mathtt{fresh}() \quad \{l' \mid s'\} = \mathtt{bind}(o, f', m, \overline{v}, \mathtt{class}(o))\end{array}}{\begin{array}{c}obj(o, a, \{l \mid x = m(e, \overline{e'})\ \mathbf{after}\ \overline{f?}; s\}, q)\ \mathbb{F}\\ \to obj(o, a, \{l' \mid s'; \mathbf{cont}(f'')\}, q \cup \{l \mid x = f'.\mathbf{get}; s\})\ fut(f', \bot)\ \mathbb{F}\end{array}}$$

$$\frac{\begin{array}{c}(\textsc{Wait-Async-Call})\\ \exists f \in \overline{f}.fut(f, v) \in \mathbb{F} \wedge v = \bot\end{array}}{\begin{array}{c}obj(o, a, \{l \mid x = !m(e, \overline{e'})\ \mathbf{after}\ \overline{f?}; s\}, q)\ \mathbb{F}\\ \to obj(o, a, \mathtt{idle}, q \cup \{l \mid x = !m(e, \overline{e'})\ \mathbf{after}\ \overline{f?}; s\})\ \mathbb{F}\end{array}}$$

$$\frac{\begin{array}{c}(\textsc{Sync-Return-Sched})\\ f'' = l(destiny)\end{array}}{\begin{array}{c}obj(o, a, \{l' \mid \mathbf{cont}(f''), q \cup \{l|s\})\\ \to obj(o, a, \{l \mid s\}, q)\end{array}}$$

$$\frac{\begin{array}{c}(\textsc{Wait-Sync-Call})\\ \exists f \in \overline{f}.fut(f, v) \in \mathbb{F} \wedge v = \bot\end{array}}{\begin{array}{c}obj(o, a, \{l \mid x = m(e, \overline{e'})\ \mathbf{after}\ \overline{f?}; s\}, q)\ \mathbb{F}\\ \to obj(o, a, \mathtt{idle}, q \cup \{l \mid x = m(e, \overline{e'})\ \mathbf{after}\ \overline{f?}; s\})\ \mathbb{F}\end{array}}$$

$$\frac{\begin{array}{c}(\textsc{Cost})\\ [\![e]\!]_{(aol)} = 0\end{array}}{\begin{array}{c}obj(o, a, \{l \mid \mathbf{cost}(e); s\}, q)\\ \to obj(o, a, \{l \mid s\}, q)\end{array}}$$

$$\frac{\begin{array}{c}(\textsc{Hold})\\ \forall (r, e) \in \overline{(r, e)}.r \in dom(res) \wedge v \geq 0\\ where\ v = res(r) - [\![e]\!]_{(aol)}\end{array}}{\begin{array}{c}obj(o, a, \{l \mid \mathbf{hold}\overline{(r, e)}; s\}, q)\ res\\ \to obj(o, a, \{l \mid s\}, q)\ res[\overline{r \mapsto v}]\end{array}}$$

$$\frac{\begin{array}{c}(\textsc{Release})\\ \forall (r, e) \in \overline{(r, e)}.r \in dom(res)\\ \wedge v = res(r) + [\![e]\!]_{(aol)}\end{array}}{\begin{array}{c}obj(o, a, \{l \mid \mathbf{release}\overline{(r, e)}; s\}, q)\ res\\ \to obj(o, a, \{l \mid s\}, q)\ res[\overline{r \mapsto v}]\end{array}}$$

Fig. 4. A selection of semantics – Part 1

$$(\text{TICK})$$

$$\frac{\text{strongstable}_t(cn)}{cn \to \Phi(cn, t)}$$

$where, \Phi(cn, t) =$

$$\begin{cases} obj(o, a, \{\ l' \mid \mathbf{cost}(k); s\}, q) \ \Phi(cn', t) & \text{if } cn = obj(o, a, \{l \mid \mathbf{cost}(e); s\}, q) \ cn' \\ & \text{and } k = [\![e]\!]_{(aol)} - t \\ obj(o, a, \{l \mid \mathbf{hold}\overline{(r, e)}; s\}, q) \ \Phi(cn', t) & \text{if } cn = obj(o, a, \{l \mid \mathbf{hold}\overline{(r, e)}; s\}, q) \ cn' \\ obj(o, a, \{l \mid x = e.\mathbf{get}; s\}, q) \ \Phi(cn', t) & \text{if } cn = obj(o, a, \{l \mid x = e.\mathbf{get}; s\}, q) \ cn' \\ obj(o, a, \mathtt{idle}, q) \ \Phi(cn', t) & \text{if } cn = obj(o, a, \mathtt{idle}, q) \ cn' \\ cn & \text{otherwise.} \end{cases}$$

Fig. 5. A selection of semantics – Part 2

Rule WAIT-FALSE suspends the active process, leaving the object idle if f is not resolved, otherwise WAIT-TRUE consumes $\mathbf{wait}(f)$. Rule NEW-OBJECT creates a new object. Rule GET retrieves the value of future f if it is resolved; the reduction on this object is blocked otherwise.

Rules ASYNC-CALL and SYNC-CALL handle the communication between objects through method invocations. To ensure the task dependencies between method calls, the rules first check if all the futures on which the method call depends exists, i.e., if $\overline{f}$ can be found in $\mathbb{F}$ and check if they are resolved. Rule ASYNC-CALL creates an invocation message to o' with a fresh unresolved future f', method name m, and actual parameters $\overline{v}$. Rule SELF-SYNC-CALL directly transfers control of the object from the caller to the callee. After the execution of invoked method is completed, rule SYNC-RETURN-SCHED reactivates the caller. Rule SYNC-CALL specifies a synchronous call to another object, which is replaced by an asynchronous call followed by a $\mathbf{get}$ statement. In case one of the futures that a synchronous (or asynchronous) method invocations depends on is not yet resolved, the process will be suspended (see Rules (WAIT-ASYNC-CALL) and (WAIT-SYNC-CALL)). Rules HOLD and RELEASE control the resource acquisition and return. Note that it is required to have all the acquired resources to be available in order to consume the $\mathbf{hold}$ statement; otherwise, the process will be blocked.

In $\mathcal{R}$PL, the unique statement that consumes time is $\mathbf{cost}(e)$. Rule COST specifies a trivial case when e evaluates to 0. When the configuration cn reaches a *stable state*, no other transition is possible except those evaluating the $\mathbf{cost}(e)$ statement where e evaluates to some $t \le 0$, then time advances by the smallest value required to let at least one process execute. To formalize this semantics, we first define stability in Definition 1.

Definition 1. *A configuration is t-stable for some $t > 0$, denoted as* $\mathtt{stable}_t(cn)$, *if every object in cn is in one of the following forms:*

1. $obj(o, a, \{l \mid x = e.\mathbf{get}; s\}, q)$ where $[\![e]\!]_{(aol)} = f$ and $fut(f, \perp) \in cn$,
2. $obj(o, a, \{l \mid \mathbf{cost}(e); s\}, q)$ where $[\![e]\!]_{(aol)} \geq t$,
3. $obj(o, a, \{l \mid \mathbf{hold}(r, e); s\}, q)$ with $res \in cn$,
   where $\exists (r, e) \in \overline{(r, e)}$ s.t. $r \in dom(res)$ and $res(r) - [\![e]\!]_{(aol)} \leq 0$,
4. $obj(o, a, \mathtt{idle}, q)$ and if
   (a) $q = \emptyset$, or,
   (b) $\forall p \in q$ and if
      i. $p = \{l \mid \mathbf{wait}(f); s\}$ and $fut(f, \perp) \in cn$, or,
      ii. $p = \{l \mid x = m(e, \overline{e'}) \textbf{ after } \overline{f?}; s\}$, or $p = \{l \mid x = \,!m(e, \overline{e'}) \textbf{ after } \overline{f?}; s\}$, where $\exists f \in \overline{f}$ s.t. $fut(f, \perp) \in cn$.

A configuration cn is *strongly t-stable*, written as $\mathtt{strongstable}_t(cn)$, if it is t-stable and there is an object $obj(o, a, \{l \mid \mathbf{cost}(e); s\}, q)$ with $[\![e]\!]_{(aol)} = t$. Note that both t-stable and strongly t-stable configurations cannot proceed anymore because every object is stuck either on a $\mathbf{cost}(e)$, on unresolved futures, or waiting for some resources. Rule TICK in Fig. 5 handles time advancement when cn is strongly t-stable by advancing time in cn for t units using $\Phi(cn, t)$.

The *initial configuration* of an $\mathcal{R}$PL program with main method $\{\overline{T\ x}; s\}$ is

$$obj(o_{main}, \varepsilon, \{[destiny \mapsto f_{initial}, \overline{x} \mapsto \perp], q)$$

where o_{main} is object name, and $f_{initial}$ is a fresh future name. Normally, $\rightarrow^*$ is the reflexive and transitive closure of $\rightarrow$ and $\overset{t}{\Rightarrow}$ is $\rightarrow^* \overset{t}{\rightarrow} \rightarrow^*$. A computation is $cn \overset{t_1}{\Rightarrow} \ldots \overset{t_n}{\Rightarrow} cn'$; that is, cn' is a configuration reachable from cn with either transitions $\rightarrow$ or $\overset{t}{\Rightarrow}$. When the time labels of transitions are not necessary, we also write $cn \Rightarrow^* cn'$.

Definition 2. *The computational time of* $cn \overset{t_1}{\Rightarrow} \ldots \overset{t_n}{\Rightarrow} cn'$ *is* $t_1 + \cdots + t_n$.

The computational time of a configuration cn, written as $\mathtt{time}(cn)$, is the maximum computational time of computations starting at cn. The computational time of an $\mathcal{R}$PL program is the computational time of its initial configuration.

3 Analysis of $\mathcal{R}$PL Program

In this section, we describe the cost analysis for an $\mathcal{R}$PL program, which translates an $\mathcal{R}$PL program into a set of cost equations that can be fed to a constraint solver. The solution to the resulting constraint set is an over-approximation of the execution time of the $\mathcal{R}$PL program. We use the example in Fig. 6 to illustrate the idea of the analysis. Our analysis assumes all $\mathcal{R}$PL programs terminate and all invoked methods are synchronised. It extends the analysis presented in [21] and to handle a more expressive language with explicit notion of task dependencies and resource allocations.

A cost equation results in a cost expression exp that has the following syntax:

$$exp ::= k \mid c_m \mid max(exp, exp) \mid exp + exp$$

```
1   [r₁ ↦ 2, r₂ ↦ 3, r₃ ↦ 2]              12   class B {
2   class A {                             13     Unit m₃(B x, Int k) {
3     Unit m₁(A x, B y, Int k) {          14       hold(r₁, 2);
4       Fut<Unit> g₁;                     15       cost(k);
5       g₁ = !m₃(y, k) after;             16       release(r₁, 2);} }
6       wait(g₁);                         17   {
7       g₁.get;}                          18     Int k₁; Int k₂; Int k₃;
8     Unit m₂(A x, B y, Int k) {          19     Fut<Unit> f₁; Fut<Unit> f₂;
9       Fut<Unit> h₁; Unit z;             20     A a₁ = new A; B b₁ = new B;
10      h₁ = !m₃(y, k) after;             21     cost(k₁);
11      z = m₁(this, y) after h₁?;} }     22     f₁ = !m₂(a₁, b₁, k₃) after;
                                          23     cost(k₂);
                                          24     f₂ = !m₃(b₁, k₃) after;
                                          25     f₁.get;
                                          26     f₂.get;}
```

Fig. 6. A running example of an $\mathcal{R}$PL program.

A cost expression may have natural numbers k, the cost c_m of executing a method m, the maximum and the sum of two cost expressions.

Given an $\mathcal{R}$PL program $\mathcal{P}$, the analysis iterates over every method definition $B\ m(\overline{T\ y})\{\overline{T\ x};\ s\}$ in each class in $\mathcal{P}$, and translates it into a cost equation of the form $eq_m = exp$, where exp corresponds to an upper bound of the computational time of m. The analysis performs this translation by considering the process pool of every object associated with the execution of method m, computing an upper bound for the finishing time of all of its processes, which gives rise to an upper bound to the computational time of the method itself.

In the following, we describe the two significant structures, namely, *synchronisation schema* and *accumulated costs*, used in the analysis to handle the complexity of considering process pools.

3.1   Synchronisation Schema

We will first describe synchronisation sets, an element of synchronisation schema, and proceed with the function that is used to manipulate the schema. A synchronisation set [21], ranged over $O, O', \ldots$, is a set of object identifiers whose processes have implicit dependencies; that is, the processes of these objects may reciprocally influence the process pools of the other objects in the same set through method invocations and synchronisations.

A *synchronisation schema*, ranged over $S, S', \ldots$, is a set of pairwise disjoint synchronisation sets. Let $B\ m(C\ o, \overline{C'\ o'}, \overline{T\ x})\ \{\overline{T'\ x'};\ s\}$ be an $\mathcal{R}$PL method declaration. The synchronisation schema of m, denoted as S_m, can be seen as a distribution of the objects used in that method into synchronisation sets, where $S_m = \texttt{sschem}(\{\{o, \overline{o'}\}\}, s, o)$, which is defined in Definition 3.

Definition 3 (Synchronisation Schema Function). *Let S be a synchronisation schema, s a statement and o a carrier object which is executing s.*

$$\mathbf{sschem}(S, s, o) = \begin{cases} S \oplus \{o', \overline{o''}\} & \text{if } s \text{ is } x = m(o', \overline{o''}, \overline{e}) \text{ after } \overline{f?} \\ & \text{or, } x = !m(o', \overline{o''}, \overline{e}) \text{ after } \overline{f'?} \\ \mathbf{sschem}(S, s_1, o) & \text{if } s \text{ is if } e \ \{s_1\} \\ \mathbf{sschem}(\mathbf{sschem}(S, s', o), s'', o) & \text{if } s \text{ is } s'; s'' \\ S & \text{otherwise.} \end{cases}$$

where

$$S \oplus O = \begin{cases} O & \text{if } S = \emptyset \\ (S' \oplus O) \cup O' & \text{if } S = S' \cup O' \text{ and } O' \cap O = \emptyset \\ S' \oplus (O' \cup O) & \text{if } S = S' \cup O' \text{ and } O' \cap O \neq \emptyset \end{cases}$$

The term $S(o)$ represents the synchronisation set containing o in the synchronisation schema S. The function $S \oplus O$ merges a schema S with a synchronisation set O. If none of the objects in O belongs to a set in S, the function reduces to a simple set union. For example, let $S = \{\{o_1, o_2\}, \{o_3, o_4\}\}$. Then $S \oplus \{o_2, o_5\}$ is equal to $(\{\{o_1, o_2\}\} \oplus \{o_2, o_5\}) \cup \{\{o_3, o_4\}\}$, resulting $\{\{o_1, o_2, o_5\}, \{o_3, o_4\}\}$. To perform cost analysis later, a synchronisation schema will be constructed for each method m. The synchronisation schemas of methods defined in Fig. 6 are $S_{m_1} = \{\{x, y\}\}$, $S_{m_2} = \{\{x, y\}\}$, $S_{m_3} = \{\{x\}\}$, $S_{main} = \{\{o_{main}\}, \{a_1, b_1\}\}$.

3.2 Accumulated Costs

The syntax of *exp* is extended to express (an over-approximation of) the time progressions of processes in the same synchronisation set. We call this extension *accumulated cost* [21], denoted as $\mathcal{E}$, which is defined as follows:

$$\mathcal{E} ::= exp \mid \mathcal{E} \cdot \langle c_m, exp \rangle \mid \mathcal{E} \parallel exp .$$

Let o be a carrier object and o' an object that does not belong to the same synchronisation set of o, i.e., $o' \notin S(o)$. The term *exp* represents the starting time of a process running on o'. The term $\mathcal{E} \cdot \langle c_m, exp \rangle$ describes the starting time of a method invoked asynchronously on object o'. For example, when o invokes a method m on o' using $f = !m(o', \overline{o''}, \overline{e})$ **after** $\overline{f?}$, the accumulated cost of the synchronisation set of o' is $\mathcal{E} \cdot \langle c_m, 0 \rangle$, where $\mathcal{E}$ is the cost accumulated up to that point and c_m is the cost of executing method m. Statement **cost**(e) in the process of the carrier o not only advances time in o, but also updates the starting time of succeeding method invocations on object o' to $\mathcal{E} \cdot \langle c_m, e \rangle$, indicating that the starting time of the subsequent method invocation on the synchronisation set of o' is after the time expressed by $\mathcal{E}$ plus the maximum between c_m and e. The term $\mathcal{E} \parallel exp$ expresses the time advancement in the carrier object o when a method running on an object o' in another synchronisation set is synchronised. In this situation, the time advances by the maximum between the current time exp in o and $\mathcal{E}$ the time in o'. The evaluation function for the accumulated cost, denoted as $[\![\mathcal{E}]\!]$, computes the starting time of the next process in the synchronisation set whose cost is $\mathcal{E}$ as follows:

$$[\![exp]\!] = exp , \quad [\![\mathcal{E} \cdot \langle c_m, exp \rangle]\!] = [\![\mathcal{E}]\!] + max(c_m, exp) , \quad [\![\mathcal{E} \parallel exp]\!] = max([\![\mathcal{E}]\!], exp) .$$

$$\mathcal{T}_{S_m}(I, \Psi, o, t_a, t, s) =$$

$$\begin{cases}
1.\ \mathcal{T}_{S_m}(I', \Psi', o, t'_a, t', s'') & \text{if } s \text{ is } s'; s'', \text{and} \\
& (I', \Psi', t'_a, t') = \mathcal{T}_{S_m}(I, \Psi, o, t_a, t, s') \\[4pt]
2.\ (I, \Psi + e, t_a, t + e) & \text{if } s \text{ is } \textbf{cost}(e) \\[4pt]
3.\ (I', \Psi', t'_a, t' + c_{m'}) & \text{if } s \text{ is } o = m'(o', \overline{e}) \textbf{ after } \overline{f?}, \text{ and} \\
& (I', \Psi', t'_a, t') = \textbf{trans}_{S_m}(I, \Psi, o, t_a, t, \overline{f}) \\[4pt]
4.\ (I'[f \mapsto S_m(o)], \Psi', t'_a + c_{m'}, t') & \text{if } s \text{ is } f =! m'(o', \overline{e}) \textbf{ after } \overline{f'?}, \ o' \in S_m(o), \text{and} \\
& (I', \Psi', t'_a, t') = \textbf{trans}_{S_m}(I, \Psi, o, t_a, t, \overline{f'}) \\[4pt]
5.\ (I'[f \mapsto S_m(o')], \Psi'[S_m(o') \mapsto \mathcal{E} \cdot \langle c_{m'}, 0 \rangle], t'_a, t') & \\
& \text{if } s \text{ is } f = m'(o', \overline{e}) \textbf{ after } \overline{f'?}, \ o' \notin S_m(o), \text{and} \\
& (I', \Psi', t'_a, t') = \textbf{trans}_{S_m}(I, \Psi, o, t_a, t, \overline{f'}), \text{where} \\
& \mathcal{E} = \begin{cases} \Psi'(S_m(o')) & \text{if } S_m(o') \in dom(\Psi') \\ t' & \text{otherwise.} \end{cases} \\[4pt]
6.\ (I', \Psi', t'_a, t') & \text{if } s \text{ is } f.\textbf{get} \text{ or } \textbf{wait}(f), \text{ and} \\
& (I', \Psi', t'_a, t') = \textbf{trans}_{S_m}(I, \Psi, o, t_a, t, \{f\}) \\[4pt]
7.\ (I', \Psi', max(t_a, t_{a_1}), max(t, t_1)) & \text{if } s \text{ is } \textbf{if } e \ \{s_1\}, \text{and} \\
& (I_1, \Psi_1, t_{a_1}, t_1) = \mathcal{T}_{S_m}(I, \Psi, o, t_a, t, s_1) \\
& I' = I \cup I_1, \text{ and} \\
& \Psi' = \textbf{upd}(\Psi, \Psi_1, I', dom(I')) \\[4pt]
8.\ (I, \Psi, t_a, t) & \text{otherwise.}
\end{cases}$$

Fig. 7. The translation function

The table below shows the accumulated costs of some of the statements declared in Fig. 6. The accumulated cost of Line 24 evaluates to $k_1 + max(c_{m_2}, k_2) + c_{m_3}$, which is the cost expression of the *main* method (c_{main}).

Method	Line	Accumulated Cost	Method	Line	Accumulated Cost
m_1	5	$0 \cdot \langle c_{m_3}, 0 \rangle$	*main*	22	$k_1 \cdot \langle c_{m_2}, 0 \rangle$
m_2	10	$0 \cdot \langle c_{m_3}, 0 \rangle$	*main*	23	$k_1 \cdot \langle c_{m_2}, k_2 \rangle$
m_3	15	k	*main*	24	$k_1 \cdot \langle c_{m_2}, k_2 \rangle \cdot \langle c_{m_3}, 0 \rangle$

3.3 Translation Function

This section defines the translation function that computes the cost of a method by analysing all possible synchronisation sets and synchronisations made on it. Given an $\mathcal{R}$PL method m and a synchronisation schema S_m computed based on Sect. 3.1, the translate function analyses the body of the method m by parsing each of its statements sequentially and recording the accumulated costs of synchronisation sets in a translation environment.

Definition 4 (Translation Environment). *Translation environments, ranged over $\Psi, \Psi', \ldots$, is a mapping from synchronisation sets to their corresponding accumulated costs ($S_m(o) \mapsto \mathcal{E}$).*

$\mathbf{trans}_{S_m}(I, \Psi, o, t_a, t, F) =$

$$\begin{cases}
(a)\ (I, \Psi, t_a, t) & \text{if } F = \emptyset \\
(b)\ \mathbf{trans}_{S_m}(I \setminus F'', \Psi + t_a, o, 0, t + t_a, F') & \text{if } F = F' \cup f \text{ and } o \in I(f) \text{ and} \\
& \qquad F'' = \{f' \mid I(f') = S_m(o)\} \\
(c)\ \mathbf{trans}_{S_m}(I \setminus F'', (\Psi \parallel t') \setminus I(f), o, 0, t', F') & \\
& \text{if } F = F' \cup f \text{ and } o \notin I(f) \text{ where} \\
& \qquad F'' = \{f' \mid I(f') = S_m(o) \vee I(f') = I(f)\} \\
& \quad \text{and } t' = max(t + t_a, \llbracket \Psi(I(f)) \rrbracket) \\
(d)\ \mathbf{trans}_{S_m}(I \setminus F'', \Psi + t_a, o, 0, t + t_a, F') & \text{if } F = F' \cup f \text{ and } f \notin dom(I) \text{ where} \\
& \qquad F'' = \{f' \mid I(f') = S_m(o)\}
\end{cases}$$

Fig. 8. The auxiliary translation function

Given a synchronisation schema of a method m, S_m, the translation function $\mathcal{T}_{S_m}(I, \Psi, o, t_a, t, s)$ defined in Fig. 7 takes six parameters: I is a map from future names to synchronisation sets, Ψ a translation environment, o is the carrier object, t_a a cost expression that computes the cost of the methods invoked on objects belonging to the same synchronisation set of carrier o and but not yet synchronised, t a cost expression that computes the computational time accumulated from the start of the method execution, and a statement s.

The function returns a tuple of four elements: an updated map I', an updated translation environment Ψ', the updated cost of asynchronously running objects t_a', and the updated current cost t'. Each case of the function is explained below.

Case 1: Each statement in a sequential composition is translated recursively.

Case 2: When s is a **cost**(e) statement, the function updates the current cost t and the accumulated cost Ψ by adding the cost e to them.

Case 3: If s is a synchronous method invocation $m'(o', \overline{e})$ **after** $\overline{f}?$, since the method can only be invoked after the futures $\overline{f}$[1] have been resolved, we need to first compute the cost of all methods associating to $\overline{f}?$ with the auxiliary function $\mathbf{trans}_{S_m}(I, \Psi, o, t_a, t, \overline{f})$ in Fig. 8 (see below for explanation). After computing the cost of executing the methods associating to $\overline{f}$, the cost of method m', $c_{m'}$, is added to the accumulated cost t'.

Case 4 and 5: The next two cases corresponds to s as an asynchronous method invocation $!m'(o', \overline{e})$ **after** $\overline{f}?$. Similar to **Case 3**, we first compute the cost of all methods associating to $\overline{f}?$. **Case 4** handles the situation if carrier o and callee o' are in the same synchronisation set. We add the cost of method m to t_a' and update I' with the binding $f \mapsto S_m(x)$. If o' is not in the same synchronisation set of carrier o, as in **Case 5**, we add the binding $f \mapsto S_m(y)$ to I' and update the Ψ' by adding the cost of method m' to the accumulated cost of $S_m(y)$.

Case 6: When s is either f.**get** or **wait**(f) statement, we compute the cost by utilising function $\mathbf{trans}_{S_m}(I, \Psi, x, t_a, t, \{f\})$.

---

[1] We refer $\overline{f}$ to a (possibly empty) set of futures by overloading the overline notation.

$\mathrm{upd}(\Psi_1, \Psi_2, I, F) =$

$$\begin{cases} \Psi_1 & \text{if } F = \emptyset \ \vee \ \Psi_2 = \emptyset \\ \Psi_2 & \text{if } \Psi_1 = \emptyset \\ \mathrm{upd}(\Psi_1[I(f) \mapsto max(\Psi_1(I(f)), \Psi_2(I(f)))], \Psi_2, I, F') \\ \qquad \text{if } F = F' \cup f \wedge I(f) \in dom(\Psi_1) \wedge I(f) \in dom(\Psi_2) \\ \mathrm{upd}(\Psi_1, \Psi_2, I, F') & \text{if } F = F' \cup f \wedge I(f) \in dom(\Psi_1) \wedge I(f) \notin dom(\Psi_2) \\ \mathrm{upd}(\Psi_1[I(f) \mapsto \Psi_2(I(f))], \Psi_2, I, F') & \text{if } F = F' \cup f \wedge I(f) \notin dom(\Psi_1) \wedge I(f) \in dom(\Psi_2) \end{cases}$$

Fig. 9. The auxiliary update function

Case 7: To handle conditional statements, we first calculate the cost of executing the statements in the conditional branch. Since the conditional branch may be executed at runtime, to over-approximate the cost, we update t_a with the maximum of t_a and t_{a_1}, and the current cost t with the maximum of t and t_1. The resulting I' is the union of I and I_1. We further update the translation environment with the auxiliary update function defined in Fig. 9.

The trans Function. The auxilary function **trans** in Fig. 8 also takes six arguments. While the first five are the same as those of $\mathcal{T}$, the last one is a set of futures F. This function recursively calculates the cost of each method associated to the futures in F as follows:

(a): It is trivial if F is an empty set, where I, Ψ, t_a, and t remain unchanged.

(b): This corresponds to the case where F contains a future f associated to a method call whose callee belongs to same synchronisation set of the carrier x. Since it is non-deterministic when this method will be scheduled for execution, to over-approximate the cost, we sum the cost of the methods invoked on the objects that are in $S_m(o)$, which is stored in t_a, and add it to the cost t accumulated so far. We then reset t_a to 0 and remove all the corresponding futures from I since the related costs have been already considered.

(c): When F contains a future associated to a method call whose callee (say o') does not belong to $S_m(o)$. Since objects o and o' reside in separate synchronisation sets, the method running on o' runs in parallel with o. Therefore, the cost is the maximum between the total cost of all methods invoked on the objects in $S_m(o)$ and that in $S_m(o')$. Since we over-approximating the cost, the cost of all methods invoked on the objects in $S_m^*(o)$ and $S_m(o')$ have already been computed. Therefore, we remove $S_m(o')$ from Ψ, as well as all the futures associated with $S_m(o)$ and $S_m(o')$ from I.

(d): When F contains a future f that does not belong to I, it indicates that the cost of the method corresponding to f has been already calculated. Since it can happen that other methods may be invoked after this computation, the actual termination of the method invocation corresponding to f may happen after the completion of these invocations. To take this into account, we add the cost of all methods whose callee belongs to $S_m(o)$, which has been stored in t_a, to the cost accumulated so far.

Example 1. We show how the translation function can be applied on the methods defined in Fig. 6. Let $S = \{\{o\}, \{a_1, b_1\}\}$, $S_1 = \{\{x, y\}\}$, $S_2 = \{\{x, y\}\}$ and $S_3 = \{\{x\}\}$ (as computed in Sect. 3.2). We use s_i to indicate the sequence of statements of a method body starting from line i.

Translation of method m_1 :
$\quad \mathcal{T}_{S_1}(\emptyset, \emptyset, x, 0, 0, g_1 = \,!m_3(y, k)\ \textbf{after}; s_6)$
$\quad = \mathcal{T}_{S_1}(\{g_1 \mapsto \{x, y\}\}, \emptyset, x, c_{m_3}, 0, \textbf{wait}(g_1); s_7)$
$\quad = \mathcal{T}_{S_1}(\emptyset, \emptyset, x, 0, c_{m_3}, g_1.\textbf{get})$
$\quad = (\emptyset, \emptyset, 0, \boxed{c_{m_3}})$

Translation of method m_2 : $\mathcal{T}_{S_2}(\emptyset, \emptyset, x, 0, 0, h_1 = \,!m_3(y, k)\ \textbf{after}; s_{11})$
$\quad = \mathcal{T}_{S_2}(\{h_1 \mapsto \{x, y\}\}, \emptyset, x, c_{m_3}, 0, z = m_1(\textbf{this}, y)\ \textbf{after}\ h1?)$
$\quad = (\emptyset, \emptyset, 0, \boxed{c_{m_3} + c_{m_1}})$

Translation of method m_3 : $\mathcal{T}_{S_3}(\emptyset, \emptyset, x, 0, 0, \textbf{hold}(r_1, 2); s_{15})$
$\quad = \mathcal{T}_{S_3}(\emptyset, \emptyset, x, 0, 0, \textbf{cost}(k); s_{16})$
$\quad = \mathcal{T}_{S_3}(\emptyset, \emptyset, x, 0, k, \textbf{release}(r_1, 2))$
$\quad = (\emptyset, \emptyset, 0, \boxed{k})$

Translation of method $main$:
$\quad \mathcal{T}_S(\emptyset, \emptyset, o, 0, 0, \texttt{A}\ a_1 = \textbf{new A};\ \texttt{B}\ b_1 = \textbf{new B}; s_{21})$
$= \mathcal{T}_S(\emptyset, \emptyset, o, 0, 0, \textbf{cost}(k_1); s_{22})$
$= \mathcal{T}_S(\emptyset, \emptyset, o, 0, k_1, f_1 = \,!m_2(a_1, b_1, k_3)\ \textbf{after}; s_{23})$
$= \mathcal{T}_S(\{f_1 \mapsto \{a_1, b_1\}\}, \{\{a_1, b_1\} \mapsto k_1 \cdot \langle c_{m_2}, 0\rangle\}, o, 0, k_1, \textbf{cost}(k_2); s_{24})$
$= \mathcal{T}_S(\{f_1 \mapsto \{a_1, b_1\}\}, \{\{a_1, b_1\} \mapsto k_1 \cdot \langle c_{m_2}, k_2\rangle\}, o, 0,$
$\qquad\qquad\qquad k_1 + k_2, f_2 = \,!m_3(b_1, k_3)\ \textbf{after}; s_{25})$
$= \mathcal{T}_S(\{f_1 \mapsto \{a_1, b_1\}, f_2 \mapsto \{a_1, b_1\}\}, \{\{a_1, b_1\} \mapsto k_1 \cdot \langle c_{m_2}, k_2\rangle \cdot \langle c_{m_3}, 0\rangle\}, o, 0,$
$\qquad\qquad\qquad k_1 + k_2, f_1.\textbf{get}; s_{26})$
$= \mathcal{T}_S(\emptyset, \emptyset, o, 0, max(k_1 + k_2, k_1 \cdot \langle c_{m_2}, k_2\rangle \cdot \langle c_{m_3}, 0\rangle), f_2.\textbf{get})$
$= (\emptyset, \emptyset, 0, \boxed{max(k_1 + k_2, k_1 \cdot \langle c_{m_2}, k_2\rangle \cdot \langle c_{m_3}, 0\rangle)})$

We notice that for each method the resulting translation environment Ψ is always empty, and t_a is always equal to 0 because every asynchronous method invocation is always synchronised within the caller method body.

4 Properties

The correctness of our analysis relies on the property that the execution time never rises throughout transitions. Therefore, the cost of the program in the initial configuration over-approximates the cost of each computation.

Cost Program. The cost of a program is calculated by solving a set of equations. Let a cost program be an equation system of the form:

$$eq_{m_i} = exp_i$$
$$eq_{main} = exp_{main}$$

where m_i are the method names and $1 \leq i \leq n$, exp_i and exp_{main} are cost expressions. The solution of the above cost program is the closed-form upper bound for the equation eq_{main}, which is a main method of the program.

Definition 5 (Cost of Program). *Let* $\mathcal{P} = (R\,\overline{C}\,\{\overline{T\ x};\ s\})$ *be an* $\mathcal{R}$PL *program, where* $\overline{C} = $ **class** $C_1\,\{\overline{T\ x};\ B\ m_1(\overline{T\ y})\{\overline{T'\ x};\ s_1\}\dots\}$

$\qquad$ **class** $C_j\,\{\overline{T\ x};\ B\ m_k(\overline{T\ y})\{\overline{T'\ x};\ s_1\}\dots\ B\ m_n(\overline{T\ y})\{\overline{T'\ x};\ s_n\}\}$
Then for every $1 \le i \le n$ *and* $1 \le j \le m$, *let*

1. $S_i = \mathtt{sschem}(\{\{o_i, \overline{o'}\}\}, s_i, o_i)$
2. $eq_{m_i} = t_i$, *where* $\boldsymbol{T}_{S_i}(\emptyset, \emptyset, o_i, 0, 0, s_i) = (I_i, \Psi_i, t_a, t_i)$
3. $S_{main} = \mathtt{sschem}(\{\{o_{main}\}\}, s, o_{main})$ *and*
   $\boldsymbol{T}_{S_{main}}(\emptyset, \emptyset, o_{main}, 0, 0, s) = (I, \Psi, t_a, t_{main})$

Let $eq(\mathcal{P})$ *be the cost program* $(eq_{m_1} = t_1, \dots, eq_{m_n} = t_n, eq_{main} = t_{main})$. *A cost solution of* $\mathcal{P}$, *named* $\mathcal{U}(\mathcal{P})$, *is the closed-form solution of the equation* eq_{main} *in* $eq(\mathcal{P})$.

For all methods, we produce cost equations that associates the method's cost to the cost of its last statement, $eq_{m_i} = t_i$. Similarly, we produce one additional equation for the cost of the main method eq_{main} and its closed-form solution over-approximates the computational time of $\mathcal{R}$PL program.

Example 2. The cost program of Fig. 6 is shown as follows, where each cost expression is computed in Example 1.

$$eq_{m_1} = c_{m_3}, \quad eq_{m_2} = c_{m_3} + c_{m_1}, \quad eq_{m_3} = k,$$
$$eq_{main} = max(k_1 + k_2, k_1 \cdot \langle c_{m_2}, k_2 \rangle \cdot \langle c_{m_3}, 0 \rangle).$$

Correctness Property. The correctness of our analysis follows the theorem below.

Theorem 1 (Correctness of Analysis). *Let* $\mathcal{P}$ *be an* $\mathcal{R}$PL *program, whose initial configuration is* cn, *and* $\mathcal{U}(\mathcal{P})$ *be the closed-form solution of* $\mathcal{P}$. *If* $cn \Rightarrow^* cn'$, *then* $\mathtt{time}(cn') \le \mathcal{U}(\mathcal{P})$.

Proof (Sketch). The proof is similar to the one proven in [21]. The main idea is to first extend function $\boldsymbol{T}$ for runtime configurations, and to define the cost of a computation $cn \Rightarrow^* cn'$, written as $\mathtt{time}(cn \Rightarrow^* cn')$, to be the sum of the labels of the transitions, and to show that $\mathcal{U}(\mathcal{P})$ is a solution of $\boldsymbol{T}(cn)$, then $\mathcal{U}(\mathcal{P}) - \mathtt{time}(cn \Rightarrow^* cn')$ is a solution of $\boldsymbol{T}(cn')$.

5   Related Work

Comprehensive research has been performed on modelling business process workflows: BPEL [22] is an executable language for simulating process behaviour, whereas BPMN [24] uses a graphical notation to represent business process descriptions. Petri-nets [1] has been used to formalize both BPEL and BPMN [9,17]. Different formal approches based on e.g., pi-calculus [3], timed automata [16], CSP [25] have been developed to analyse and reason about models of business process workflows. Compared to our proposed approach, the main focus of these techniques is on intra-organisational workflows and have limited support for coordinating tasks and resources in workflows that are across organisational.

Approaches have been proposed to merge business process models, e.g., [15] presents an approach to merge two business processes based on Event-driven Process Chains [23], which has been implemented in the process mining framework ProM [11], and [20] describes a technique that generates a configurable business process with a pair of business processes as input. To the best of our knowledge, these techniques do not consider connecting workflows across organisations.

Numerous techniques have been introduced for static cost analysis. For example, [6] presents the first approach to the automatic cost analysis of object-oriented bytecode programs, [18] proposes the first automatic analysis for deriving bounds on the worst-case evaluation cost of parallel first-order functional programs. In [21], authors define a concurrent actor language with time. Also, they define a translation function that uses synchronisation sets to compute a cost equation function for each method definition. Compared to this techniques, this paper handles a more expressive language that is sensitive to task dependencies and resource consumption.

6   Conclusion

We have presented in this paper a formal language $\mathcal{RPL}$ that can be used to model cross-organisational workflows consisting of concurrently running workflows. We use an example to show how the language can be employed to couple these concurrent workflows by means of resources and task dependencies. We also proposed a static analysis to over-approximate the computational time of an $\mathcal{RPL}$ program. We also presented a proof sketch of the correctness of the proposed analysis.

As for the immediate next steps, we plan to enrich the language such that the resource features, e.g., the experience and specialities, can be explicitly specified, and to extend the analysis to handle non-terminating programs. We also plan to develop an approach to associate workflow resources to ontology models. Furthermore, we intend to develop verification techniques to ensure the correctness of workflow models in $\mathcal{RPL}$ for cross-organisational workflows. A reasonable starting point is to investigate how to extend KeY-ABS [10], a deductive verification tool for ABS, to support $\mathcal{RPL}$.

The presented language is intended to be the first step towards the automation of cross-organisational workflow planning. To achieve this long-term goal, we plan to implement a workflow modelling framework with the support of cost analysis. In this framework, planners can design and update workflows modelled in $\mathcal{RPL}$, and simulate the execution of the workflows. By connecting the cost analysis to a constraint solver, the planner can estimate the overall execution time of collaborative workflows and see the effect of any changes in the resource allocation and task dependency. We foresee that such framework can eventually contribute to automating planning for cross-organisational workflows.

References

1. van der Aalst, W.M.: The application of Petri nets to workflow management. J. Circuits, Syst. Comput. **8**(01), 21–66 (1998)
2. van der Aalst, W.M.: Loosely coupled interorganizational workflows: modeling and analyzing workflows crossing organizational boundaries. Inf. Manag. **37**(2), 67–75 (2000)
3. Abouzaid, F.: A mapping from pi-calculus into BPEL. Front. Artif. Intell. Appl. **143**, 235 (2006)
4. Agha, G.A.: Actors: A Model of Concurrent Computation in Distributed Systems. Tech. rep, Massachusetts Inst of Tech Cambridge Artificial Intelligence Lab (1985)
5. Albert, E., Arenas, P., Genaim, S., Puebla, G.: Closed-form upper bounds in static cost analysis. J. Autom. Reason. **46**(2), 161–203 (2011)
6. Albert, E., Arenas, P., Genaim, S., Puebla, G., Zanardini, D.: Cost analysis of object-oriented bytecode programs. Theor. Comput. Sci. **413**(1), 142–159 (2012)
7. Ali, M.R., Pun, V.K.I.: Cost Analysis for an Actor-Based Workflow Modelling Language (long version). In: Research Report 15, Western Norway University of Applied Sciences (2021)
8. Rizwan Ali, M., Ka I Pun, V.: Towards a resource-aware formal modelling language for workflow planning. In: Bellatreche, L., Chernishev, G., Corral, A., Ouchani, S., Vain, J. (eds.) MEDI 2021. CCIS, vol. 1481, pp. 251–258. Springer, Cham (2021). https://doi.org/10.1007/978-3-030-87657-9_19
9. Dijkman, R.M., Dumas, M., Ouyang, C.: Formal semantics and analysis of BPMN process models using Petri nets. In: Queensland Univ. of Technology, Tech. Rep. pp. 1–30 (2007)
10. Din, C.C., Bubel, R., Hähnle, R.: KEY-ABS: a deductive verification tool for the concurrent modelling language ABS. In: Felty, A.P., Middeldorp, A. (eds.) CADE 2015. LNCS (LNAI), vol. 9195, pp. 517–526. Springer, Cham (2015). https://doi.org/10.1007/978-3-319-21401-6_35
11. van Dongen, B.F., de Medeiros, A.K.A., Verbeek, H.M.W., Weijters, A.J.M.M., van der Aalst, W.M.P.: The ProM framework: a new era in process mining tool support. In: Ciardo, G., Darondeau, P. (eds.) ICATPN 2005. LNCS, vol. 3536, pp. 444–454. Springer, Heidelberg (2005). https://doi.org/10.1007/11494744_25
12. Dourish, P.: Process descriptions as organisational accounting devices: the dual use of workflow technologies. In: Proceedings of the 2001 Intl. ACM SIGGROUP Conference on Supporting Group Work, pp. 52–60 (2001)
13. Dumas, M., van der Aalst, W.M., Ter Hofstede, A.H.: Process-aware information systems: bridging people and software through process technology. Wiley, Hoboken (2005)
14. Flores-Montoya, A., Hähnle, R.: Resource analysis of complex programs with cost equations. In: Garrigue, J. (ed.) APLAS 2014. LNCS, vol. 8858, pp. 275–295. Springer, Cham (2014). https://doi.org/10.1007/978-3-319-12736-1_15
15. Gottschalk, F., van der Aalst, W.M.P., Jansen-Vullers, M.H.: Merging event-driven process chains. In: Meersman, R., Tari, Z. (eds.) OTM 2008. LNCS, vol. 5331, pp. 418–426. Springer, Heidelberg (2008). https://doi.org/10.1007/978-3-540-88871-0_28
16. Gruhn, V., Laue, R.: Using timed model checking for verifying workflows. Comput. Support. Act. Coord. **2005**, 75–88 (2005)

17. Hinz, S., Schmidt, K., Stahl, C.: Transforming BPEL to petri nets. In: van der Aalst, W.M.P., Benatallah, B., Casati, F., Curbera, F. (eds.) BPM 2005. LNCS, vol. 3649, pp. 220–235. Springer, Heidelberg (2005). https://doi.org/10.1007/11538394_15

18. Hoffmann, J., Shao, Z.: Automatic static cost analysis for parallel programs. In: Vitek, J. (ed.) ESOP 2015. LNCS, vol. 9032, pp. 132–157. Springer, Heidelberg (2015). https://doi.org/10.1007/978-3-662-46669-8_6

19. Johnsen, E.B., Hähnle, R., Schäfer, J., Schlatte, R., Steffen, M.: ABS: a core language for abstract behavioral specification. In: Aichernig, B.K., de Boer, F.S., Bonsangue, M.M. (eds.) FMCO 2010. LNCS, vol. 6957, pp. 142–164. Springer, Heidelberg (2011). https://doi.org/10.1007/978-3-642-25271-6_8

20. La Rosa, M., Dumas, M., Uba, R., Dijkman, R.: Merging business process models. In: Meersman, R., Dillon, T., Herrero, P. (eds.) OTM 2010. LNCS, vol. 6426, pp. 96–113. Springer, Heidelberg (2010). https://doi.org/10.1007/978-3-642-16934-2_10

21. Laneve, C., Lienhardt, M., Pun, K.I., Román-Díez, G.: Time analysis of actor programs. J. Logical Algebraic Method Program. 105, 1–27 (2019)

22. Juric, M., Benny Mathew, P.S.: Business Process Execution Language for Web Services BPEL and BPEL4WS. Packt Publishing (2006)

23. Mendling, J.: Event-driven process chains (EPC). In: Metrics for Process Models. LNBIP, vol. 6, pp. 17–57. Springer, Heidelberg (2008). https://doi.org/10.1007/978-3-540-89224-3_2

24. OMG, B.P.M.: Notation (BPMN) Version 2.0 (2011)

25. Wong, P.Y., Gibbons, J.: Property specifications for workflow modelling. Sci. Comput. Program. 76(10), 942–967 (2011)

26. Xu, L., Liu, H., Wang, S., Wang, K.: Modelling and analysis techniques for cross-organizational workflow systems. Syst. Rcs. Behav. Sci. Official J. Intl. Federation Syst. Res. 26(3), 367–389 (2009)

Minimization of the Number of Clocks for Timed Scenarios

Neda Saeedloei[1]([⊠]) and Feliks Kluźniak[2]

[1] Towson University, Towson, USA
nsaeedloei@towson.edu
[2] LogicBlox, Atlanta, USA
feliks.kluzniak@logicblox.com

Abstract. We present a new optimization algorithm for timed scenarios that achieves the minimal number of clocks when timed scenarios are viewed as timed automata.

1 Introduction

Using scenarios for specification and implementation of complex systems (including real time systems), and synthesizing formal models of systems from scenarios have been active areas of research for several decades [2,5,7–11,15,16].

In our earlier work [12] we developed, from first principles, a formal, yet simple notation for timed scenarios. We want to use such scenarios to automatically synthesize formal models in the form of timed automata.

For a timed automaton with $|K|$ clocks, the number of clock regions is at most $R = |K|! 4^{|K|} \Pi_{x \in K}(\mu_x + 1)$, where μ_x is the maximum constant with which clock x is compared [4]. Verification of a timed automaton can be computationally expensive, and the cost depends on the number of regions of the automaton.

So, we want the value of R in our synthesized automaton to be as low as possible. Before tackling that problem it behooves us to study it in the more limited setting of a single scenario: this is the topic of the current paper.

As part of our earlier work [12] we obtained a canonical representation (a "stable distance table") for the entire class of scenarios that are equivalent to a given one. We used stable tables as a linchpin of a very simple algorithm for "optimizing" scenarios ("optimization" was used in the sense of "improvement", but did not necessarily lead to a result that was optimal in some sense).

The goal of that algorithm was to decrease the number of constraints as well as the maximum constants appearing in constraints.

In our later work [13] we studied optimization of scenarios in more depth and developed a general algorithm that would optimize scenarios according to some given strategy. Our main goal was to minimise the maximum constants associated with the clocks that would be needed after converting a scenario to a timed automaton, while decreasing the number of clocks. Similarly to our earlier algorithm, this new algorithm relied on some particular ordering of constraints. While we had more control over—and insight into—how the algorithm worked,

© Springer Nature Switzerland AG 2021
O. Campos and M. Minea (Eds.): SBMF 2021, LNCS 13130, pp. 122–139, 2021.
https://doi.org/10.1007/978-3-030-92137-8_8

we did not obtain an entirely satisfactory result: we did not achieve minimality in the number of clocks.

The current paper summarizes our final approach to optimizing scenarios. Given a scenario, our new optimization algorithm replaces the time constraints of the scenario, represented by a stable distance table, with an equivalent set that would require the smallest number of clocks in the entire class of equivalent scenarios, when the scenarios are viewed as timed automata.

2   Preliminaries

2.1   Timed Automata

A *timed automaton* [3] is a tuple $\mathcal{A} = \langle \Sigma, Q, q_0, Q_f, C, T \rangle$, where Σ is a finite alphabet, Q is the (*finite*) set of locations, $q_0 \in Q$ is the initial location, $Q_f \subseteq Q$ is the set of final locations, C is a finite set of *clock* variables (clocks for short), and $T \subseteq Q \times Q \times \Sigma \times 2^C \times 2^{\Phi(C)}$ is the set of transitions. In each transition $(q, q', e, \lambda, \phi)$, λ is the set of clocks to be reset with the transition and $\phi \subseteq \Phi(C)$ is a set of clock constraints over C of the form $c \sim a$ (where $\sim \in \{\leq, <, \geq, >, =\}$, $c \in C$ and a is a constant in the set of rational numbers, $\mathbb{Q}$).

A *clock valuation* ν for C is a mapping from C to $\mathbb{R}^{\geq 0}$. ν satisfies a set of clock constraints ϕ over C iff every clock constraint in ϕ evaluates to true after each clock c is replaced with $\nu(c)$. For $\tau \in \mathbb{R}$, $\nu + \tau$ denotes the clock valuation which maps every clock c to the value $\nu(c) + \tau$. For $Y \subseteq C$, $[Y \mapsto \tau]\nu$ is the valuation which assigns τ to each $c \in Y$ and agrees with ν over the rest of the clocks.

A *timed word* over an alphabet Σ is a pair (σ, τ) where $\sigma = \sigma_1 \sigma_2...$ is a finite [1,6] or infinite [3] word over Σ and $\tau = \tau_1 \tau_2...$ is a finite or infinite sequence of (time) values such that (i) $\tau_i \in \mathbb{R}^{\geq 0}$, (ii) $\tau_i \leq \tau_{i+1}$ for all $i \geq 1$, and (iii) if the word is infinite, then for every $t \in \mathbb{R}^{\geq 0}$ there is some $i \geq 1$ such that $\tau_i > t$.

A run ρ of $\mathcal{A}$ over a timed word (σ, τ) is a sequence of the form $\langle q_0, \nu_0 \rangle \xrightarrow[\tau_1]{\sigma_1} \langle q_1, \nu_1 \rangle \xrightarrow[\tau_2]{\sigma_2} \langle q_2, \nu_2 \rangle \xrightarrow[\tau_3]{\sigma_3} \ldots$, where for all $i \geq 0$, $q_i \in Q$ and ν_i is a clock valuation such that (i) $\nu_0(c) = 0$ for all clocks $c \in C$ and (ii) for every $i > 1$ there is a transition in T of the form $(q_{i-1}, q_i, \sigma_i, \lambda_i, \phi_i)$, such that $(\nu_{i-1} + \tau_i - \tau_{i-1})$ satisfies ϕ_i, and ν_i equals $[\lambda_i \mapsto 0](\nu_{i-1} + \tau_i - \tau_{i-1})$. The set $inf(\rho)$ consists of $q \in Q$ such that $q = q_i$ for infinitely many $i \geq 0$ in the run ρ.

A run over a finite timed word is *accepting* if it ends in a final location [6]. A run ρ over an infinite timed word is *accepting* iff $inf(\rho) \cap Q_f \neq \emptyset$ [3]. The *language* of $\mathcal{A}$, $L(\mathcal{A})$, is the set $\{(\sigma, \tau) \mid \mathcal{A}$ has an accepting run over $(\sigma, \tau)\}$.

2.2   Timed Scenarios

(This subsection briefly recounts our earlier work [12,13]).

Let Σ be a finite set of symbols called *events*. A *behaviour*[1] over Σ is a sequence $(e_0, t_0)(e_1, t_1)(e_2, t_2)\ldots$, such that $e_i \in \Sigma$, $t_i \in \mathbb{R}^{\geq 0}$ and $t_{i-1} \leq t_i$ for

---

[1] The notion of "behaviour" is equivalent to that of Alur's "timed word" [3].

$$L_0 : a;$$
$$L_1 : b;$$
$$L_2 : c \ \{L_0 \leq 9, L_0 \geq 9, L_1 \leq 3\};$$
$$\quad d \ \{L_2 \leq 2\}.$$

$$L_0 : a;$$
$$\quad b \ \{L_0 \geq 6\};$$
$$L_2 : c \ \{L_0 \leq 9, L_0 \geq 9\};$$
$$\quad d \ \{L_2 \leq 2\}.$$

	1	2	3
0	(6, 9)	(9, 9)	(9, 11)
1		(0, 3)	(0, 5)
2			(0, 2)

$$\xi \qquad\qquad \eta$$

Fig. 1. Two equivalent scenarios with their stable table

$i \in \{1, 2 \dots\}$. For a finite behaviour $\mathcal{B} = (e_0, t_0)(e_1, t_1) \dots (e_{n-1}, t_{n-1})$ of length n, and for any $0 \leq i < j < n$, we use $t_{ij}^{\mathcal{B}}$ to denote the *distance*, in time units, of event j from event i in $\mathcal{B}$. That is, $t_{ij}^{\mathcal{B}} = t_j - t_i$.

Given a natural number n, we use $\Phi(n)$ to denote the set of *constraints* of the form $b \sim a$, where b is the symbol $\tau_{i,j}$ (for some integers $0 \leq i < j < n$), $\sim \in \{\leq, \geq\}^2$ and a is a constant in the set of rational numbers, $\mathbb{Q}$. A *timed scenario* (*scenario* for short) of length $n \in \mathbb{N}$ over Σ is a pair $(\mathcal{E}, \mathcal{C})$, where $\mathcal{E} = e_0 e_1 \dots e_{n-1}$ is a sequence of events, and $\mathcal{C} \subset \Phi(n)$ is a finite set of constraints.

A scenario will be written as a sequence of events, separated by semicolons and terminated by a period. If the scenario contains a constraint such as $\tau_{i,j} \leq a$, then event i in the sequence will be labelled by a unique symbol L_i, and event j will be annotated with a set of constraints that contains $L_i \leq a$. We refer to this as the external representation of the scenario. η in Fig. 1 is the external representation of scenario $(abcd, \{\tau_{0,1} \geq 6, \tau_{0,2} \leq 9, \tau_{0,2} \geq 9, \tau_{2,3} \leq 2\})$.

A behaviour $\mathcal{B} = (e_0, t_0)(e_1, t_1) \dots (e_{n-1}, t_{n-1})$ over Σ is *allowed* by scenario $\xi = (\mathcal{E}, \mathcal{C})$ iff $\mathcal{E} = e_0 \dots e_{n-1}$ and every $\tau_{i,j} \sim a$ in $\mathcal{C}$ evaluates to true after $\tau_{i,j}$ is replaced by $t_{ij}^{\mathcal{B}}$.

The constraints $\tau_{i,j} \geq 0$ and $\tau_{i,j} \leq \infty$, which always evaluate to true after we replace them with some $t_{ij}^{\mathcal{B}}$, will be called *default constraints*.

The *semantics* of scenario ξ, denoted by $[\![\xi]\!]$, is the set of behaviours that are allowed by ξ. For scenario η in Fig. 1 $[\![\eta]\!] = \{(a, t_0)(b, t_1)(c, t_2)(d, t_3) \mid t_3 \geq t_2 \geq t_1 \geq t_0 \wedge t_1 - t_0 \geq 6 \wedge t_2 - t_0 \leq 9 \wedge t_2 - t_0 \geq 9 \wedge t_3 - t_2 \leq 2\}$.

A scenario ξ is *consistent* iff $[\![\xi]\!] \neq \emptyset$. It is *inconsistent* iff $[\![\xi]\!] = \emptyset$.

If $\xi = (\mathcal{E}, \mathcal{C})$ is a scenario of length n, and $\mathcal{C}$ contains a constraint $\tau_{i,j} \sim a$ for some $0 \leq i < j < n$, then the index i is an *anchor*. We sometimes say constraint $\tau_{i,j} \sim a$ "begins" at anchor i. For an anchor i, if $0 < j < n$ is the largest number such that $\tau_{i,j} \sim a$ is a constraint in $\mathcal{C}$, then $[i, j]$ is the *range* of anchor i. If i_1 and i_2 are two anchors with ranges $[i_1, j_1]$ and $[i_2, j_2]$ in ξ, then the two ranges *overlap* iff $i_1 < i_2 < j_1$ or $i_2 < i_1 < j_2$.

An anchor i in ξ corresponds to a referenced label in the external representation of ξ. For example, in scenario η of Fig. 1, i.e., $(abcd, \{\tau_{0,1} \geq 6, \tau_{0,2} \leq 9, \tau_{0,2} \geq 9, \tau_{2,3} \leq 2\})$, the anchors 0 and 2 correspond to labels L_0 and L_2, respectively. The range of 0 is $[0, 2)$ and the range of 2 is $[2, 3)$: these are non-overlapping.

By $Anch_\xi$ we denote the set of anchors of ξ. We assume the existence of a set X of clock variables. A clock allocation for ξ is a relation $alloc_\xi \subset Anch_\xi \times X$.

---

[2] To keep the presentation compact, equality is expressed in terms of $\leq$ and $\geq$ [12].

Fig. 2. Two equivalent timed automata corresponding to the scenarios of Fig. 1

$alloc_\xi$ is *complete* iff for every anchor $i \in Anch_\xi$ there is a clock $x \in X$ such that $(i, x) \in alloc_\xi$. $alloc_\xi$ is *incorrect* iff there exist two different anchors i and j in $Anch_\xi$ whose ranges overlap, such that $(i, x) \in alloc_\xi$ and $(j, x) \in alloc_\xi$ for some $x \in X$. $alloc_\xi$ is *correct* iff it is not incorrect. A correct and complete clock allocation is *optimal* if there is no other correct and complete allocation that uses fewer clocks.

$\{(0, x), (2, x)\}$ is an optimal clock allocation for scenario η of Fig. 1.

For a scenario $\xi = (e_0 e_1 \ldots e_{n-1}, \mathcal{C})$ and an optimal clock allocation $alloc_\xi$, its corresponding timed automaton, $\mathcal{A}_\mathcal{C}$, is defined as follows: $\{l_0, l_1, \ldots l_n\}$ is the set of locations of $\mathcal{A}_\xi$; l_0 is the initial location and l_n is the final location; there is a transition r_i from l_i to l_{i+1} labeled with e_i, for each $0 \leq i < n$; $K = \{x \mid \exists_{i \in Anch_\xi} (i, x) \in alloc_\xi\}$ is the set of clocks of $\mathcal{A}_\xi$; if $(i, x) \in alloc_\xi$, then there is a clock reset $x := 0$ on transition r_i; if $\tau_{i,j} \sim a$ is a constraint in $\mathcal{C}$ and $(i, x) \in alloc_\xi$, then there is a clock constraint $x \sim a$ on transition r_j.

The two automata of Fig. 2 correspond to scenarios of Fig. 1.

For a consistent scenario ξ of length n, and for $0 \leq i < j < n$, we define $m_{ij}^\xi = min\{t_{ij}^\mathcal{B} \mid \mathcal{B} \in [\![\xi]\!]\}$ and $M_{ij}^\xi = max\{t_{ij}^\mathcal{B} \mid \mathcal{B} \in [\![\xi]\!]\}$. If there is no upper bound for i and j we will use $M_{ij}^\xi = \infty$. We will often write just m_{ij} and M_{ij} when ξ is understood. Obviously, for any behaviour in $[\![\xi]\!]$, $0 \leq m_{ij} \leq t_{ij} \leq M_{ij} \leq \infty$.

For a consistent scenario ξ of length n, and for any $0 \leq i < j < k < n$ the following inequations hold:

$$m_{ij} + m_{jk} \leq m_{ik} \leq \begin{Bmatrix} m_{ij} + M_{jk} \\ M_{ij} + m_{jk} \end{Bmatrix} \leq M_{ik} \leq M_{ij} + M_{jk} \qquad (1)$$

Let $\xi = (\mathcal{E}, \mathcal{C})$ be a scenario of length n, such that, for any $0 \leq i < j < n$, $\mathcal{C}$ contains at most one constraint of the form $\tau_{i,j} \geq c$ and at most one of the form $\tau_{i,j} \leq c$. A *distance table* for ξ is a representation of $\mathcal{C}$ in the form of a triangular matrix $\mathcal{D}^\xi$. For $0 \leq i < j < n$, $\mathcal{D}_{ij}^\xi = (l_{ij}, h_{ij})$, where l_{ij} and h_{ij} are rational numbers. If $\tau_{i,j} \geq c \in \mathcal{C}$ then $l_{ij} = c$, otherwise $l_{ij} = 0$; if $\tau_{i,j} \leq c \in \mathcal{C}$ then $h_{ij} = c$, otherwise $h_{ij} = \infty$. (See the example in Fig. 3).

A distance table of size n is *valid* iff $l_{ij} \leq h_{ij}$, for all $0 \leq i < j < n$. A table that is not valid is *invalid*. If $\mathcal{D}^\xi$ is invalid, then ξ is obviously inconsistent.

A distance table of size n is *stable* iff, for all $0 \leq i < j < k < n$, the inequations in (1) hold when m_{ij}, m_{jk}, m_{ik} are replaced by l_{ij}, l_{jk}, l_{ik} and M_{ij}, M_{jk}, M_{ik} are replaced by h_{ij}, h_{jk}, h_{ik}. If $\mathcal{D}^\xi$ is stable then ξ is consistent.

| L_0 : e; |
| L_1 : f; |
| L_2 : $g\ \{L_0 \le 10, L_0 \ge 10\}$; |
| $\quad h\ \{L_1 \le 8, L_1 \ge 8,$ |
| $\quad\quad L_2 \le 2\}$. |

	1	2	3
0	$(0, \infty)$	$(10, 10)$	$(0, \infty)$
1		$(0, \infty)$	$(8, 8)$
2			$(0, 2)$

	1	2	3
0	$(2, 4)$	$(10, 10)$	$(10, 12)$
1		$(6, 8)$	$(8, 8)$
2			$(0, 2)$

Fig. 3. A scenario, its initial distance table and its stable distance table

To *stabilise* $\mathcal{D}^\xi$ we repeatedly apply the following six rules until the table becomes either invalid or stable.

$$l_{ij} + l_{jk} > l_{ik} \longrightarrow l_{ik} := l_{ij} + l_{jk} \qquad l_{ik} > l_{ij} + h_{jk} \longrightarrow l_{ij} := l_{ik} - h_{jk}$$
$$l_{ik} > h_{ij} + l_{jk} \longrightarrow l_{jk} := l_{ik} - h_{ij} \qquad l_{ij} + h_{jk} > h_{ik} \longrightarrow h_{jk} := h_{ik} - l_{ij}$$
$$h_{ij} + l_{jk} > h_{ik} \longrightarrow h_{ij} := h_{ik} - l_{jk} \qquad h_{ik} > h_{ij} + h_{jk} \longrightarrow h_{ik} := h_{ij} + h_{jk}$$

At least one of these rules is applicable if and only if some inequation in (1) does not hold. The purpose of each rule is to tighten a constraint just enough to establish a particular inequation.

A stabilised distance table has two properties. First, all the constraints represented by the table are as *tight* as possible, i.e., $l_{ij} = m_{ij}$ and $h_{ij} = M_{ij}$ for every $0 \le i < j < n$. Second, as a result of applying the rules above, the table includes all the constraints that are "implied" by the initial set of constraints.

The right hand side of Fig. 1 shows the stable distance table obtained from the constraints of either of the two scenarios in the figure (which shows that they are equivalent). The right-hand side of Fig. 3 shows the result of stabilising the original distance table (shown in the middle).

Given a scenario ξ with its stable distance table $\mathcal{D}_s^\xi$, we use $\mathcal{C}(\mathcal{D}_s^\xi)$ to denote the set of constraints represented by $\mathcal{D}_s^\xi$.

Definition 1. *Let ξ be a scenario of length n, $\mathcal{D}_s^\xi$ be its stable table, $c \in \mathcal{C}(\mathcal{D}_s^\xi)$ be a non-default constraint, $S \subset \mathcal{C}(\mathcal{D}_s^\xi)$, and $0 \le i < j < k < n$. We say that c is directly supported by S, denoted by $S \rightsquigarrow c$, iff c and S satisfy one of the following six conditions:*

1. $c = \tau_{i,k} \ge u$, $S = \{\tau_{i,j} \ge v, \tau_{j,k} \ge w\}$, and $u = v + w$.
2. $c = \tau_{i,j} \ge u$, $S = \{\tau_{i,k} \ge v, \tau_{j,k} \le w\}$, and $u = v - w$.
3. $c = \tau_{j,k} \ge u$, $S = \{\tau_{i,k} \ge v, \tau_{i,j} \le w\}$, and $u = v - w$.
4. $c = \tau_{j,k} \le u$, $S = \{\tau_{i,k} \le v, \tau_{i,j} \ge w\}$, and $u = v - w$.
5. $c = \tau_{i,j} \le u$, $S = \{\tau_{i,k} \le v, \tau_{j,k} \ge w\}$, and $u = v - w$.
6. $c = \tau_{i,k} \le u$, $S = \{\tau_{i,j} \le v, \tau_{j,k} \le w\}$, and $u = v + w$.

Each of the cases in the definition corresponds to one of the six rules above. For example, if $l_{13} = 3$, $l_{36} = 4$ and $l_{16} = 0$ (i.e., the corresponding constraint is missing), then the first rule will force l_{16} to be 7. In other words, the constraint $l_{16} = 7$ is directly supported (i.e., "implied") by the other two constraints.

Definition 2. *(quasi-transitivity) Let $\mathcal{D}_{\hat{s}}^{\xi}$ be a stable table. $\leadsto^+ \subset 2^{\mathcal{C}(\mathcal{D}_{\hat{s}}^{\xi})} \times \mathcal{C}(\mathcal{D}_{\hat{s}}^{\xi})$ is the smallest relation that satisfies the following two conditions:*

1. *If $S \leadsto c$ then $S \leadsto^+ c$;*
2. *If $S \leadsto^+ c$ and there is a constraint $d \in S$ such that, for some S', $S' \leadsto^+ d$ and $c \notin S'$, then $(S \setminus \{d\}) \cup S' \leadsto^+ c$.*

When $S \leadsto^+ c$, we say that c is supported *by S. S is then called a* support *of c.*

We sometimes say that c *has a support*, when there is no need to specify S.

Intuitively, if a constraint d has a supporting set, then d can be removed from the scenario, because stabilisation of the distance table will restore it: d is implied by its support. The removed d can be a member of the supports of other constraints, e.g., d can appear in a set S that supports c. As long as d has a support S' that does not include c, S can be updated by replacing d with S'. The relation $\leadsto^+$ captures all the possible supports for the constraints in $\mathcal{C}(\mathcal{D}_{\hat{s}}^{\xi})$. As constraints are removed, the set of constraints will decrease and $\leadsto^+$ (as well as other relation derived from it) should be understood as restricted to the current set of constraints: we will not be pedantic about capturing it in the notation.

Observation 1. *If $S \leadsto^+ c$, then $c \notin S$.*

3   A New Optimization Algorithm

Given a collection of scenarios, our ultimate goal is to synthesize a timed automaton [3] whose language would be the set of behaviours allowed by appropriate combinations of the scenarios [14]. The first step towards that goal is optimization of single scenarios.

A timed scenario ξ can be trivially converted to a simple timed automaton $\mathcal{A}_\xi$ (Sect. 2.1). An equivalent scenario η would yield a timed automaton $\mathcal{A}_\eta$. $\mathcal{A}_\xi$ and $\mathcal{A}_\eta$ will be language-equivalent, but each of them might have a different number of clocks. As an example consider the two equivalent scenarios of Fig. 1 along with their corresponding equivalent automata shown in Fig. 2. Notice that $\mathcal{A}_\eta$ has only one clock, while $\mathcal{A}_\xi$ requires two clocks.

Our task is as follows: given a timed scenario ξ, find an equivalent scenario ξ' such that the number of clocks in $\mathcal{A}_{\xi'}$ is minimal in the class of automata that are obtained from all scenarios equivalent to ξ.

We do so by starting from a scenario that contains $\mathcal{C}(\mathcal{D}_{\hat{s}}^{\xi})$ (i.e., all the constraints that are implied by the constraints of the original scenario ξ), and then successively removing constraints that are implied by other constraints. From a bird's eye perspective, the process can be described as follows (see Sect. 3.5 for details):

- Let $C = \mathcal{C}(\mathcal{D}_{\hat{s}}^{\xi})$;
- While there is a $c \in C$ such that $\exists_{S \subset C}(S \leadsto^+ c)$:
  - remove c from C;
- C is the solution, i.e., the final set of constraints.

This involves making choices, and the solution may depend on how these choices are made. For example, removing constraint a may prevent us from removing constraint b, and vice versa.

In the remainder of this section we carefully analyze the situations that may arise during this process, and formulate a set of rules that, when applied, guarantee reaching a solution that is optimal in terms of the number of clocks.

We begin by examining cyclic dependencies, because it turns out they are the only source of those choices that actually affect the outcome.

3.1 Cyclic Dependencies

Definition 3. *Let $\mathcal{D}_s^\xi$ be a stable table and let a and b be constraints in $\mathcal{C}(\mathcal{D}_s^\xi)$. A support of b with respect to a, denoted by $S_a^{\triangleright b}$, is any set $S \subset \mathcal{C}(\mathcal{D}_s^\xi)$ such that $a \in S$ and $S \rightsquigarrow^+ b$.*

Given a and b, $S_b^{\triangleright a}$ need not be unique. Notice that $a \notin S_b^{\triangleright a}$ (Observation 1).

Definition 4. *If there is some $S_a^{\triangleright b}$, then we say that b depends on a, and write $a \rightarrow b$.*

Observation 2. *Let a, b and c be three different constraints in $\mathcal{C}(\mathcal{D}_s^\xi)$, such that $a \rightarrow b$ and $b \rightarrow c$. If there is some $S_a^{\triangleright b}$ that does not contain c, then $a \rightarrow c$.*

Proof. The above follows directly from Definitions 2, 3 and 4. □

Definition 5. *We say that a and b are in a cyclic dependency, denoted by $a \leftrightarrow b$, if $a \rightarrow b$ and $b \rightarrow a$.*

As an example consider scenario ξ of Fig. 1 along with its distance table. Let $a = \tau_{0,1} \geq 6$, $b = \tau_{1,2} \leq 3$ and $c = \tau_{1,3} \leq 5$. $\{\tau_{0,2} \leq 9, \tau_{0,1} \geq 6\} \rightsquigarrow \tau_{1,2} \leq 3$, so we have a $S_a^{\triangleright b}$, hence $a \rightarrow b$. Moreover, $\{\tau_{1,2} \leq 3, \tau_{2,3} \leq 2\} \rightsquigarrow \tau_{1,3} \leq 5$, so we have a $S_b^{\triangleright c}$, hence $b \rightarrow c$. Since we have a $S_a^{\triangleright b}$ that does not contain c, we can conclude that $a \rightarrow c$.

Also, $a \leftrightarrow b$: let $S_a^{\triangleright b}$ be $\{\tau_{0,2} \leq 9, \tau_{0,1} \geq 6\}$ and let $S_b^{\triangleright a}$ be $\{\tau_{0,2} \geq 9, \tau_{1,2} \leq 3\}$.

Observation 3. *Let a, b and c be three different constraints in $\mathcal{C}(\mathcal{D}_s^\xi)$, such that $a \rightarrow b$ and $b \rightarrow c$. If, additionally, for every pair of constraints x and y, $x \not\leftrightarrow y$, then $a \rightarrow c$.*

Proof. Assume the condition of Observation 2 is not satisfied, i.e., c is present in every $S_a^{\triangleright b}$. There is at least one $S_a^{\triangleright b}$, but if it includes c then it is also $S_c^{\triangleright b}$. Therefore $b \leftrightarrow c$: a contradiction. □

Observation 4. *Let $\mathcal{D}_s^\xi$ be a stable distance table. Let a, b and c be three different constraints in $\mathcal{C}(\mathcal{D}_s^\xi)$ such that $a \leftrightarrow b$ and $b \leftrightarrow c$. Then $a \leftrightarrow c$ if there is some $S_a^{\triangleright b}$ that does not contain c and some $S_c^{\triangleright b}$ that does not contain a.*

Proof. This follows directly from Observation 2 and Definition 5. □

In the scenario of Fig. 3 let $a = \tau_{0,1} \leq 4$, $b = \tau_{1,2} \geq 6$, and $c = \tau_{2,3} \leq 2$.

$\{\tau_{0,2} \leq 10, \tau_{1,2} \geq 6\} \leadsto \tau_{0,1} \leq 4$, and $\{\tau_{0,2} \geq 10, \tau_{0,1} \leq 4\} \leadsto \tau_{1,2} \geq 6$. So we have a $S_b^{\triangleright a}$ and a $S_a^{\triangleright b}$. That is, $a \leftrightarrow b$. On the other hand, we also have a $S_c^{\triangleright b}$ and a $S_b^{\triangleright c}$: $\{\tau_{1,3} \geq 8, \tau_{2,3} \leq 2\} \leadsto \tau_{1,2} \geq 6$ and $\{\tau_{1,3} \leq 8, \tau_{1,2} \geq 6\} \leadsto \tau_{2,3} \leq 2$. So $b \leftrightarrow c$. Notice that the $S_a^{\triangleright b}$ does not include c, while the $S_c^{\triangleright b}$ does not include a. By Observation 4, $a \leftrightarrow c$. Indeed, $S_c^{\triangleright a}$ and $S_a^{\triangleright c}$ exist: $\{\tau_{0,2} \leq 10, \tau_{1,3} \geq 8, \tau_{2,3} \leq 2\} \leadsto^+ \tau_{0,1} \leq 4$ and $\{\tau_{1,3} \leq 8, \tau_{0,2} \geq 10, \tau_{0,1} \leq 4\} \leadsto^+ \tau_{2,3} \leq 2$.

Observation 5. *Let $\mathcal{D}_s^\xi$ be a stable distance table. Let a, b and c be three different constraints in $\mathcal{C}(\mathcal{D}_s^\xi)$ such that $a \leftrightarrow b$ and $a \nleftrightarrow c$. If $a \to c$, then, after a is removed, c is still supported.*

Proof. $a \leftrightarrow b$, so there is some $S_b^{\triangleright a}$: call it S_1. Clearly, $c \notin S_1$, otherwise we would have $c \to a$, and therefore $a \leftrightarrow c$.

$a \to c$, so there is a set $S \subset \mathcal{C}(\mathcal{D}_s^\xi)$ such that $a \in S$ and $S \leadsto^+ c$. $c \notin S$ (by Observation 1). So, by Definition 2, $(S \setminus \{a\}) \cup S_1 \leadsto^+ c$. □

In other words: if two constraints a and b are in a cyclic dependency and during the course of optimization one of them, say a, is removed, then all the constraints that were previously supported by a continue to be supported. The only exception is b: if b has only one support which is its support with respect to a, then b can no longer be removed after the removal of a.

Obviously, if two constraints are in a cyclic dependency, either one of them can be removed. However, both of them cannot be removed unless at least one of them has a support other than its supports with respect to the other constraint.

Observation 6. *Let $\mathcal{D}_s^\xi$ be a stable distance table. Let a and b be two constraints in $\mathcal{C}(\mathcal{D}_s^\xi)$ such that $a \leftrightarrow b$. If there is some $S \subset \mathcal{C}(\mathcal{D}_s^\xi)$ such that $S \leadsto a$ and $b \notin S$, then both a and b can be removed.*

Proof. $a \leftrightarrow b$, so there is a $S_a^{\triangleright b}$: call it S_1.

We consider two cases:

(1) If a is removed first, then, by Definition 2, $(S_1 \setminus \{a\}) \cup S \leadsto^+ b$. Since b has a support, it can be removed.

(2) If b is removed first, then a is supported by S and can be removed. □

In the example of Fig. 1 $\tau_{0,1} \geq 6$ and $\tau_{1,2} \leq 3$ do not have any supports other than their supports with respect to each other, so one of them must be retained. Scenario η of Fig. 1 shows an equivalent scenario where $\tau_{0,1} \geq 6$ is retained. Observe that after removal of $\tau_{1,2} \leq 3$ label L_1 is no longer needed.

Theorem 1. *Let $\mathcal{D}_s^\xi$ be a stable distance table. Let a, b and c be three constraints in $\mathcal{C}(\mathcal{D}_s^\xi)$ such that $a \to b$, $b \to c$, $a \nleftrightarrow b$, and $b \nleftrightarrow c$. Then $c \nrightarrow a$, and therefore $a \nleftrightarrow c$.*

Proof. Assume that $c \to a$. Then there must exist some $S_c^{\triangleright a}$. It cannot contain b, otherwise we would have $b \to a$, and therefore $a \leftrightarrow b$. But if so, then by Observation 4 we would have $c \to b$, and therefore $b \leftrightarrow c$: a contradiction. □

Intuitively, Theorem 1 states that there is no cycle of length three consisting of members of $\mathcal{C}(\mathcal{D}_s^\xi)$ between which there is no cyclic dependency. Moreover, because of the quasi-transitivity of $\leadsto^+$ (Definition 2), it follows that there are then also no cycles of length greater than three.

3.2 Cyclic Dependencies and Equality Constraints

Henceforth, we will refer to the pair of constraints, $\tau_{i,j} \leq a$ and $\tau_{i,j} \geq a$, for some a, as an *equality constraint* $\tau_{i,j} = a$.

It turns out that if there is a cyclic dependency among the constraints in $\mathcal{C}(\mathcal{D}_s^\xi)$, then there must be at least one equality constraint in $\mathcal{C}(\mathcal{D}_s^\xi)$.

Observation 7. *Let ξ be a scenario of length n and $\mathcal{C}(\mathcal{D}_s^\xi)$ be the set of constraints in its stable distance table. If $\forall_{0 \leq i < j < n}(\tau_{i,j} \geq u \in \mathcal{C}(\mathcal{D}_s^\xi) \wedge \tau_{i,j} \leq v \in \mathcal{C}(\mathcal{D}_s^\xi) \implies u \neq v)$, then there is no cyclic dependency between the members of $\mathcal{C}(\mathcal{D}_s^\xi)$.*

Proof. First, we show that there is no "cyclic dependency of length one", i.e., for any two constraints a and b in $\mathcal{C}(\mathcal{D}_s^\xi)$, there are no $S_a^{\triangleright b}$ and $S_b^{\triangleright a}$ such that $S_a^{\triangleright b} \leadsto b$ and $S_b^{\triangleright a} \leadsto a$ (note that $\leadsto$ is the direct support relation: see Definition 1). The general observation then follows from Theorem 1.

Assume that there are two constraints a and b such that $a \leftrightarrow b$ and that there is a $S_a^{\triangleright b}$ and a $S_b^{\triangleright a}$ such that $S_a^{\triangleright b} \leadsto b$ and $S_b^{\triangleright a} \leadsto a$.

We show the proof for the case when constraint a is of type minimum. Then there are three cases to consider:

1. Assume a is of the form $\tau_{i,k} \geq u$, and $S_b^{\triangleright a} = \{\tau_{i,j} \geq v, \tau_{j,k} \geq w\}$, where $i < j < k$ and $u = v + w$ (pt. 1. of Definition 1). One of the two constraints in $S_b^{\triangleright a}$ must be b.
   (a) Assume $b = \tau_{i,j} \geq v$. Since $a \in S_a^{\triangleright b}$, $S_a^{\triangleright b} = \{\tau_{i,k} \geq u, \tau_{j,k} \leq w'\}$ for some w' such that $v = u - w'$ (pt. 2. of Definition 1). But then $v + w = v + w'$, which implies $w = w'$. Therefore both $\tau_{j,k} \geq w$ and $\tau_{j,k} \leq w$ are constraints (in $S_b^{\triangleright a}$ and $S_a^{\triangleright b}$, respectively). But this contradicts the assumptions of Observation 7.
   (b) Assume $b = \tau_{j,k} \geq w$. Since $a \in S_a^{\triangleright b}$, $S_a^{\triangleright b} = \{\tau_{i,k} \geq u, \tau_{i,j} \leq w'\}$ for some w' such that $w = u - w'$ (pt. 3. of Definition 1). But then $v + w = w + w'$, which implies $v = w'$. Therefore both $\tau_{i,j} \geq v$ and $\tau_{i,j} \leq v$ are constraints (in $S_b^{\triangleright a}$ and $S_a^{\triangleright b}$, respectively). But this is a contradiction.
2. Assume a is of the form $\tau_{i,j} \geq u$ and $S_b^{\triangleright a} = \{\tau_{i,k} \geq v, \tau_{j,k} \leq w\}$, where $i < j < k$ and $u = v - w$ (pt. 2. of Definition 1).
   (a) If $b = \tau_{i,k} \geq v$, then $S_a^{\triangleright b} = \{\tau_{i,j} \geq u, \tau_{j,k} \geq w'\}$, where $v = u + w'$ (pt. 1. of Definition 1). So $u + w = u + w'$, hence $w = w'$ and both $\tau_{j,k} \leq w$ and $\tau_{j,k} \geq w$ are constraints: contradiction.
   (b) If $b = \tau_{j,k} \leq w$, then $S_a^{\triangleright b} = \{\tau_{i,j} \geq u, \tau_{i,k} \leq w'\}$, where $w = w' - u$ (pt. 3. of Definition 1). So $v - w = w' - w$, hence $v = w'$ and both $\tau_{i,k} \geq v$ and $\tau_{i,k} \leq v$ are constraints: contradiction.

3. Assume a is of the form $\tau_{j,k} \geq u$ and $S_b^{\triangleright a} = \{\tau_{i,k} \geq v, \tau_{i,j} \leq w\}$, where $i < j < k$ and $u = v - w$ (pt. 3. of Definition 1).

   (a) If $b = \tau_{i,k} \geq v$, $S_a^{\triangleright b} = \{\tau_{j,k} \geq u, \tau_{i,j} \geq w'\}$, where $v = u + w'$ (pt. 1. of Definition 1). So $v - w = v - w'$, hence $w = w'$, and both $\tau_{i,j} \leq w$ and $\tau_{i,j} \geq w$ are constraints: a contradiction.

   (b) If $b = \tau_{i,j} \leq w$, $S_a^{\triangleright b} = \{\tau_{j,k} \geq u, \tau_{i,k} \leq w'\}$, where $w = w' - u$ (pt. 2. of Definition 1). So $v - w = w' - w$, hence $v = w'$ and both $\tau_{i,k} \geq v$ and $\tau_{i,k} \leq v$ are constraints: a contradiction.

We omit the very similar proof for the case when a is of the form maximum. $\square$

Theorem 2. *Let ξ be a scenario and let $\mathcal{D}_s^\xi$ be its stable distance table. If, for every pair of constraints x and y in $\mathcal{C}(\mathcal{D}_s^\xi)$, $x \not\leftrightarrow y$, then $\to$ defined on $\mathcal{C}(\mathcal{D}_s^\xi)$ is a strong partial order.*

Proof. We must show that $\to$ is irreflexive, antisymmetric and transitive.

By Observation 1, $\to$ is irreflexive. To see that $\to$ is antisymmetric, we assume it is symmetric. Let a and b be two constraints in $\mathcal{C}(\mathcal{D}_s^\xi)$ such that $a \to b$. Then $b \to a$, therefore $a \leftrightarrow b$: a contradiction.

For transitivity, let a and b be two constraints in $\mathcal{C}(\mathcal{D}_s^\xi)$ such that $a \to b$ and $b \to c$. There are no cyclic dependencies: $a \to c$ follows from Observation 3. $\square$

Intuitively, in the absence of cyclic dependencies $(\mathcal{C}(\mathcal{D}_s^\xi), \to)$ is a partially ordered set. Since $\mathcal{C}(\mathcal{D}_s^\xi)$ is finite, it has at least one minimal element, i.e., an element that does not have any support and hence cannot be removed. The set of such minimal elements is equivalent to the set of constraints represented by $\mathcal{C}(\mathcal{D}_s^\xi)$. Moreover, this is the smallest set equivalent to $\mathcal{C}(\mathcal{D}_s^\xi)$: any scenario equivalent to ξ must include this minimal set in its set of constraints.

It should be obvious that when a scenario with just this minimal set of constraints is converted to a timed automaton, the latter has the smallest number of clocks in the class of all equivalent timed automata.

Another important consequence of Theorem 2 is that if $\mathcal{C}(\mathcal{D}_s^\xi)$ does not include cyclic dependencies, then all of its members that do have supports can be removed in any order.

3.3 $\mathcal{C}(\mathcal{D}_s^\xi)$ with Cyclic Dependencies

$\mathcal{C}(\mathcal{D}_s^\xi)$ can include equality constraints which might give rise to cyclic dependencies (Observation 7). In that case $(\mathcal{C}(\mathcal{D}_s^\xi), \to)$ is not a partially ordered set. We could then have $a \leftrightarrow b$ such that we can remove a or b, but not both. As a result there could be more than one minimal set of constraints equivalent to $\mathcal{C}(\mathcal{D}_s^\xi)$.

To avoid this we will introduce a set of rules that would make the choice for removal between two constraints that are in a cyclic dependency deterministic. More importantly, the choice will result in a set of constraints that would require the smallest number of clocks in the class of all timed automata that are obtained from scenarios that are equivalent to ξ. These rules are presented below.

3.4   Resolving Cyclic Dependencies

We consider all the cases that give rise to cyclic dependencies. These cases (which involve equality constraints) are summarized as observations in the remainder of this subsection.

Observation 8. *Let $i < j$ be some event indices such that $(\tau_{i,j} = a) \in \mathcal{C}(\mathcal{D}_s^\xi)$ and, for any $i < p < j$, a_1 and a_2, $(\tau_{i,p} = a_1) \notin \mathcal{C}(\mathcal{D}_s^\xi)$ and $(\tau_{p,j} = a_2) \notin \mathcal{C}(\mathcal{D}_s^\xi)$. Then the clock allocated to anchor i can always be allocated to anchor j if needed.*

Proof. We consider the following three cases (see Fig. 4):

1. If every constraint that begins at i is of the form $\tau_{i,r} \geq c$ (or $\tau_{i,r} \leq c$), for some $r < j, c \leq a$, then the ranges of i and j will be non-overlapping, so one clock can be allocated to both.
2. If there is a constraint of the form $\tau_{i,k} \geq c$, for some $k > j, c \geq a$, then we must have $\{\tau_{i,j} \geq a, \tau_{j,k} \geq c - a\} \rightsquigarrow \tau_{i,k} \geq c$ (pt. 1 of Definition 1) and $\{\tau_{i,k} \geq c, \tau_{i,j} \leq a\} \rightsquigarrow \tau_{j,k} \geq c - a$ (pt. 3 of Definition 1). That is, $\tau_{i,k} \geq c \leftrightarrow \tau_{j,k} \geq c - a$. In this case, $\tau_{i,k} \geq c$ can be removed, while $\tau_{j,k} \geq c - a$ is retained. Then the ranges of i and j are non-overlapping.
   Similarly, if there is a constraint of the form $\tau_{i,k} \leq c$, for some $k > j, c \geq a$, then $\tau_{i,k} \leq c \leftrightarrow \tau_{j,k} \leq c - a$ and $\tau_{i,k} \leq c$ can be removed.
3. If there is a constraint of the form $\tau_{i,k} = c$, for some $k > j, c \geq a$, then we must also have $\tau_{j,k} = c - a$. According to Definition 1 the direct supports of these three equality constraints (six constraints in $\mathcal{C}(\mathcal{D}_s^\xi)$) are

$$\{\tau_{i,j} \leq a, \tau_{j,k} \leq c - a\} \rightsquigarrow \tau_{i,k} \leq c, \qquad \{\tau_{i,j} \geq a, \tau_{j,k} \geq c - a\} \rightsquigarrow \tau_{i,k} \geq c,$$
$$\{\tau_{i,k} \leq c, \tau_{i,j} \geq a\} \rightsquigarrow \tau_{j,k} \leq c - a, \qquad \{\tau_{i,k} \geq c, \tau_{i,j} \leq a\} \rightsquigarrow \tau_{j,k} \geq c - a,$$
$$\{\tau_{i,k} \leq c, \tau_{j,k} \geq c - a\} \rightsquigarrow \tau_{i,j} \leq a, \text{ and } \{\tau_{i,k} \geq c, \tau_{j,k} \leq c - a\} \rightsquigarrow \tau_{i,j} \geq a.$$

   Observe that $\tau_{i,j} \leq a \leftrightarrow \tau_{j,k} \geq c - a \leftrightarrow \tau_{i,k} \geq c \leftrightarrow \tau_{i,j} \geq a \leftrightarrow \tau_{j,k} \leq c - a \leftrightarrow \tau_{i,k} \leq c \leftrightarrow \tau_{i,j} \leq a$.
   The dependencies can be resolved by removing some of the constraints. We can remove $\tau_{i,k} \geq c$, then $\tau_{i,j} \geq a$ and $\tau_{j,k} \geq b$ will both lose their direct supports. If we follow this by removing $\tau_{i,k} \leq c$, then $\tau_{i,j} \leq a$ and $\tau_{j,k} \leq b$ will lose their direct supports. That is, the equality between i and k can be removed as long as the equalities between i and j, and between j and k remain. Then the ranges of i and j become non-overlapping.   □

It is worth noticing that resolving the cyclic dependencies as described in case 3 of Observation 8 (see the diagram on the left of Fig. 5) leads to the most satisfactory result: the other possibility, where the equality between j and k is retained (shown in the diagram on the right of Fig. 5), would require two clocks associated with anchors i and j.

   Observe also that, for example, $\tau_{i,j} \leq a \not\leftrightarrow \tau_{i,k} \geq c$: Observation 4 cannot be applied, because $\tau_{j,k} \geq b$ has only one support, and that includes both $\tau_{i,j} \leq a$ and $\tau_{i,k} \geq c$.

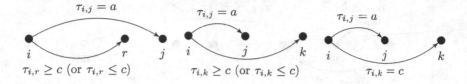

Fig. 4. Observation 8

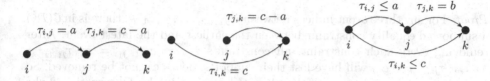

Fig. 5. Alternatives of case 3 of Observation 8   **Fig. 6.** Observation 10

Observation 0. *An equality constraint can only be supported by a pair of equality constraints.*

Proof. This is a direct consequence of Definition 1 (see the discussion above). □

In the first diagram of Fig. 5 (after $\tau_{i,k} = c$ has been removed) neither $\tau_{i,j} = a$, nor $\tau_{j,k} = c - a$ can be removed.

Observation 10. *Let $i < j < k$ be some event indices such that $(\tau_{j,k} = b) \in \mathcal{C}(\mathcal{D}_s^\xi)$ and, for any $j < p < k$, b_1 and b_2, $(\tau_{j,p} = b_1) \notin \mathcal{C}(\mathcal{D}_s^\xi)$ and $(\tau_{p,k} = b_2) \notin \mathcal{C}(\mathcal{D}_s^\xi)$. Moreover, either (a) $\tau_{i,j} \leq a$, and $\tau_{i,k} \leq c$, or (b) $\tau_{i,j} \geq a$, and $\tau_{i,k} \geq c$, such that $a + b = c$. If there is no unsupported constraint of the form $\tau_{i,l} \sim d$ such that $l > j$, then one clock can be associated with both anchors i and j.*

Proof. In case (a), illustrated in Fig. 6, from Definition 1 (pts. 6. and 5.) we have $\{\tau_{i,j} \leq a, \tau_{j,k} \leq b\} \rightsquigarrow \tau_{i,k} \leq c$ and $\{\tau_{i,k} \leq c, \tau_{j,k} \geq b\} \rightsquigarrow \tau_{i,j} \leq a$. So $\tau_{i,k} \leq c \leftrightarrow \tau_{i,j} \leq a$. After removing $\tau_{i,k} \leq c$, if there is no unsupported constraint of the form $\tau_{i,l} \sim d$, such that $l > j$, then the ranges for i and j will be non-overlapping and one clock can be assigned to both i and j. Otherwise ranges for i and j will overlap and two clocks will be needed.

Case (b) is very similar.   □

Observation 11. *Let ξ be a scenario of length n and $\mathcal{D}_s^\xi$ be its stable table. Let $i < j_1 < j_2 < \cdots < j_{m-1} < k$ (where $0 \leq i, k \leq n, m > 1$) be indices of events and $\tau_{i,k} = c$, $\tau_{i,j_1} = a_1, \tau_{j_1,j_2} = a_2, \ldots, \tau_{j_{m-1},k} = a_m$ be constraints in $\mathcal{C}(\mathcal{D}_s^\xi)$, such that $a_1 + a_2 + \ldots a_m = c$. Moreover, for any $i < p < k$, such that $p \neq j_l$ $(1 \leq l \leq m - 1)$, and for any b_1, b_2, $\mathcal{C}(\mathcal{D}_s^\xi)$ contains no constraints of the form $(\tau_{i,p} = b_1)$ or $(\tau_{p,k} = b_2)$. Then, after all the supported constraints have been removed, an allocation to anchors $i, j_1, j_2, \ldots, j_{m-1}$ will require only one clock.*

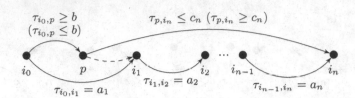

Fig. 7. An illustration of Observation 12

Proof. For any three event indices between $i, j_1, j_2, \ldots, j_{m-1}, k$, there is in $\mathcal{C}(\mathcal{D}_s^\xi)$ a supported equality constraint between the earliest and the latest event. After removing every such constraint, all constraints $\tau_{i,k} = c$, $\tau_{i,j_1} = a_1, \tau_{j_1,j_2} = a_2, \ldots, \tau_{j_{m-1},k} = a_m$ will have lost their supports, hence cannot be removed. So anchors $i, j_1, j_2, \ldots, j_{m-1}$ must be allocated clocks. But by Observation 8 the ranges of all these anchors are non-overlapping, therefore the same clock can be allocated to all of them. □

By Observation 11 the only unsupported constraints that begin at anchors $i, j_1, j_2, \ldots, j_{m-1}$ are the equality constraints between any two adjacent events. The next two observations consider the constraints that begin at other anchors.

Observation 12. *Let $i_0 < i_1 < i_2 < \cdots < i_{n-1} < i_n$ (where $n \geq 1$) be indices of events and $\tau_{i_0,i_1} = a_1, \tau_{i_1,i_2} = a_2, \ldots, \tau_{i_{n-1},i_n} = a_n$ be constraints in $\mathcal{C}(\mathcal{D}_s^\xi)$. Let $i_0 < p < i_1$ be an arbitrary event index such that $\tau_{i_0,p} \geq b$ (or $\tau_{i_0,p} \leq b$). Then, after all the supported constraints have been removed, an allocation to anchors $i_0, p, i_1, \ldots, i_{n-1}$ will require at most two clocks.*

Proof. Let us assume $\tau_{i_0,p} \geq b$. (We omit the very similar case of $\tau_{i_0,p} \leq b$.)

Then *for every i_m such that $1 \leq m \leq n$ we must have $\tau_{p,i_m} \leq c_m$, where c_m* satisfies $a_1 + a_2 + \cdots + a_m = b + c_m$ (see the diagram in Fig. 7).
By Definition 1 pts. 4. and 2. (with $i = i_0$, $j = p$ and $k = i_1$):

$$\{\tau_{i_0,i_1} \leq a_1, \tau_{i_0,p} \geq b\} \rightsquigarrow \tau_{p,i_1} \leq c_1$$
$$\{\tau_{i_0,i_1} \geq a_1, \tau_{p,i_1} \leq c_1\} \rightsquigarrow \tau_{i_0,p} \geq b$$

By Definition 1 pts. 4. and 2. (with $i = i_0$, $j = p$ and $k = i_m$) and Definition 2:

$$\{\tau_{i_0,i_1} \leq a_1, \tau_{i_1,i_2} \leq a_2, \ldots, \tau_{i_{m-1},i_m} \leq a_m, \tau_{i_0,p} \geq b\} \rightsquigarrow^+ \tau_{p,i_m} \leq c_m$$
$$\{\tau_{i_0,i_1} \geq a_1, \tau_{i_1,i_2} \geq a_2, \ldots, \tau_{i_{m-1},i_m} \geq a_m, \tau_{p,i_m} \leq c_m\} \rightsquigarrow^+ \tau_{i_0,p} \geq b$$

By Definition 1 pts. 5. and 6. (with $i = p$, $j = i_1$ and $k = i_m$) and Definition 2:

$$\{\tau_{p,i_m} \leq c_m, \tau_{i_1,i_2} \geq a_2, \ldots, \tau_{i_{m-1},i_m} \geq a_m\} \rightsquigarrow^+ \tau_{p,i_1} \leq c_1$$
$$\{\tau_{p,i_1} \leq c_1, \tau_{i_1,i_2} \leq a_2, \ldots, \tau_{i_{m-1},i_m} \leq a_m\} \rightsquigarrow^+ \tau_{p,i_m} \leq c_m$$

That is, $\tau_{i_0,p} \geq b \leftrightarrow \tau_{p,i_1} \leq c_1$, $\tau_{i_0,p} \geq b \leftrightarrow \tau_{p,i_m} \leq c_m$, and $\tau_{p,i_1} \leq c_1 \leftrightarrow \tau_{p,i_m} \leq c_m$. By Observation 6, two of the constraints among the three can be removed (for any $1 \leq m \leq n$). Observe that $\tau_{p,i_1} \leq c_1$ and $\tau_{p,i_m} \leq c_m$ begin at anchor p. We consider three cases:

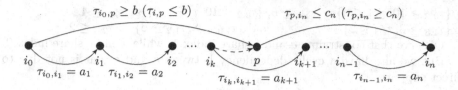

Fig. 8. An illustration of Observation 13

1. If there are in $\mathcal{C}(\mathcal{D}_s^\xi)$ no other constraints that begin at p, then after removing $\tau_{p,i_1} \leq c_1$ and $\tau_{p,i_m} \leq c_m$, p is no longer an anchor.
2. If there are in $\mathcal{C}(\mathcal{D}_s^\xi)$ some other constraints of the form $\tau_{p,j} \leq d$ or $\tau_{p,j} \geq d$ (where $j > p$, $j \neq i_m$ and $1 \leq m \leq n$) and they are all supported, then, after removing $\tau_{p,i_1} \leq c_1$ and $\tau_{p,i_m} \leq c_m$, they continue to be supported (Observation 5). So all all the constraints that begin at p can be removed and p is no longer an anchor.
3. If there is in $\mathcal{C}(\mathcal{D}_s^\xi)$ an unsupported constraint of the form $\tau_{p,j} \leq d$ or $\tau_{p,j} \geq d$ (where $j > p$, $j \neq i_m$, and $1 \leq m \leq n$), then after removing $\tau_{p,i_1} \leq c_1$ and $\tau_{p,i_m} \leq c_m$ p is still an anchor p.

If p is no longer an anchor, then by Observation 11 an allocation to anchors $i_0, i_1, \ldots, i_{n-1}$ requires exactly one clock. If p remains an anchor, we will need an extra clock for p.   □

Observation 13. *Let $i_0 < i_1 < i_2 < \cdots < i_{n-1} < i_n$ (where $n \geq 1$) be indices of events and $\tau_{i_0,i_1} = a_1, \tau_{i_1,i_2} = a_2, \ldots, \tau_{i_{n-1},i_n} = a_n$ be constraints in $\mathcal{C}(\mathcal{D}_s^\xi)$. Let $i_k < p < i_{k+1}$ (where $1 \leq k < n$) be an arbitrary event index such that $\tau_{i_0,p} \geq b$ (or $\tau_{i_0,p} \leq b$). Then, after all the supported constraints have been removed, an allocation to anchors $i_0, i_1, \ldots, i_{n-1}, p$ will require at most two clocks.*

Proof. Let us assume $\tau_{i_0,p} \geq b$. Then for every i_m such that $1 < m \leq n$ we must have $\tau_{p,i_m} \leq c_m$, where c_m satisfies $a_1 + a_2 + \cdots + a_m = b + c_m$ (see the diagram in Fig. 8).

The argument is quite similar to that for Observation 12. It can be shown that $\tau_{i_0,p} \geq b \leftrightarrow \tau_{p,i_m} \leq c_m$, $\tau_{p,i_m} \leq c_m \leftrightarrow \tau_{i_k,p} \geq d_k$, and $\tau_{i_k,p} \geq d_k \leftrightarrow \tau_{i_0,p} \geq b$, for $k < m$, $d_k < a_m$, and $d_k < b$. By Observation 6, two of the constraints among the three can be removed (for any $1 \leq m \leq n$). It is not difficult to see that retaining $\tau_{i_k,p} \geq d_k$ is the best choice and that at most two clocks will be needed.   □

In all the cases that we have considered so far in this section (Observations 8–13), the cyclic dependencies are between constraints of the form $\tau_{r_1,r_2} \sim c$ and $\tau_{l_1,l_2} \sim d$ (for some c and d) such that either $r_2 = l_1$, or $r_2 = l_2$, or $r_1 = l_1$. That is, the two constraints "shared" an event index. But other forms of cyclic dependencies might exist.

As an example consider the scenario in Fig. 3 along with its stable table. As we mentioned before, $a = \tau_{0,1} \leq 4 \leftrightarrow b = \tau_{1,2} \geq 6$ and $b \leftrightarrow c = \tau_{2,3} \leq 2$:

$\{\tau_{0,2} \geq 10, \tau_{0,1} \leq 4\} \leadsto \tau_{1,2} \geq 6, \{\tau_{0,2} \leq 10, \tau_{1,2} \geq 6\} \leadsto \tau_{0,1} \leq 4,$
$\{\tau_{1,3} \geq 8, \tau_{2,3} \leq 2\} \leadsto \tau_{1,2} \geq 6,$ and $\{\tau_{1,3} \leq 8, \tau_{1,2} \geq 6\} \leadsto \tau_{2,3} \leq 2.$

Observe that constraints a and b share index 1, while b and c share index 2.

But we also have a cyclic dependency between a and c that is not due to direct support:

$\{\tau_{0,2} \leq 10, \tau_{1,3} \geq 8, \tau_{2,3} \leq 2\} \leadsto^+ \tau_{0,1} \leq 4,$
$\{\tau_{1,3} \leq 8, \tau_{0,2} \geq 10, \tau_{0,1} \leq 4\} \leadsto^+ \tau_{2,3} \leq 2.$

So $\tau_{0,1} \leq 4 \leftrightarrow \tau_{2,3} \leq 2$. Only one of them can be removed, and the question is: which one? To answer this question we evaluate the two options by comparing the number of clocks that would be needed if one converted the resulting scenarios to their corresponding automata.

In this particular example removing either one of the constraints would result in the same outcome: two clocks are needed. But this might not always be the case. In general:

Observation 14. *Let $i < j < k < l$ be some event indices.*

1. *If there is a cyclic dependency between one of $\tau_{i,j} \geq a/\tau_{i,j} \leq a$ and one of $\tau_{k,l} \geq b/\tau_{k,l} \leq b$ (for some a and b), and if $\tau_{i,k} = c$ for some c, then we remove $\tau_{k,l} \geq b$ (or $\tau_{k,l} \leq b$): i is needed as an anchor for the equality.*
2. *If there is a cyclic dependency between one of $\tau_{i,k} \geq a/\tau_{i,k} \leq a$ and one of $\tau_{j,l} \geq b/\tau_{j,l} \leq b$ (for some a and b), and if $\tau_{i,j} = c$ for some c, then by Observation 6 we remove both, because $\tau_{i,k} \geq a/\tau_{i,k} \leq a$ will be supported (Observation 8) and the support does not include $\tau_{j,l} \geq b/\tau_{j,l} \leq b$.*
3. *If there is a cyclic dependency between one of $\tau_{i,l} \geq a/\tau_{i,l} \leq a$ and one of $\tau_{j,k} \geq b/\tau_{j,k} \leq b$ (for some a and b), and if $\tau_{i,j} = c$ for some c, then we remove $\tau_{i,l} \geq a$ (or $\tau_{i,l} \leq a$): this will shorten the range of anchor i.*

After resolving the cyclic dependencies in $\mathcal{C}(\mathcal{D}_s^\xi)$ by removing some of the constraints, we have obtained a smaller set $C_{acyclic} \subset \mathcal{C}(\mathcal{D}_s^\xi)$. The dependency relation $\rightarrow$, when restricted to $C_{acyclic}$, is a partial order (Observation 2). The set of the minimal elements of this partial order will be equivalent to $\mathcal{C}(\mathcal{D}_s^\xi)$.

We are now ready to present our new optimization algorithm, which is based upon our previous algorithm [13].

3.5   The Optimization Algorithm

Given a scenario $\xi = (\mathcal{E}, \mathcal{C})$, our goal is to find $\mathcal{C}' \subseteq \mathcal{C}(\mathcal{D}_s^\xi)$ that is equivalent to $\mathcal{C}(\mathcal{D}_s^\xi)$, such that, if $\xi' = (\mathcal{E}, \mathcal{C}')$, then the number of clocks in $\mathcal{A}_{\xi'}$ is the smallest in the entire class of language-equivalent timed automata.

We define the *direct support relation on* $\mathcal{C}(\mathcal{D}_s^\xi)$ by $DSupp = \{(c, S) \mid S \leadsto c\}$ and the *support relation on* $\mathcal{C}(\mathcal{D}_s^\xi)$ by $Supp = \{(c, S) \mid S \leadsto^+ c\}$.

If (c, S) is a member of $Supp$, then $\mathcal{C}(\mathcal{D}_s^\xi) \setminus \{c\}$ is equivalent to $\mathcal{C}(\mathcal{D}_s^\xi)$.

The optimization algorithm uses three data structures, C, WS, and CD. C represents the current set of constraints, WS ("working support") contains information about whether and how the constraints are supported by subsets of

C, while CD ("cyclic dependencies") contains information about constraints in C that are in cyclic dependencies with other constraints in C.

We initialize C to $\mathcal{C}(\mathcal{D}_s^\xi)$, WS to $DSupp$, and CD to $\leftrightarrow$ restricted to WS.

The optimization process is carried out in two phases. During the first phase the algorithm takes pairs of constraints from CD, one at a time, and resolves the cyclic dependency between the elements of the pair (see Sect. 3.4). This involves removing the appropriate constraint from C, updating WS with the supports of this constraint (see below) and removing the entry from CD. As WS is updated, new cyclic dependencies may be uncovered and added to CD.

This phase consists of two steps. First, the algorithm examines dependencies that are described by Observation 11 and removes every equality constraint that is supported by a pair of equality constraints on smaller distances. In the second step it resolves dependencies described by Observations 8, 10 and 12–14.

At the end of this step CD becomes empty: there is no cyclic dependency between the members of C, hence there is a partial order on C (Theorem 2).

Then the algorithm proceeds to the second phase, where it takes any constraint that has a support in WS, removes it from C and updates WS. The order in which the constraints are considered for removal does not matter. Observe that CD remains empty during this phase.

The algorithm terminates once WS becomes empty. At this point C includes the final minimal set of constraints equivalent to $\mathcal{C}(\mathcal{D}_s^\xi)$.

The four important invariants are:

1. C is equivalent to $\mathcal{C}(\mathcal{D}_s^\xi)$;
2. WS is a subset of $Supp$, the support relation associated with $\mathcal{C}(\mathcal{D}_s^\xi)$;
3. WS contains only those tuples in $Supp$ that do not contain constraints from outside C(but not necessarily all such tuples);
4. CD contains only tuples with constraints that appear as the first elements of some tuples in WS.

Clearly, the initialization establishes these invariants.

Thanks to the second and third invariant, a constraint c that has support in WS can be removed from C without violating the first invariant. The resulting new version of C will not contain c, therefore WS must be updated to restore the third invariant, in a way that does not violate the second invariant. CD must also be updated accordingly.

Every time that a supported constraint c is removed from C:

1. For each $(c', S') \in WS$, such that $c \in S'$:
   - remove (c', S') from WS;
   - for each $(c, S) \in WS$, if $c' \notin S$, add $(c', S' \setminus \{c\} \cup S)$ to WS.
2. Remove from WS every tuple whose first element is c.
3. Remove from CD every tuple whose first or second element is c.

Notice that the first step above generates new tuples in WS according to pt. 2 of Definition 2.

It should be clear that this method of updating ensures that WS remains within $Supp$ (restricted to the current C) and that we do not lose information about indirect supports in C. Moreover, every constraint that appears in some tuple in CD must also appear as the first element of some tuple in WS.

Termination is assured, because at each step we remove a constraint from a finite set of constraints. Correctness is ensured by the invariants.

Scenario η of Fig. 1, obtained by our algorithm, is equivalent to ξ.

In summary, every time there is a choice between constraints that are involved in a cyclic dependency, we retain the one that will reduce the number of anchors, or—if that is impossible—reduce the number of overlapping ranges of anchors (Observations 8–14). This process does not remove supports from those constraints that are not involved in cyclic dependencies (Observation 5).

Once the cyclic dependencies are resolved, we retain only those of the remaining constraints that have no support, and that must therefore be included in all the equivalent sets of constraints. It follows that the number of clocks required for the resulting automaton cannot be decreased by choosing another equivalent set of constraints.

This can be summarized as follows.

Theorem 3. *Let $\xi = (\mathcal{E}, \mathcal{C})$ be a scenario and $\mathcal{D}_s^\xi$ be its stable distance table. Let $\mathcal{C}_{opt}$ be the set of constraints obtained from $\mathcal{C}(\mathcal{D}_s^\xi)$ by our optimization algorithm. Then $\mathcal{A}_{\xi'}$, where $\xi' = (\mathcal{E}, \mathcal{C}_{opt})$, has the smallest number of clocks in the entire class of timed automata that are language equivalent to $\mathcal{A}_\xi$.*

4   Conclusions

We present a new optimization algorithm that achieves the minimal number of clocks when timed scenarios are viewed as timed automata.

That is, given a scenario $\xi = (\mathcal{E}, \mathcal{C})$, the algorithm finds a set of constraints, $\mathcal{C}'$, such that $\xi' = (\mathcal{E}, \mathcal{C}')$ is equivalent to ξ, and the automaton derived from ξ' has the smallest number of clocks in the entire class of equivalent timed automata.

References

1. Abdulla, P.A., Deneux, J., Ouaknine, J., Worrell, J.: Decidability and complexity results for timed automata via channel machines. In: Caires, L., Italiano, G.F., Monteiro, L., Palamidessi, C., Yung, M. (eds.) ICALP 2005. LNCS, vol. 3580, pp. 1089–1101. Springer, Heidelberg (2005). https://doi.org/10.1007/11523468_88
2. Akshay, S., Mukund, M., Kumar, K.N.: Checking coverage for infinite collections of timed scenarios. In: Caires, L., Vasconcelos, V.T. (eds.) CONCUR 2007. LNCS, vol. 4703, pp. 181–196. Springer, Heidelberg (2007). https://doi.org/10.1007/978-3-540-74407-8_13
3. Alur, R., Dill, D.L.: A theory of timed automata. Theor. Comput. Sci. **126**(2), 183–235 (1994)
4. Alur, R., Madhusudan, P.: Decision problems for timed automata: a survey. In: Bernardo, M., Corradini, F. (eds.) SFM-RT 2004. LNCS, vol. 3185, pp. 1–24. Springer, Heidelberg (2004). https://doi.org/10.1007/978-3-540-30080-9_1

5. Alur, R., Martin, M., Raghothaman, M., Stergiou, C., Tripakis, S., Udupa, A.: Synthesizing finite-state protocols from scenarios and requirements. In: Yahav, E. (ed.) HVC 2014. LNCS, vol. 8855, pp. 75–91. Springer, Cham (2014). https://doi.org/10.1007/978-3-319-13338-6_7
6. Baier, C., Bertrand, N., Bouyer, P., Brihaye, T.: When are timed automata determinizable? In: Albers, S., Marchetti-Spaccamela, A., Matias, Y., Nikoletseas, S., Thomas, W. (eds.) ICALP 2009. LNCS, vol. 5556, pp. 43–54. Springer, Heidelberg (2009). https://doi.org/10.1007/978-3-642-02930-1_4
7. Bollig, B., Katoen, J.-P., Kern, C., Leucker, M.: Replaying play in and play out: synthesis of design models from scenarios by learning. In: Grumberg, O., Huth, M. (eds.) TACAS 2007. LNCS, vol. 4424, pp. 435–450. Springer, Heidelberg (2007). https://doi.org/10.1007/978-3-540-71209-1_33
8. Chandrasekaran, P., Mukund, M.: Matching scenarios with timing constraints. In: Asarin, E., Bouyer, P. (eds.) FORMATS 2006. LNCS, vol. 4202, pp. 98–112. Springer, Heidelberg (2006). https://doi.org/10.1007/11867340_8
9. Harel, D., Kugler, H., Pnueli, A.: Synthesis revisited: generating statechart models from scenario-based requirements. In: Kreowski, H.-J., Montanari, U., Orejas, F., Rozenberg, G., Taentzer, G. (eds.) Formal Methods in Software and Systems Modeling. LNCS, vol. 3393, pp. 300–324. Springer, Heidelberg (2005). https://doi.org/10.1007/978-3-540-31847-7_18
10. Heitmeyer, C.L., et al.: Building high assurance human-centric decision systems. Autom. Softw. Eng. 22(2), 159–197 (2014). https://doi.org/10.1007/s10515-014-0157-z
11. Saeedloei, N., Kluźniak, F.: From scenarios to timed automata. In: Cavalheiro, S., Fiadeiro, J. (eds.) SBMF 2017. LNCS, vol. 10623, pp. 33–51. Springer, Cham (2017). https://doi.org/10.1007/978-3-319-70848-5_4
12. Saeedloei, N., Kluźniak, F.: Timed scenarios: consistency, equivalence and optimization. In: Massoni, T., Mousavi, M.R. (eds.) SBMF 2018. LNCS, vol. 11254, pp. 215–233. Springer, Cham (2018). https://doi.org/10.1007/978-3-030-03044-5_14
13. Saeedloei, N., Kluźniak, F.: Optimization of timed scenarios. In: Carvalho, G., Stolz, V. (eds.) SBMF 2020. LNCS, vol. 12475, pp. 119–136. Springer, Cham (2020). https://doi.org/10.1007/978-3-030-63882-5_8
14. Saeedloei, N., Kluźniak, F.: Synthesizing clock-efficient timed automata. In: Dongol, B., Troubitsyna, E. (eds.) IFM 2020. LNCS, vol. 12546, pp. 276–294. Springer, Cham (2020). https://doi.org/10.1007/978-3-030-63461-2_15
15. Somé, S., Dssouli, R., Vaucher, J.: From scenarios to timed automata: building specifications from users requirements. In: Proceedings of the Second Asia Pacific Software Engineering Conference. APSEC 1995, pp. 48–57. IEEE Computer Society (1995)
16. Uchitel, S., Kramer, J., Magee, J.: Synthesis of behavioral models from scenarios. IEEE Trans. Softw. Eng. 29(2), 99–115 (2003)

Author Index

Printed in the United States
by Baker & Taylor Publisher Services